AMILCAR

THE COMPLETE STORY

AMILCAR

THE COMPLETE STORY

CHRIS MARTIN

THE CROWOOD PRESS

120 KLM A L'HEURE
Le GRAND SPORT
AMILCAR
S^té N^le POUR L'AUTOMOBILE "AMILCAR" 31 à 47 B^d ANATOLE FRANCE St DENIS

CONTENTS

INTRODUCTION

As I had always been interested in old cars, racing and most things French, it was probably inevitable I would become interested in Amilcars; consequently, I am currently running a restored 1925 CS and working on rebuilding an early C4. Having the chance to write the history of these cars has also been an interesting journey, researching the ups and downs, the various models and where they are today.

First, I should explain the problems with researching a subject that started over 100 years ago and for which there are no primary sources – first-hand witnesses – still alive. Yes, today we are fortunate to have the resources of the internet available to all, and true, there is much information there, but much of it is not properly verified. It is all too easy to publish something online that is just a repetition of rumour, hearsay and incorrect theories, such that if a statement is repeated often enough it becomes accepted as fact. Even so, there are some resources that are indeed well researched and valuable for checking details. I have included an appendix listing all of the sources I have referred to, as there has been a lot already written by respected writers, historians and experts in the field, but even those writers do not always agree. Where there may be a discrepancy in the stated facts, I have added reference notes that may offer alternate explanations.

This book aims to cover the Amilcar story from the start in 1921 through to the demise of the marque in 1939. I start with a brief explanation of the situation in France and the French automobile industry after World War I to give some background as to how and why the Amilcar was born.

The following chapters deal with the history in a chronological order where possible, detailing the models and their place in the market as well as their results in competition, although some specifics will be dealt with in their own chapters. Each model is illustrated by both period photos and a story or two about survivors that have been restored and are still giving their lucky owners enjoyment on the road today.

After the 6-cylinder racers the competition department was wound up and Amilcar went through several changes of management, trying to find their place in the medium car market but with limited success; the relevant chapters cover this period with more detail regarding the financial struggles and changes of management and direction until the end in 1939.

Later chapters cover the rival brands, the Amilcar in international markets, period road tests and press reports, related ephemera and a few odd Amilcar tales. In each chapter I have also added some occasional historical notes not specifically about Amilcar but relevant to the times. These are intended to help paint a picture of cultural and historical events that would have had an influence on the city of Paris, the rest of France and its neighbouring countries through the inter-war period.

Several of the Amilcars illustrated in these pages are in Australia. I make no apology for this and it is not just because I now live 'down under'; the Amilcar was always a popular car here, selling in large numbers especially in the southern states, and there is still a healthy interest among the many owners who keep about 100 of these delights on the road. I have also included several cars from the Netherlands, where there is a particularly healthy Amilcar community, as well as contributions from British, French and German Amilcar owners.

After the chapters covering the full story in chronological order there are appendices with competition results, technical specifications, the suppliers of outsourced parts, and information about clubs, and a bibliography.

Were they really just a 'Poor Man's Bugatti' as the old cliché says, or do Amilcars deserve to be recognised initially as an affordable sporting car followed by a significant racing machine and later making cars of some merit in what were difficult times? Amilcar started by making a cheap utilitarian small car that could take advantage of the new cyclecar regulations, with no initial ideas of sporting use, while Bugatti were already having competition success with the Brescia Type 22/23. When Morel and others took to the tracks Amilcars were not competing with the Bugatti Type 35, which was probably the most successful Grand Prix car of all time. By the time Amilcar made a real racing car, the C6, it cost *more* than the Bugatti Type 37, which was the nearest Bugatti ever got to an affordable sports car for the amateur driver.

In the 1930s Bugatti's glamorous models were made for the exclusive and expensive end of the market, while the Amilcars of the same period were aimed at the middle classes who by 1934 were buying the Citroën Traction in their thousands. Read on and unravel the ups and downs of the Amilcar story. *Amilcar Un Jour, Amilcar Toujours!*

TIMELINE

1919 André Morel meets Edmond Moyet at the Excelsior restaurant. Émile Akar and Joseph Lamy agree to finance the new car.

1920 New premises at 34, Rue du Chemin–Vert; work begins on new car, for now called the Borie Cyclecar.

1921 19 July: The name Amilcar is registered.
29 September: Articles of the company Société Nouvelle pour l'Automobile (SNPA) published.
6 October: Amilcar CC launched at the Paris Salon.
23 October: Morel 1st in class for the flying kilometre at an average speed of over 90km/h.
Marcel Sée joins as technical director.

1922 19 February: Victory for Munch in the Forest of Marly near Versailles leads to setting up an official Competition Department.
27–29 May: Morel wins the Bol d'Or.
2 July: Morel sets flying kilometre record for 1100cc class at 120km/h.
17 September: Morel crowned 1922 Speed Champion of France and Amilcar win Constructors Champion of France in the 1100cc class.
CV and C4 shown at the Paris Salon. 10CV E Type announced for 1923.

1923 The CS and GCS launched at the Paris Salon and patent applied for front wheel braking system.

1924 16 May: Patent issued for front wheel braking system.
Competition Department expanded and renamed Racing Department.
Amilcar moved to a new factory in Saint-Denis.
CGS3 added to the range.
2 October: Paris Salon – Amilcar launch the 7CV G Type and the 10CV J Type.

1925 Morel wins the Bol d'Or again.
Marius Mestivier killed at Le Mans.
Racing debut for the 6-cylinder CO.
Amilcar buys Margyl coachworks.
Morel sets flying kilometre record for 1100cc class at 147.42km/h.
Paris Salon – The CGSs replaces the CGS.

1926 25 September: Martin, Duray, Morel finish 1,2,3 at Brooklands JCC 200 Miles.
At the Paris Salon, the first showing of the C6 to be available for the next year.

1927 15 January: Marcel Lefebrve-Despeaux wins the Monte Carlo Rally in an Amilcar G Type.
New 'Offset' version of the CO racer.
SNPA in liquidation. The new company Société Anonyme Française d'Automobile (SAFA) takes over with Marcel Sée and Albert Neubauer in charge. Akar and Lamy leave.
L Type replaces the G Type at the Paris Salon.

1928 Larger 1270cc version of the CO engine developed for the 1500cc class.
Amilcar announces deal with Durant Motors to sell Amilcars in the USA.
Eight-cylinder C8 chassis and M Type introduced at the Paris Salon.
Racing Department closed down.

1929 André Morel leaves the company.
Last official outing for any works Amilcar racers.
Jules Moriceau enters the Indianapolis 500.
Wall Street Crash ends the Amilcar Durant alliance.
M2 replaces the M Type and C8 and CS8 announced at the Paris Salon.
Clément Auguste Martin buys remaining team racing cars.

1931 Paris Salon showed only the M3 and CS8 models.

1932 5CV C Type introduced alongside the M3 at the Salon.

1933 Administrators André Briès and Marcel Sée set up new holding company, Société Financière pour l'Automobile, (SOFIA) to raise finance.
CS8 dropped, C Type updated as the C3. New M4 introduced.
Edmond Moyet leaves Amilcar.

1934 C5 replaces the C3 and aerodynamic updates offered for the M3 and M4.
Prototype Pégase shown at the October Paris Salon.

1935 Pégase goes on sale with ten body styles offered.

1936 Pégase range reduced to just four models. Hotchkiss buys into Amilcar.

1937 Hotchkiss takes over Amilcar. Pégase production ends. Amilcar Compound B38 shown at the Paris Salon in October.

1938 Production of the Compound started in April 1938 with new 1185cc engine.

1939 Compound B67 announced with new 1349cc engine.

1940–1942 Sales of Amilcars stop when Germany occupies Paris. A few last Compound chassis were built as vans and ambulances.

CHAPTER 1

FRANCE 1920

To fully understand how and why the Amilcar marque came to be, and why the new model was the right idea at the right time, it is useful to summarise the historical context that helps to set the scene at the time of the creation of these wonderful cars. Several circumstances contributed to the birth of the Amilcar, the coincidental timing of which was critical.

There had been a phenomenon known as the 'Cyclecar' around for a few years, but it took hold in France in the early 1920s. There was already a well-established car manufacturing industry in France; it could be said this country was probably one of the first to embrace the new-fangled automobile in any quantity, although Britain, Germany and America were not far behind. To give some background to this story, what follows is a brief description of the economic, political, industrial and sociological conditions in France at the time followed by a brief overview of the local motor industry, particularly the people and companies that were to play a part in the birth of the Amilcar.

FRANCE AFTER THE GREAT WAR

Following the 1914–18 war France found itself in a dire economic state. Despite the intentions of the Treaty of Versailles to ensure Germany should pay for all restoration of the damaged infrastructure, industry and agricultural land, France received nothing from a country that was in an even worse financial state. Added to the problems of rebuilding factories, mines and farms, there was a chronic shortage of manpower. Over 1.5 million French soldiers were killed and many more left with disabilities. This alone meant there was a significant reduction in the number of workers who would otherwise have been employed in the French car industry. Prior to the war, immigration was not regulated in any way to be advantageous to either industry or the local population and workers were needed in both the growing industries as well as France's widespread agricultural interests. There was a desire by 1920 to enact some laws to control immigration. This was so that skilled labour could be encouraged while the flow of unskilled people was restricted – particularly those from the colonies. During the war years, many of the latter had been found unsuitable for general labour. There was also a desire to prevent cheap labour from driving down wages for the indigenous population. In the early 1920s, some 20,000 Belgians were already employed, mostly in mining and agriculture, and much of the shortfall of skilled workers under the new regulations would be taken up by immigrants from Czechoslovakia, Italy and Poland. These were followed by Portuguese and Spanish immigrants for less skilled work. By 1924, over a million foreign workers had come to France and this influx of imported labour was an important component of the economic growth of France in the decade following the war.

Politically, the mood of the country remained conservative: the peasants who had continued to farm the land were profiting well enough from their markets and what socialist attempts there were to unionise the labour force were fruitless; France had been taking notice of the recent Bolshevik revolution in Russia and wanted no such thoughts to influence its workers. Widespread strikes by the unions in May 1920 were crushed by the government supported by the majority. In 1919 Prime Minister Georges Clemenceau had implemented the eight-hour working day for most trades (excluding farmers) and working conditions had improved across the board. Clemenceau had been Prime Minister throughout the war and was a prominent author of the Treaty of Versailles. He had wanted Germany to be punished, but other influences were at work to bring peace to Europe and even to help Germany get back on its feet. All of this weakened Clemenceau's position and, after his defeat in the presidential election in January 1920 by Paul Deschanel, he took no further part in politics. He was replaced as Prime Minister by Alexandre Millerand, who in turn became President in September that year after the resignation of Deschanel, but the general political climate remained largely conservative.

Increased taxes on consumers had been a worrying burden since the war – necessary in order to fund the government's policies – but output in both manufacturing industry and agriculture was still considerably lower than it had been prior to 1914. Exports in 1920 were indeed much increased over the previous year, but any benefits were negated by the falling value of the French franc against other currencies, which combined with higher taxes to cause a steep rise in the cost of living.

The necessary reforms resulting in the Finance Law of 30 July 1920 had been planned as far back as 1919, but other parliamentary business held up the required ratification. Through that period Louis Lucien Klotz was the Finance Minister from 1917 through the war years until January 1920, when he was replaced by Frédéric François-Marsal, so it is not clear who was responsible for drawing up the final draft. It is often thereafter referred to as the 'Le Trocquer Law' after Yves Le Trocquer, the Minister of Public Works with responsibilities for transport policies who pushed for an incentive to give a boost to the car industry and at the same time encouraged more people to gain motorised mobility. It may have seemed an odd move to be going against the pattern of increased taxes of the previous two years, but it was a priority of the government to help reinstate the once prosperous motor industry at least at the cheaper end of the market. Certainly, there was also a keen demand among the French population to become mobile and join the motoring classes.

WHAT IS A CYCLECAR?

In the early years of the automobile industry there was no standard specification, and most of the engineers responsible were still finding their way with various choices of large-capacity engines capable of pulling the luxurious coach-built limousines and tourers down to the most basic single-cylinder runabouts. Petrol power had by no means a monopoly, with steam and electric cars also improving as viable alternatives.

The trend for smaller, affordable cars created what were to become 'cyclecars' in most of the bigger markets, Britain, France, Germany and the USA from around 1910. These were usually very basic lightweight cars or tricycles with single- or twin-cylinder motorcycle engines and, on 14 December 1912, the Federation Internationale des Clubs Moto Cycliste announced an international classification of cyclecars that was adopted by Austria, Belgium, Canada, France, Germany, Italy, the Netherlands, the United Kingdom and the United States. This defined a cyclecar as a single- or two-seater weighing not more than 350kg (772lb) with an engine capacity not exceeding 1100cc. Some were no more than a light frame with three or four wheels and a motorcycle engine, often a single- or twin-cylinder unit, which had to work hard to move anything close to the maximum weight. Extreme cases might include the Smith Flyer (later sold as the Briggs & Stratton Flyer), the Dudly Bug and the Scripps-Booth Rocket in the USA and in the UK the Morgan three-wheelers, the AC Sociable and the GN were moderately successful. Others came and went in Europe, particularly in Germany and Italy, but France was the most prolific in terms of cyclecar manufacturers. Many of these came under a loose definition of what was known as a cyclecar, but it was the new 'Le Trocquer Law' that gave the French car industry a clear incentive to build small cars that complied to a workable set of rules.

One peculiarity of the laws governing the registration and tax liability of motor vehicles in early twentieth-century France was that this all fell under the responsibility of the 'Service des Mines' who applied their own formulae for calculating the taxable horsepower, or the CV figure. This probably came about as the mining industry had, since the nineteenth century, some expertise and familiarity with powered machinery. Although in modern times France has streamlined its bureaucracy and government departments, a car registration plate is still often referred to as a *'plaque minéralogique'*.

The new tax regulations provided for a reduced tax of 100 francs per year for cyclecars, the same rate as for motorcycles at the time. An explosion of small manufacturers resulted, but most of these were nothing more than assemblers of bought-in components; axles, engines and gearboxes all sourced from proprietary suppliers of varying quality and efficiency. Most of these small workshops were situated in the industrial area stretching from Boulogne in the west of Paris to Saint-Denis in the north, encompassing Puteaux, Levallois-Perret, Courbevoie and Asnières-sur-Seine, all place names that will be familiar to anyone with an interest in vintage French cars.

The better-equipped manufacturers such as Mathis, Peugeot and Salmson, however, were able to build complete cars using parts made in house and, from the start, Amilcar also fell into this latter category.

In 1920 there were 814 cyclecars registered in France and the demand quickly grew such that by 1924 there were 29,542 happy *cyclecaristes* paying the reduced rate, but their days were soon to be numbered. An amendment to the finance law in April 1924 raised the tax to 120 francs and at the same time lowered the voiturette rate for cars with engines of less than 1500cc to 180 francs. There was already a reduced demand for these basic machines and the lower cyclecar tax was abolished altogether in 1925.

The original definition of a cyclecar in 1920 that limited the weight to 350kg was for the basic rolling chassis with minimal bodywork and excluded accessories like lights, spare wheel and starter, all of which of course were available from the dealer to be installed after the car was registered. A contemporary report said:

The French have always been rebellious and worked to subvert the law. So, the buyer received two invoices, one for the car, stripped of lighting, roof and spare wheel, the other for whatever accessories he had ordered.

If the cars had been delivered fully equipped, they could never have met the 350kg limit. Although Amilcars and many others continued to be known as cyclecars for many years after, they only qualified under the regulations until 1923, by which time they were classified as voiturettes due to the increased weight of the improved models designed to appeal to a wider market.

THE FRENCH MOTOR INDUSTRY IN 1920

It would be useful here to understand the main players of the French car industry following the 1914–18 war; for various reasons, major changes were about to take place. Many of the established brands would continue making cars based on the earlier veteran models that had served them well enough through the first fifteen or twenty years of the pioneering days of motoring, but they would soon be pushed aside by new names that had benefited from the war and started afresh with more modern ideas. While the automobile had been the preserve of the wealthy few with a taste for adventure back in the pre-war days, it was soon to become an affordable and reliable alternative to the horses or bicycles the ordinary working man had been used to. New thinking was needed: where previously such machines had been handmade by skilled engineers, production line mass production, as had been demonstrated by Ford in America, would be needed to meet the emerging market.

Once great names like Delaunay Belleville lost their way and diverted into making trucks before fading away; Berliet likewise suffered problems in the 1920s and did better with their commercials. Many other established names like the once mighty De Dion Bouton struggled through the 1920s, the last passenger car being produced in 1932, although the name survived with a few commercials until 1950. Darracq was absorbed by Talbot and the name was lost after 1922; Unic lasted until 1938, by then best known for their taxis, although again a few commercials carried the name until a takeover by Simca in 1953. Léon Bollée was taken over by Morris in 1924 and Clément-Bayard was bought out by Citroën in 1922, as was Mors in 1925, in both cases to increase factory capacity. Chenard & Walcker faded away during the 1930s and was taken over by the Chausson company and then Peugeot in the late 1940s. Mathis stumbled on until a merger with Ford in 1934 to form the Matford brand, which itself did not survive the 1939–45 war.

Ford had already had a presence in the French market since before the war; French agent Henri Depasse had set up a venture, with Model Ts being assembled at a factory at Bordeaux. This was taken over by the newly set up Ford SAF and manufacture increased when they moved to a larger factory at Asnières-sur-Seine in 1925. Because of the heavy taxation on the original 2.9-litre engine, Ford introduced a sleeved-down 2-litre version for the European markets. The simplicity of manufacture and subsequent sales success had a lasting influence on the French automobile industry.

Hotchkiss had long been established as an armaments manufacturer since 1867 and had already made a name for themselves with some luxury cars since 1903. Post-war investment in new factories in France and Britain and the new AM series launched in 1923 would continue the name into the 1930s when they too struggled to sell new models, but the name continued until 1970, making trucks and military vehicles. Hotchkiss will reappear in the Amilcar story later.

Many of these manufacturers had profited well from military contracts during World War I but were not prepared for the new market demands of the 1920s. Two exceptions were of course Peugeot and Renault, who had been among the first established motor companies with a sound pedigree in competition since the early years. Peugeot's small cars: the Ettore Bugatti-designed Bébé launched in 1912 and the later Type 161 Quadrilette and the 10hp Type 163 of the 1920s establishing the name as a popular brand. Likewise, Renault, who continued after the war with a strong line of medium to large cars, although through this period they did not have a share of the now popular market for small cars of the 5hp to 7hp range.

Le Zèbre

One more of the French car manufacturers that was at a loose end after the war was the small Le Zèbre company.

Jules Salomon began his career as a young engineer working for Georges Richard, one of the many motoring pioneers of the late nineteenth century who had graduated from making bicycles. Richard sold out to Brasier and went on to start Unic in 1905 with Jacques Bizet (son of the famous composer Georges). In 1909, Salomon teamed up with Bizet to start up their own company, which they called Le Zèbre. One story suggests this was a nickname for a fellow employee at Unic, the office boy who was known to run fast on errands, which may seem a fairly tenuous connection, but another theory was that it was fashionable at the time to name car marques after animals: Licorne (Unicorn); Lion-Peugeot; Ours (Bear); Sphinx and so on, but whatever the origins the name stuck. Another story has it that it was the name of a dray horse used

Le Zèbre advertisement.

Le Zèbre Torpédo Type A 1913.

to haul goods at the Unic factory. The first cars were made at the Unic factory in Puteaux before the Le Zèbre company was formally set up as a separate identity. With capital from the banker Henri de Rothschild, who also had a stake in Unic, and Bizet in charge of the finances and presumably the management of the business, the company was initially registered as Bizet Constructions, and Jules Salomon was the engineering brains responsible for the design of the Type A, launched in 1909. Featuring a 630cc single-cylinder engine and two-speed gearbox, it was something of a bargain with a price of 3,000 francs, well below the average cost of the competition. These had been immediately well received, making Le Zèbre a popular brand.

The leading motoring journalist of the time, Louis Baudry de Saunier, who contributed to the weekly magazine *L'Illustration* and was the publisher of *Omnia*, a monthly motoring magazine, was impressed and often wrote favourable reports extolling the virtues of Le Zèbre cars, although it has been suggested that he may have also had a financial interest. In 1911 the company was registered as Société Anonyme Le Zèbre. The business soon attracted investment from two prominent businessmen, Emile Akar and Joseph Lamy, the latter having already invested in the Taximètres Unic de Monaco business with Bizet and Rothschild. There was now sufficient finance for a new factory to be built at Puteaux, which in turn allowed for production to meet the demand, and Lamy took on the role of Commercial Director. The Type B, a larger 4-cylinder model, followed in 1912. Rated at 10CV and priced at 6,000 francs, this was also a lot of car for the money compared to the competition. The Type C appeared soon after, another smaller 4-cylinder car with a lightweight two-seater body. Luckily, the military also approved of these strong but light and nimble cars, resulting in orders for 40 cars per month for army use, which meant Le Zèbre was one of the few car factories continuing to make cars through the war while also having to adapt to manufacturing hardware and machinery for other military supply contracts. Moving again to a bigger factory at Suresnes in 1914 to meet the demand, Le Zèbre also rented a small workshop owned by a Monsieur Borie at 34 Rue du Chemin-Vert near the Bastille and established the head office and showrooms near the Champs Elysées, the preferred sales area for all car manufacturers of note.

Through the war Jules Salomon remained in charge of production under the Service Technique des Armées, which is how he was introduced to André Citroën, who had become a major supplier for the army by a mutual acquaintance, a M. Nieder. As early as February 1917, Citroën had asked Salomon if he could come up with a design for a small car, but at the

JULES SALOMON, 1873–1963

Although never an employee of Amilcar, Jean-Marie-Jules Salomon obviously had quite an influence on the design of the early cars.

He was born 1 February 1873, in Cahors, and graduated at the School of Commerce and Industry in Bordeaux. From there he started his career at engine manufacturers Rouart Brothers. He then worked at several other jobs, apparently impatient and unable to settle down (the shortest stay of his career was two hours at Delaunay-Belleville), before arriving at Georges Richard, where he met Jacques Bizet (son of composer Georges Bizet). The pair formed a partnership in 1909 to manufacture his new car design, which became Le Zèbre.

The first model, Type A, was well received and attracted investment from businessmen Émile Akar and Joseph Lamy. Further models were also successful and during World War I they secured contracts to supply the army. Salomon, however, was a hardworking and pragmatic engineer while Bizet was reported to be too easy going and lacking discipline, so it was no surprise that they eventually went their separate ways.

Jules Salomon.

After a brief stay at Charron, Salomon joined André Citroën's new company in charge of designing the new Types A and B models. The smaller Type C, the design of which he had delegated to Edmond Moyet, became very successful and was to have an influence on the Amilcars that followed.

In 1925 Salomon found his power and influence diminished, as the company had adopted the American Budd system of making all-steel bodies, and he left Citroën. Not to be unemployed for long, he was then hired by rival Peugeot, but that only lasted two years when he moved again to Rosengart, where he remained until 1939.

He also found time around 1927 to make a prototype of another light car to be built under his own name. The little two-seat Salomon was based on a Rosengart LR2 chassis and powered by a two-stroke single cylinder engine of 386cc with a basic aluminium body, a curious return to the now out of fashion cyclecar principles. Presumably plans to produce copies never eventuated and the sole prototype, which was not registered until 1931, still exists in a museum in France.

Despite offers of work after peace returned in 1945, Salomon remained retired to pursue other interests. He died on 31 December 1963, in Suresnes.

same time Salomon was becoming frustrated by Bizet's lack of direction for any post-war plans and took a position with Charron responsible for their army contracts. This did not last long, as his discussions with Citroën resulted in Salomon being recruited by the latter in July the same year to head the design office in charge of the new models planned for when peace returned.

In 1919 several changes were made to the management at Le Zèbre; Jacques Bizet resigned as a director though retaining a financial stake in the company now registered as Société Anonyme des Automobiles Le Zèbre, and new management was installed under administrator Albert Hainon, who had been one of their major suppliers since the beginning in 1909. The Type D, another 4-cylinder, this time rated at 8CV, was launched and André Morel was taken on as sales manager for the south of France. Morel had been employed as a test driver at Berliet and brought valuable experience too, but when engineer Edmond Moyet left to join Salomon at Citroën where he had responsibility for the design of the new 5CV Type C, it would soon be the beginning of the end for Le Zèbre. Morel himself would be moving on in early 1921 to what would become Amilcar. Meanwhile, Le Zèbre tried again with the Type Z, the chassis for which were assembled ironically at the Amilcar factory, but sales dwindled and the marque finally closed its doors in 1931 after producing a total of around 9,500 cars since 1909.

Citroën

There was, however, one other engineering company that invested their war profits wisely by entering car manufacture with new ideas and modern designs. André Citroën had ambitious plans. Profiting well from the war, Citroën now had a large well-equipped factory at the Quai de Javel on the banks of the Seine in the west of Paris. At the height of the war, the Quai de Javel factory was turning out more than 35,000 shells every day, staffed with over 12,000 workers. With his previous experience with the Mors company and influenced by his visit to the Ford factory in Detroit in 1913, he decided as early as 1916 that he would enter the automobile business as soon as peace returned. Initial plans were for a larger 18hp model, possibly to be sold as a Mors, to be drawn up by Ernest Artault and Louis Dufresne, who he had poached from Panhard, but this was soon shelved, and that design was sold to Gabriel Voisin as the basis for his new C1 model in 1919. Citroën had a change of heart, reportedly on the advice of his doctor, who reminded him how many lives ordinary cheap cars had saved during the war and, learning from the Ford example, he decided a small practical and reliable car that could be produced in large numbers from the start was what the market wanted. With a smaller 10hp engine designed by Jules Salomon, Citroën came up with the all-new Model A. Announced to the press in March 1919, the first examples left the Quai de Javel factory in May that year, soon establishing the marque as one of France's most successful.

Salmson

On a smaller scale, Salmson had also been a major player in the supply of war materials, making complete aircraft as well as supplying thousands of aircraft engines, and they too entered the car market in 1919, initially building the small British GN cyclecar under licence. We will return to Salmson later.

THE 1920s

Citroën and Peugeot continued to grow their market share with their small-to-medium models, Renault continued to offer a wider range, also sticking with their larger 40CV, while many of the other marques that were slow to adapt to the changing times after the war would be less fortunate and eventually disappear. Others with more modern ideas would soon step up to replace them.

So now the scene is set for the optimism that returned to the French people and a market developed for a new type of small but lively car that would soon populate the roads, and in many cases, the racetracks of the country.

While working for Citroën designing the new 5CV under Salomon, Moyet had also been busy drawing plans for another new car. It is probable he had started this in 1919 or earlier with Salomon for what would be a new model for Le Zèbre, but after moving to Citroën, he continued to work on this secret project in the evenings at home. The new design was for a light car smaller than the Citroën 5CV, with some similarities to the previous Le Zèbre Type C, to be powered by a 4-cylinder side-valve engine; it seems the chassis and engineering drawings were already well advanced by 1920. A commonly repeated story has it that André Morel was introduced to Edmond Moyet at the Excelsior Restaurant in Paris by Voisin dealer Maurice Puech. However, Morel had joined Le Zèbre late in 1918 after the war and other sources suggests Moyet was already working at Le Zèbre at that time and only left to join Salomon at Citroën in 1919, so it is probable that they already knew of each other.[1] Whatever the truth of that meeting, Morel and Moyet discussed the latter's design for a new car and plotted how to get it into production. Morel, an experienced salesman by this time, had ambitions of becoming a racing driver, and Moyet probably also saw some sporting potential in his new machine; it would appear the two got along well.

Morel knew he needed some solid finance to get the project going and presented his case to Akar and Lamy, whom of course he already knew as the backers of Le Zèbre. The pair were impressed by the case presented by Morel and Moyet and agreed to support the project. To finance the new company Akar and Lamy convinced some of the Le Zèbre dealers to join them in the new venture, raising initial capital totalling three million francs. These dealers were represented on the board by M. Dumond of Lyon. The Dumond brothers had a successful garage business and were agents for Delaunay-Belleville, Lorraine-Dietrich, Talbot-Darracq as well as Le Zèbre. The defections of Akar, Lamy and Morel and the loss of several dealers would certainly impact the well-being of Le Zèbre. Further, the new company took over the premises previously occupied by Le Zèbre at 34, Rue du Chemin-Vert to assemble the new Amilcars.

The name 'Amilcar' is thought to be a contorted anagram of the two main partners' names Akar and Lamy; according to motoring historian Paul Yvelin, this was suggested by Voisin agent Maurice Puech. Other theories have said it is a shortened phonetic version of Emil Akar, others have linked it to a play on the name of the great Carthaginian warrior

Hamilcar, father of Hannibal. Whatever the origins of the name the car was initially known during 1921 as the '*Borie Cyclecar*' after the landlord of the small factory in the 11th arrondissement in Paris. The name Amilcar was registered in the Seine Commercial Court on 19 July 1921, but it was not until September that the articles of the company Société Nouvelle pour l'Automobile (SNPA) were published with Akar named as Deputy General Manager and Lamy as Commercial Manager. André Morel had joined, taking the role of Sales Manager for the south, and at some point, in the middle of 1921 Moyet was named Chief Engineer.

The Amilcar was on its way.

JOSEPH LAMY, 1881–1947

Joseph Lamy was born in Courtomer in the Orne department of north-west France on 20 July 1881. He was the eldest son of a family of farmers. The family was poor, and with little prospect of betterment he left for Russia in 1900 in search of work.

He must have had a talent for languages, as he learned Russian in a few months and went on to become a professor of French at the University of Saint Petersburg. He also took up a position as a correspondent for *L'Ouest-Éclair*, a newspaper covering north-west France for which he submitted several reports, including an adventurous trip on the Trans-Siberian Railway to Macedonia and another to Korea.

Upon returning to France in 1908, he became a director of a Monaco taxi company, and the next year he joined Le Zèbre as Commercial Director, also investing some of the starting capital of the company.

In 1921, he formed a partnership with financier Émile Akar to start the new Amilcar company, taking the position of Commercial Manager and later Managing Director. At the same time, he owned a fashionable restaurant and night club on Rue Caumartin, Paris.

Joseph Lamy.

Despite earning great wealth, a salary said to be 300,000 francs in 1925 alone, and moving in society circles, he was not seen to be extravagant and kept in contact with the village where he was born, giving to local charities, and later serving on the municipal council; there is even today a street in Courtomer named after Joseph Lamy.

After he was ousted from Amilcar in 1927, Lamy set up business as a Hudson and Essex dealer until 1935, during which time he also entered the Tour de France Automobile with his old friend André Morel driving.

From 1935 to 1940, Lamy was interested in improving cleaner, less polluting exhaust systems and synthetic fuel (is there nothing new?), all of which caused him to lose money. He was also involved in a project to develop a Brazilian rubber forest at the mouth of the Amazon.

From 1941 to 1945, he created a gasifier business, a common practice in wartime Europe in which wood or charcoal is heated to produce gas as an alternative to rationed petrol. Using the brand '*Le Français*' he was more successful with this project. He died on 3 June 1947, in the 17th arrondissement of Paris after an unknown illness.

ÉMILE AKAR, 1876–1940

Émile Akar.

Émile Akar was born on 27 March 1876, the son of a wealthy Parisian clothes manufacturer. His three brothers were all successful in business and he graduated from the Ecole des Hautes Etudes Commerciales. He married Clémence Cahen (1892–1979) and they had one son, Robert, born in 1911. Akar's father-in-law, M. Albert Cahen, had built up a business from selling packets of coffee on the streets of Paris, creating a coffee roasting and grinding factory and a chain of shops across France under the name 'Planteur de Caïffa'. At some point Émile joined this business and in 1911 he also invested some capital in the Le Zèbre car company.

Before the 1914–18 war Akar also owned a horse-drawn transport company. This had been linked to supplying the coffee shops, but when all horses were requisitioned for the war effort, he established another business repairing military uniforms.

When he met Morel and Moyet to discuss the Amilcar project, he gave them 100,000 francs for the manufacture of two prototypes.

Émile Akar was very fond of luxury and the Parisian social life. A close friend of André Citroën, he was also passionate about shooting and luxury cars, and alongside the inevitable Amilcar, he also owned a Voisin, a Chrysler and a Hispano-Suiza, with a chauffeur on the staff.

At the start of the Amilcar affair, he lived in a small mansion on Rue Berlioz in Paris, but with the success of the Amilcar he moved into a large house on the Rue Jean-Goujon near the Grand Palais. He also owned a country property in Sologne.

When he was ousted from Amilcar in 1927, Émile Akar sold a large part of his property to compensate his creditors and returned to his old businesses and started some new ones, usually successfully.

In April 1936, Akar bought the Château de l'Écluse, in Salbris, Loir-et-Cher near Orléans. During World War II, Akar, being of Jewish descent, fled the Nazi-occupied north, and died in Marseille trying to escape the country on 16 November 1940. In 1941 the wartime Vichy government confiscated the chateau. This was followed by the death of his son Robert two years later without leaving any other heirs.

CHAPTER 2

1921 – THE FIRST AMILCARS

To say the Amilcar was created by the convenient marriage of a design by Edmond Moyet, the persuasive ambitions of Morel with the capital, and the business skills of Emile Akar and Joseph Lamy would be to oversimplify the case. First, there is the conundrum of Edmond Moyet's employment in 1921, for a period certainly in the early part of that year he was working for both Citroën and his future employers at Amilcar. Since joining Jules Salomon on the design of the new Citroën Type A in 1919 (and later he probably had some influence on the Type B which replaced it in June 1921), Moyet alone had been tasked with the design of the Type C, although Salomon probably once again designed the engine. This was to be a small car rated at 5CV that was to prove very popular, with over 80,000 examples sold between 1922 and 1926. The Citroën Type C was launched at the Paris Salon on 6 October 1921, all within the timeframe of the gestation of what was to become the Amilcar CC, which must have kept Moyet busy. The basic design of the engine for the new Amilcar at least was ready first, probably also started by Salomon when still at Le Zèbre, but nevertheless Moyet must have been burning some midnight oil to see both projects through.

EDMOND MOYET, 1893–1954

Edmond Moyet.

Edmond Paul Moyet was born in Toulon on 30 March 1893. Moyet began his career as a draughtsman at Borie & Cie and collaborated with Jules Salomon on cyclecar design for Le Zèbre.

After Salomon went to Citroën in 1917 to head the design department, he recruited Moyet to join him. While Salomon was responsible for the first Citroën models, the small 5CV Type C is credited as the work of Moyet, who worked at the research department in the Rue du Théatre alongside Salomon. The 5CV filled a gap in the market for a small car somewhere between a cyclecar and full-size automobile. It was immediately successful, selling about 80,000 examples between 1922 and 1926.

Moyet left Citroën to take charge as Chief Engineer at Amilcar some time in 1921, which must have been a busy year for him. Both the 5CV and the Amilcar CC were presented to the public for the first time in October 1921 at the Paris Salon.

Moyet left Amilcar in 1934, along with many other staff when Marcel Sée closed the Saint-Denis factory in August of that year, and he returned to work at Citroën taking Marcel Chinon, former head of the drawing office, to start work on the design of what would become the legendary 2CV under Pierre Boulanger and André Lefebvre.

Moyet was granted a few patents, two published on 24 July 1929: FR-661360-A for 'Improvements to the control devices for the rockers and cam valves of internal combustion engines' and FR-661361-A for 'Improvements to internal combustion engines including those fitted in motor vehicles'. Another on 28 February 1934 was published as FR-760670-A for 'Improvements to chassis of vehicles including motor vehicles'.

Moyet died in Paris on 9 November 1954.

Records do not say exactly when Moyet left Citroën, but by the time the new Amilcar appeared at the same Paris Salon in October he was an employee of the new company. Akar and Lamy appear to not have been bothered by taking their respective investments out of Le Zèbre while at the same time poaching their dealers. They must have preferred what they had seen of Morel and Moyet and the design of the new car over the existing situation at Le Zèbre. Similarly, taking over the workshop premises at 34 Rue du Chemin-Vert from the latter did not appear to trouble anyone's conscience. The date of the meeting of Morel and Moyet at the Excelsior restaurant is not recorded, but it was most likely in 1919 with the business partnership agreed and work on the prototype starting in 1920 and the name Amilcar registered by July 1921.

ANDRÉ MOREL, 1884–1961

André Morel.

André Paul Victor Morel was born on 3 August 1884, in Troyes in the Aube department. The family lived nearby in Buchères, but he lost his father at the age of eleven. There were plans for him to be a priest or a butcher, which came to nothing, and he joined a local garage as an apprentice but did not settle and then cycled to Paris by bike finding work as a porter at Les Halles in Paris.

Morel next signed on as an apprentice mechanic with Corre in Levallois. He then cycled to Lyon, but without qualifications he had again to take on menial jobs. Luckily, while working as a used car salesman he was recruited to work at Berliet and was soon chief test driver for their 40hp bus chassis. He must have made a good impression, as he was also taken on as Marius Berliet's chauffeur.

At last, with some experience, he moved back to his native Aube region and in 1911 opened a garage where he became an agent for Berliet and Le Zèbre and started a bus company. The buses were taken by the military for war use but Morel himself was rejected as unfit for combat, so he returned to Berliet where the factory was turned over to making armaments and shells. He tried again and was accepted by the aviation service and soon was a qualified pilot – presumably a good one too, as he was promoted to an officer rank and became a flying instructor.

Peace eventually returned and, on 1 April 1919, Morel was hired by Le Zèbre as sales manager for 40 départements in the south-east of France. There were potential buyers and the marque still had a good reputation, but there were delays with making enough cars. Additionally, as inflation was rampant prices were rising while customers were still waiting for delivery, causing many orders to be cancelled, which was not an easy situation for a sales manager.

Morel also had ambition to get into driving competitively and possibly his first outing was at the Limonest hillclimb on 24 April 1921 in a D type Le Zèbre. His subsequent move to Amilcar is covered elsewhere, and on the circuits he had many successes with the Amilcars, Delages and Voisins without too much pain, the worst injury being burnt feet at the 1926 San Sébastian in the Delage. He also set speed records with Voisin.

When Amilcar finally closed the competition department in 1929, Morel left to work for his old partner Joseph Lamy selling Essex and Hudson cars. Thus, it was inevitable that Morel would start racing these marques with many class victories over the next two years. After a short spell at Minerva, Morel was hired by Talbot as head test driver and later helped with developing the very successful T150C, finishing third (with Jean Prenant) in the Le Mans 24-hour race in 1938. Morel raced again at Le Mans in a 4.5-litre Talbot coupé in 1949 and 1950 and an open-bodied T26GS for the next two years, after which at the age of 68 his family persuaded him to retire from racing.

André Morel died in 1961 in relative obscurity at the age of 77 in Lyon following a short illness, but is now remembered as one of the great racing drivers in his home country. Conflicting records suggest the date of his death was either 17 July or 5 October.

Keen to get going, things moved quickly, recruiting Henri-Georges-Jean Renoult as Technical Director and design staff to work under Chief Engineer Moyet in the drawing office. A significant addition to the team was Marcel Sée, brought in by Akar as Deputy Manager; Sée had already formed a coach-building and upholstery business in partnership with his cousin Gilbert Nataf, which they named Margyl as a contraction of the pair's first names. Marcel Sée would play an important role later in the Amilcar story. In what was thought to be a first for a woman in the automobile industry, Joseph Lamy's wife Thérèse was appointed General Sales Manager. Mechanics and engineers were hired to start building the first three cars under Production Manager Edmond-Louis Delmer. The articles of the parent company Sociéte Nouvelle pour l'Automobile were published by Parisian notary M. Barillot on 29 September 1921. As well as Akar and Lamy, officials included Akar's brother Jean and publisher Michel Calman-Lévy. Initially, the prototypes were called the 'Borie Cyclecar', so one could wonder if the owner of the factory had any financial interest in the new company or possibly this was just a temporary convenience while future plans were still being decided. Whatever the reason for the name, by the time of the Salon in October they were officially launched as the new Amilcar CC – the CC part of the name referring to the cyclecar identity.

The 16th Salon de l'Automobile opened on Thursday, 6 October 1921, and ran for ten days at the Grand Palais, a large glass and steel exhibition hall situated between the Avenue des Champs-Élysées and the River Seine. Opened in 1900, this was home to the annual motor shows from 1910 until 1961 and in the rush of post-war optimism the 1921 Salon was a popular attraction with many new models to tempt the public.

THE AMILCAR CC

Designed to fit the new regulations to qualify as a cyclecar, the first Amilcar was a true sports touring car in miniature with no unnecessary extras, although a customer could order

Amilcar CC bare chassis as shown at the Paris Salon October 1921.

such things as a spare wheel to be fitted after the car had been weighed at under 350kg for tax purposes. Most of the small cyclecar companies that proliferated around Paris at the time were making rather crude machines. Many of them merely assembled a collection of bought-in parts and used proprietary engines from several suppliers, the most common being Anzani, Chapuis-Dornier, the wonderfully named Compagnie Industrielle des Moteurs à Explosion (CIME), Ruby and Société de Construction Automobile Parisienne (SCAP). Briefly after the war, there were many more crude light cars built using military surplus supplies of American Harley-Davidson and Indian V-Twin motorcycle engines. Immediately distancing themselves from such machines Amilcar had planned from the start to make the entire car, save for a few accessories, in house. The basic concept was not too far removed from the previous Le Zèbre, so the Jules Salomon influence was evident, even though he was never an Amilcar employee.

The CC was powered by a simple 4-cylinder engine not too dissimilar to the existing Le Zèbre and new Citroën designs with the same 55mm bore, two-bearing crankshaft and side-valve cylinder head but with a one-piece cast-iron cylinder block and crankcase. The 95mm stroke gave a capacity of 903cc rated at 17hp. This was in unit with the three-speed sliding pinion gearbox and three-plate clutch sharing the same oil as the engine. With no pressurised oil pump fitted, lubrication to the engine components was provided by the flywheel lifting oil up into a reservoir that supplied gravity-fed troughs that fed the big-end and main bearings. This worked well enough as long as a constant oil level was maintained in the sump. The quoted power output was 17hp, although by the French tax system it qualified as a 6CV, the CV being shorthand for '*Chevaux Vapeur*', the archaic nineteenth-century formula for rating the horsepower of steam engines. Cooling was by thermo-syphon with no water pump, effective enough if there was some forward movement providing airflow to the radiator. The radiators were supplied by either Chausson or Gallay and were initially made in one piece so the outer shell was sealed to the core as an outer water tank. These were soon changed to a sealed radiator comprising a core with soldered top and bottom tanks surrounded by a separate nickel-plated shell. Final drive was via a cardan shaft enclosed in a torque tube to the rear axle. This too was a simple design with no differential, which was considered unnecessary due to the narrow 109cm track and bicycle-thin section tyres allowing enough slip when cornering without significant resistance. In fact, it was also an advantage on what were often rough roads of the time, as braking was available on whichever tyre had contact with the surface at any given time. The simple crown wheel was held on to the one-piece axle shaft by a keyway and early cars had straight tooth bevel gears. The rear axle casing comprised a cast aluminium housing with a pair of trumpet casings bolted each side which held the brake backing plates at either end. Braking was by the rear wheels only, with ribbed cast iron drums, which were operated one side by the foot pedal and the other by the hand brake; of course, with no differential both had the same effect on both wheels.

The chassis frame was very basic and was similar in principle to the previous Le Zèbre design with two channel section rails open ended at the rear and tapering towards the front with three crossmembers and a wheelbase of 2.31 metres. The quarter-elliptic springs at the rear extended back from the ends of the rails and those at the front hung from brackets outside the frame rails, their forward end being attached to the top of the front axle. The latter, on the earliest models, had a U-section pressed steel centre section reinforced by a timber insert with castings riveted at either end supporting the kingpins and stub axles. The steering box was cast bronze with worm and sector gears bolted to the right-side chassis rail with the column supported by a simple bearing at the firewall to which was also bolted the gravity-feed petrol tank. The steel brackets supporting the firewall also had four arms extending rearward to hold the plain flat dashboard, which held a simple plate for the lighting and magneto switches. As was common practice, some accessory parts were sourced from specialist suppliers; Bleriot, Ducellier and RB (Robert Bosch) supplying magnetos; acetylene lighting was standard equipment or optional electric lights came from Bleriot and Marchal, in which case a battery and generator was fitted too. Wire wheels with splined hubs came from Rudge-Whitworth or RAF, fitted with 700mm by 80mm beaded edge tyres. Friction disc shock absorbers from either Hartford or Repusseau were fitted at both ends. A single bronze sidedraught Solex carburettor fed the fuel, and radiators came from Chausson or Gallay. Instruments where fitted came from Jaeger or OS but were generally not included in the first year of the CC. The steering column was on the right as was still common in France at the time and the three pedals consisted of the brake on the right, a small accelerator in the centre and the clutch on the left. A simple choke pull closed a flat disc across the throttle of the Solex carburettor and there was no starter motor on the early cars, the driver having to use the usual handle mounted centrally below the radiator after having remembered to prime the carburettor and switch the magneto on.

The three Amilcar CC models shown on Stand 21 had bodywork made by Duval. This has been previously reported to be a convenience simply because they were based in the same street, but although both addresses were at a Rue du

Duval Carrossier body plate clearly shows the Boulogne-sur-Seine address.

Chemin-Vert, they were in fact two different streets; Amilcar were based in the 11th arrondissement near the Bastille and Duval at number 12 of another Rue du Chemin-Vert, eight kilometres west in Boulogne-sur-Seine.[(2)]

However, the connection was made. Amilcar would continue to use Duval as their preferred coachbuilder for some time, although bare chassis were also supplied for dealers and customers to have finished to their own tastes. One of the three at the Salon wore closed coupé-type coachwork, but this was not put into production; it probably also exceeded the maximum weight for a cyclecar of 350kg, which was apparently the target market for the newcomer.

The standard bodywork supplied initially was the 'Touriste' style, a basic two-seater with a single door on the left side, provision being made for the spare wheel to be mounted on the right. Simple mudguards and running boards were fitted and a top speed of 80km/h (50mph) was claimed. Priced at 9,200 francs, it was even cheaper than the Peugeot Quadrilette. The public were impressed as were the press and favourable reviews ensured orders were taken at the Salon and in the next few weeks. This must have been encouraging for the new company and in their optimism by November they had appointed Munch & Oblin of Avenue Alphand in the 16th arrondissement as their Paris agents and Lancia and Voisin dealer W.L. Stewart & Company of 26, Albemarle Street, London W1, as their English agent. This may have been a little premature, however, as although deliveries were planned to start in November there were delays in getting a production line organised, with the first cars not reaching customers until the end of the year.

AMILCAR STARTS RACING

On 23 October, soon after the Salon, the ambitious André Morel entered a speed trial on the road between Chères and Anse near Lyon and won his class for the flying kilometre at an average speed over 90km/h. He did this without the knowledge of Akar and Lamy, using one of the first cars he had taken to show the Dumond brothers in Lyon. Lamy was initially unimpressed with Morel's efforts – he may have even been unaware – but after a second victory on 19 February 1922, in the Forest of Marly near Versailles, he and Akar agreed there could be some benefit to be gained from the publicity generated by competitive results. Morel had entered three cars for the Union Motorcycle Française Endurance Trial to be driven by Mestivier, Minchin, one of the first customers, and Munch, of Paris agents Munch & Oblin. The race was open to motorcycles, sidecar combinations and cyclecars. It was conducted over 35 laps of a 7-kilometre circuit and run as a regularity trial, meaning each lap had to be within the same time. Some drivers had to slow down and check their stopwatches if they were going too fast to make sure they received no penalties. Of the 68 starters, Munch came joint 1st with no penalties, with Minchin 11th and Mestivier 13th respectively, delayed by stops for minor repairs.

An official Competition Department was immediately set up under Morel's leadership, assisted by Marius Mestivier the chief test driver at the workshop, the pair both driving in events, supported by Mestivier's brother Maurice. Another chassis tester Pierre Chan – known as 'Chanu' – became assistant to Moyet, race mechanics Burden and Fratissier were recruited from the production line and the salesman for the northern areas, Maurice Boutmy, joined them as reserve driver. The mechanics rode with the drivers to assist with running repairs, as required

An early advertisement for the Amilcar CC.

Amilcar dealer Munch at the Endurance Trial in the Marly Forest, February 1922.

A happy *Amilcariste* in an early model.

by the rules of the time. Using covered trucks which included a mobile workshop, the thoroughly prepared cars were transported to the various event locations. Engine modifications consisted of enlarging and polishing inlet and exhaust ports, larger valves, double valve springs and reprofiled camshafts. The drivers made their own way in standard touring Amilcars.

The successes that soon followed would be a great help in promoting the Amilcar name.

A VERY EARLY CC IN THE NETHERLANDS

This early CC was said to have been built in France in 1921 and exported to England where the car was first registered on 11 August 1922, with licence plate OK 4223 in the name of Bryan Fenion. Given the delay before it was registered it could have been a 1922 model, but whichever date is true it is certainly a very early example. The car then changed owners seven times, remaining in England until 2018 when it was bought by its eighth owner in the Netherlands by Jos Cox. The bodywork was restored replacing both the timber frame and the aluminium panels.

Typical of the first series of CC, it has the pressed steel U-section front axle with wooden reinforcement and the early type rear axle with the cast centre section and the aluminium cover. This was the basic cyclecar CC that weighed in at 350kg; the electric lighting would have been added later.

Another early CC belongs to Jos Cox in the Netherlands.

Typical pointed tail bodywork on Jos Cox's CC.

Although they were driving on the right, many French marques continued with right-hand drive until after World War II.

AN EARLY CC SURVIVES IN AUSTRALIA

Owned by Neil Heilbrunn of New South Wales, this CC has engine number 2806. It is thought it was sold new through T.D. Chapman, the Sydney agent, to a doctor from the Lake Macquarie area. The original two-seat body was made by E.E. Agate of Summer Hill, Sydney, but has been completely rebuilt. It is equipped with original Bleriot headlamps and a Bleriot dashboard switchplate.

It claims to be a 1921 model, but it was unlikely any reached Australia so early in production. The engine number (if the original) would date it to 1922 or 1923, but it does have the pressed steel front axle with the wood insert.

ABOVE: Neil Heilbrunn's Amilcar CC has Australian bodywork...

...now nicely restored it sees regular use.

ABOVE: **Unusually for a CC it has useful boot space.**

The engine plate of this CC shows number 2806.

CHAPTER 3

1922 – COMPETITION SUCCESSES AND THE NEW MODELS

Back at the drawing office on Rue du Chemin-Vert, Moyet was at work designing the next new models to be launched at the Paris Salon on 5 October. While the CC had already been a significant improvement over what had previously been accepted from a cyclecar, the success of the 5CV Type C Citroën had shown there was a strong market for small, economical but better-equipped cars, even if it meant paying the higher tax for exceeding the weight limit of the cyclecar class.

THE NEXT NEW MODELS

Some manufacturers continued providing basic and crudely engineered cyclecars for which there was still a small and dwindling demand, but Amilcar decided to move gradually upmarket. Moyet had by now recruited a couple of his former colleagues from Citroën, Maurice Dubois and Emmanuel Cohen, and work began on the next new cars.

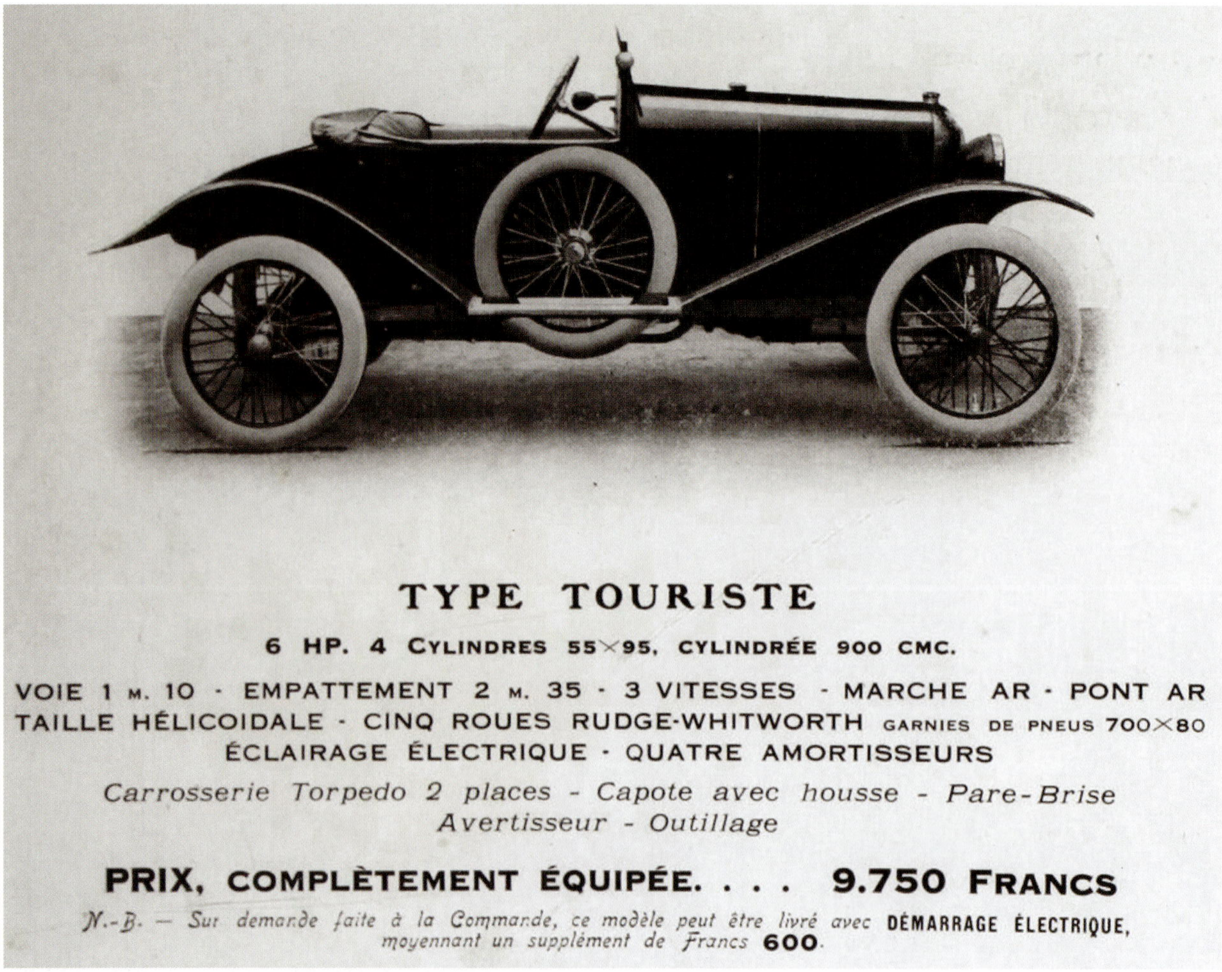

Advertisement for a CC with 'Touriste' body.

This roadster has the distinctive pointed tail profile.

The CC itself continued until 1925; later improvements included a new drop-forged solid front axle, quieter spiral bevel gears in the rear axle and the fitting of electric lighting as standard (acetylene lamps were no longer available), which then required a dynamo and battery, and thus equipped it was logical to then add an electric starter. The 'Touriste' two-seater remained the standard body offered, but there was now an optional drophead convertible in the catalogue.

These and the choices of more stylish bodies available for the customer who ordered a bare chassis meant they no longer met the maximum 350kg cyclecar limit and were now classified as voiturettes. Dumond in Lyon ordered 50 chassis to be fitted with locally made bodies, and the La Phocéenne boat-building company at 38, Avenue du Prado in Marseille offered a stylish 'Skiff' design comprising pointed tail body of longitudinal varnished mahogany strips accompanied by 'Papillon' (butterfly) mudguards and a polished aluminium bonnet.

The next new Amilcar launched at the 1922 Paris Salon was the CV; although it seems this was only a brief stop-gap between models, it was a combination of a CC chassis

A 1922 Amilcar CC Roadster, with optional electric lighting.

with an engine bored out to 57mm, giving a capacity of 985cc putting out 18hp. It was usually supplied with the pointed tail Bordino type body and made an attractive small sporty car for the amateur competitor. There was another one-off model shown, which was a modified CC with a larger engine of 1130cc named the FF. This was built for Morel and Mestivier to race but was never put into production and was probably kept at the Competition Department and duly modified again or the parts used for competition.

The standard engine was further bored out to 58mm, retaining the 95mm stroke for a capacity of 1004cc and this in 22hp form was fitted to the other new model, the C4.

Exceeding the cyclecar weight limit of 350kg, this new voiturette had a longer 2.45-metre wheelbase chassis designed to offer a wider choice of bodywork and became a strong seller, remaining in the range until 1929 with several detail changes along the way.

The CV did not last long on the catalogue and, with further improvements, the engine was replaced by the 1004cc unit from the C4 with an improved 23hp at 3,000rpm. The difference was due to altered cam timing and, with a new drop-forged front axle replacing the previous pressed steel item, it became the CS by the time of the following year's Salon. The CS used a similar chassis frame to the CC with a short extension to the rear of the chassis rails to support a new sporting body style. The car was known as the 'Petit Sport', featuring the now fashionable pointed tail and the staggered seating where the passenger seat was positioned a little behind to keep within the narrow design of the body, yet allowing enough elbow room for the driver. It was offered with either cycle type mudguards or more often sweeping one-piece mudguards combined with short running boards and pressed from a uniform flat section shape; this style acquired the nickname 'gutter guards'.

There was also a CS3 listed – basically a CS with a third seat fitted behind in the pointed tail – although the best-known of these is probably the skiff-bodied version by La Phocéenne.

As if that was not enough the prototype chassis of a new larger 10CV model to be called the E Type was shown at the Salon to be available for sale in 1923.[3]

Thérèse and the sales staff were busy again at the Salon and business was booming.

CH. DUVAL CARROSSIER

Charles Duval established his coachbuilding business, Ch. Duval Carrossier, in 1921 at 12, Rue du Chemin-Vert at Boulogne-sur-Seine in the south-west of Paris, an area crowded with many of the new factories large and small that were dedicated to the growing French automobile industry. Contrary to what had been written about the two being neighbours[2], the similarity of the address to the premises occupied by Amilcar from 1921 to 1925 is purely coincidental; the latter was in the 11th arrondissement near the Bastille.

Duval supplied the bodies for all the standard catalogued Amilcar models until 1926, when Amilcar were able to expand their Saint Denis premises to build complete cars in house. Chassis were of course, in the French tradition, available to customers to have their own preferred 'carrosserie' supply alternative designs.

The best-known of the Amilcar/Duval collaboration are the sporty models from the 'Petit Sport' and 'Grand Sport' range on CS, CGS and CGSs chassis.

Duval continued to supply Amilcar with bodies for the Sport models and expanded their customer base, creating stylish bodies on chassis from most of the French marques and several American imports, particularly known for sporty coupés. In the late 1920s, Duval moved to 93, Rue Thiers and then 86, Rue du Dôme – both also in Boulogne-sur-Seine – but, as with many such coachbuilders, Duval suffered from a drop in demand during the depression years and did not see out the 1930s, being declared bankrupt in 1939.

Charles Duval.

Advertisement for a 'Type Sport' CV.

Amilcar dealers were appearing all over France; the location of this one is unknown.

This CV is on display at the Musée Automobile de Vendée at Talmont-Saint-Hilaire, France.

The sporty Amilcar CV had a larger engine than the CC, but was later fitted with the C4 engine and became the CS.

Several early Amilcars lined up outside a dealer's garage in Charleville.

AMILCAR SHINES IN COMPETITION

1922 was a good year for Amilcar, with some early successes in competition and the introduction of new improved models.

The year saw a significant growth in interest in racing and speed events and while most weekends saw the team competing somewhere, they were even sometimes in two places at once; Morel often in the south, Mestivier racing in the Parisian area, and Boutmy who was from Amiens, often racing in the north, where he was also the sales agent. Rules at some events called for touring cars that were fitted with standard mudguards, lights and roadgoing equipment, while other racing events allowed all unnecessary accessories to be discarded in the interest of saving weight, sometimes with the driver sitting on a bare chassis. Moyet took responsibility for what could, or could not, be permitted according to the rules.

After the February event at Marly the official competition department moved up a gear to take racing seriously and entered events across the country. Morel took a lightweight CC type to the hillclimb at Limonest, which was fitted with a longer stroke engine of 1100cc, averaging 73km/h on the 3.7km climb to win the under 1500cc class. This sporting model was later shown at the 1922 Salon as the 'Type FF Grand Sport', but it seems none were made for sale.

Morel then entered the race for cyclecars organised by the Moto Club de Lyon on 21 May at Saint-André-de-Corcy, where he finished second behind a Spidos driven by Vassiaux, the constructor of these lightweight racers made in Lyon.

The first major success was at the Bol d'Or, a 24-hour race held over the weekend of 27–28 May 1922, or rather two separate races, the first open to motorcycles with sidecars with another race for cyclecars starting on the Sunday and finishing on Monday. Showing incredible stamina driving over rough roads for 24 hours, 38-year-old Morel won, completing 283 laps of the 5.1km circuit at an average speed of 60.447km/h (37.5mph), nine laps ahead of the second placed Salmson of Robert Benoist. Mestivier finished seventh, fifth in the 1100cc class, with 264 laps completed. The other official team car driven by Fardeau failed to finish, as did a fourth CC privately entered by José Scaron, the Amilcar agent for Le Havre who was accompanied by another factory mechanic, Van Parys. This was to be the start of the close-fought battles between Amilcar and Salmson that would continue through the following years, even continuing today in historic events as a friendly rivalry.

Mestivier left, and Minchin, at the Endurance Trial in the Marly Forest, February 1922.

André Morel before the start of the Bol d'Or in May 1922.

THE BOL D'OR

The start appears to be chaotic, with large crowds close to the action.

The original Bol d'Or race was organised by the Association des Anciens Motorcyclistes Militaires, a club for ex-army dispatch riders. Their President Eugene Mauve was also a manufacturer of cyclecars under the Elfe, Elfe-Anzani and Mauve brands between 1919 and 1925. Mauve donated a prize of an old, gilded fruit bowl – the Bol d'Or – that stood about a metre high, but of course the publicity that followed for any victor was worth far more. The first event was a race for motorcycles, and automobiles limited to 1100cc engine capacity, run over a triangular route of dirt roads between Clichy-sous-Bois, Livry-Gargan and Vaujours to the north-east of Paris; only one driver or rider was allowed, although there was a requirement for either a passenger or an extra 60kg (132lb) ballast to be carried in the cyclecars.

For 1923, the Bol d'Or moved to a more suitable circuit using roads around the Forest Saint-Germain, moving again to Fontainebleu in 1927 until World War II. It was revived in 1947 but in the later years run as a 24-hour race solely for motorcycles. It was held at variously Linas-Montlhéry, Le Mans, Magny-Cours and Circuit Paul Ricard. Prior to 1953 only one rider per machine was permitted, although today the rules stipulate that three riders share each bike.

Morel then recorded a speed of 120km/h (75mph) at the flying kilometre of Lyon trial in June with his car now fitted for the first time with a Point Bordino-style body; this description applied to the new trend for racing bodies that tapered to a pointed tail, named after Pietro Bordino, who raced a FIAT with a similar streamlined body. This would become a common feature of the new CS model and subsequent sporting Amilcars. July saw the team score a pair of victories on the same day; Boutmy won his class at the Crochat hillclimb south of Limoges, matched by another win for Morel at the Val de Suzon hillclimb near Dijon.

Boulogne-sur-Mer hosted a busy meeting organised by the Automobile Club du Nord over four days from 27 to 30 July including various races, sprints and hillclimbs as well as a *concours d'élégance*. The Thursday started with a 3km race in heavy rain, in which Morel won the 1100cc class. He followed that with a victory in the standing kilometre and a second in the 500 metre hillclimb. These combined results meant Morel was classified first overall with Boutmy finishing third. After the *concours d'élégance* on the Friday, the main event for the Saturday was the Grand Prix de Boulogne des Cyclecars et Petite Voitures to be run over twelve laps of a 37km route on country roads around Boulogne. This was expected to be another close encounter fought by the rival Amilcar and Salmson teams.

Of the seventeen starters, ten were in the 1100cc class including four Salmsons and the three team Amilcars crewed by Morel with Chanu as riding mechanic, Marius Mestivier with Jérôme Marcandanti, and Boutmy was accompanied by Crespel. Although it had stopped raining the roads used were narrow, hilly and twisty and in an attempt to avoid any trouble at the start the cars were sent off at one-minute intervals. Passing would still be difficult, which may have been why the Salmsons set a blistering pace straight away with Ramon Bueno clocking 96km/h (60mph) and then increasing that in the following laps. Morel was out early with a big-end failure followed by Mestivier on lap two with a similar problem, but Boutmy kept up the chase. Going into the third lap Bueno was pushing too hard and rolled his Salmson, damaging the car but not himself. Boutmy then made a mistake a lap later, skidding into a tree tearing off the back axle before crashing into a second tree, this time with more serious consequences suffering cuts and bruises to himself while poor Crespel had a fractured skull. When the doctor and priest arrived Boutmy was able to return to his hotel, but the unconscious Crespel was given the last rites and taken off to the Saint-Louis Hospital where he underwent various procedures while in a coma for three days. Luckily, he eventually made a good recovery after spending eighteen months in convalescence, before returning to assist Maurice Dubois in the drawing office and then left the company to take on the Amilcar agency at Le Mans. The race was won by Desvaux in a Salmson, with only six of the seventeen starters still running. Embarrassed to be beaten by Salmson, Amilcar put out a statement that the engine failures were due to a late switch of oil brands, but the truth was that the new experimental aluminium connecting rods were not strong enough. Not wanting to scare potential customers, these were subsequently replaced with tubular steel ones with white-metal babbit bearings. Such rushed development and testing ideas in the field was common in those days and new parts were quickly proven durable or otherwise; Amilcar found that out the hard way again when trialling new magnesium pistons.

August was busy with three hillclimbs, at the famous 22km run up Mont Ventoux on 6 August followed by Laffrey near Grenoble on 20 August and a short 1km hillclimb at Gometz-le-Châtel, 25 kilometres south-west of Paris, on 27 August. The Amilcars did not feature significantly in the results that month, the cyclecar classes being dominated by Sénéchals and three-wheel Morgans.

The next major event was the Cyclecar Grand Prix at Le Mans on 17 September. Organised jointly by the Automobile Club de l'Ouest (ACO) and the Union Motocycliste de France (UMF) the race was to be run over 22 laps of the 17.26km circuit of public roads, which would be the same route used for the following year's first running of the Le Man 24-hour race. The circuit was in better condition than most of the public roads used for racing at the time as Georges Durand, secretary of the ACO, had been pressuring government to improve roads in the area and most of the route chosen had recently been resurfaced. Amilcar entered three cars for Morel, Mestivier and Fratissier, who was standing in for Boutmy, who was still recovering from his injuries sustained at Boulogne. The cars had standard chassis with the pressed steel and wood front axle replaced by a stronger tubular steel unit. Engines were well prepared at the factory as usual with the new tubular connecting rods and improved camshafts. Salmson of course turned out in strength with three cars for Robert Benoist, Ramon Bueno and Lucien Desvaux. The four-hour race was run in heavy rain and the three Salmsons led away with a lone EHP in front of the Amilcar trio all lapping close together at over 90km/h (56mph), which increased to over 100km/h (62mph) on the second lap. The order changed with pit stops and, with Bueno crashing out, the chequered flag saw Benoist win, followed by Desvaux with the Amilcars of Fratissier and Morel third and fourth after Mestivier had retired with mechanical failure. Salmson may have had the upper hand in these recent competitions, but nevertheless Morel and Amilcar were crowned 1922 Speed Champion of France and Constructors Champion of France respectively in the 1100cc class, taking the title from what were now their closest rivals. This was mainly because Salmson had missed the qualifying Grand Prix du Moto Club de Lyon back in May, preferring instead to contest the Grand Prix of San Sebastian the same weekend.

The following week the two teams fought a close battle again at the Circuit des Routes Pavées; an endurance event for sports cars in Pont-à-Marcq in the Nord department south-east of Lille organised by the Club National d'Encouragement au Sport, the Automobile Club du Nord and the Moto-Club du Nord and the motoring newspaper *L'Auto*. The route covered a lap of 13km over paved roads surfaced with cobble stones typical of the area. A tough competition designed to test the suspension and general ruggedness of the cars, it was run to a handicap system with varying distances according to the classes and minimum lap times. The 1100cc class ran over nineteen laps covering 247km (153 miles) followed by a 500-metre sprint from a standing start. The Salmson of Desvaux narrowly beat Morel's Amilcar, one minute separating them after nearly five hours racing, but Morel won the sprint by a large margin, making him the overall winner.

A week later at the Gaillon hillclimb on 1 October, Benoist's Salmson won the 1100cc cyclecar class with Mestivier fourth and Morel fifth, but Fratissier took victory in the 1100cc Touring Car class.

Although the more experienced Salmson team were usually faster, the first year of competition had been good for Amilcar and the ensuing publicity had been good for sales. By now there were many customers who were buying Amilcars to compete in events around the country, and their reputation was also spreading outside of France.

CHAPTER 4

1923 – NEW MODELS, MORE RACING

In what had always been a busy drawing office, work had already begun on the new larger 10CV E Type model. Sources say this model first appeared at the Paris Salon in October 1922 to be available for sale in 1923.[3] It was significant for the introduction of the new four-wheel braking system designed by Edmond Moyet with help from his fellow ex-Citroën colleagues Dubois and Cohen. However, in such a competitive industry it does seem strange that Amilcar already had the front brake system on display at the Salon in 1922 when the patent was not applied for until a year later, or possibly as Moyet had previously been issued a patent in Belgium, he thought his design was safe from being copied. It is possible that in fact it was not unveiled until later, or that the brakes on the show car were not the final working system.

Whichever is the correct date, it is usually referred to as being available from 1923 and was replaced by the J-Type at the end of 1925. The E-Type featured an engine designed around the existing block but enlarged to 1486cc with a bore and stroke of 65mm by 112mm mated to a four-speed gearbox fitted to a new 3-metre wheelbase chassis fitted with the new four-wheel brakes and a spiral bevel rear axle with a differential. Suspension was by semi-elliptics at the front and cantilevered rear springs controlled by Hartford friction dampers. It was listed fitted with an open 4/5 seat tourer body and also supplied as a bare chassis, so some E-Type Amilcars had closed coachwork and other styles.

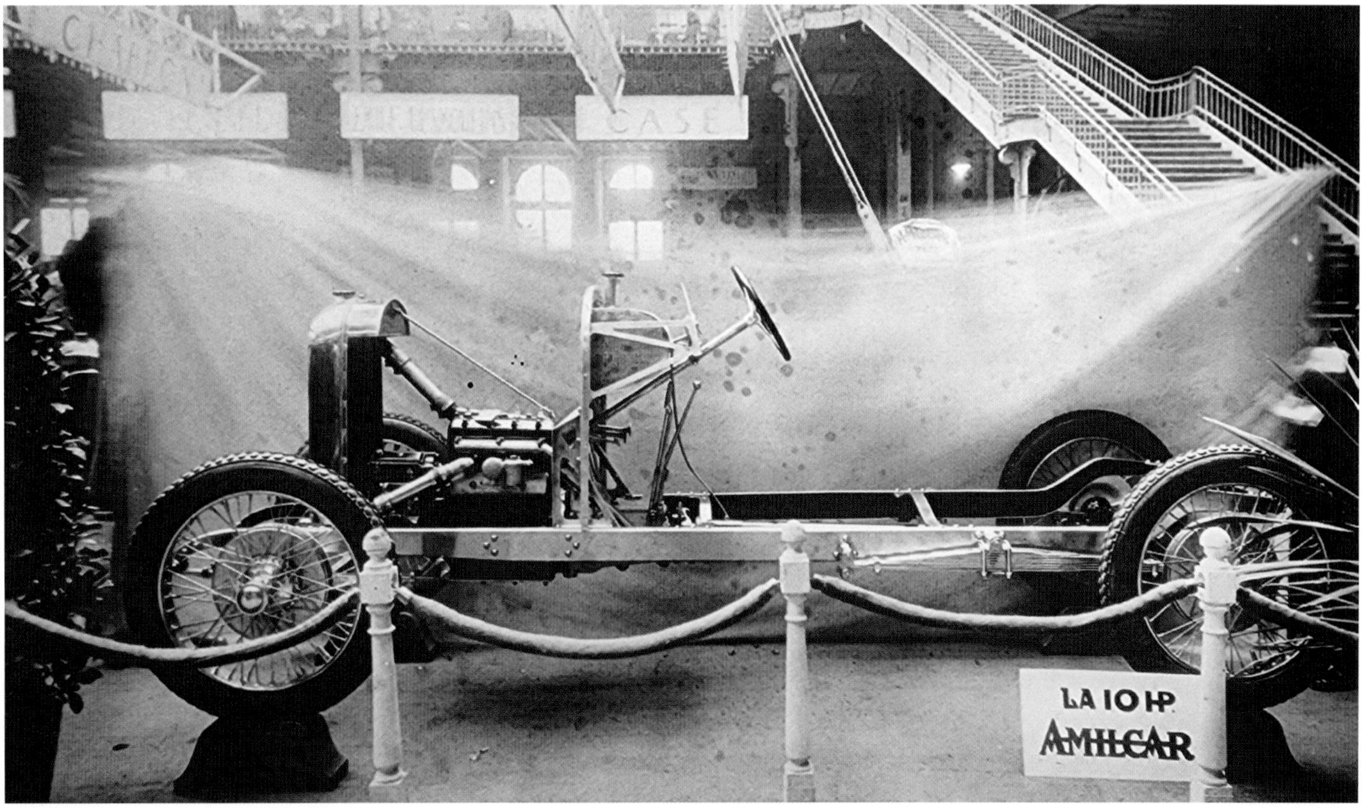

The E-Type 10CV chassis as shown at the Paris Salon, October 1922.

A standard Tourer body on the E-Type chassis.

The only known photograph of an E-Type Tourer in Australia.

THE AMILCAR FRONT BRAKES

A major improvement introduced on the new E-Type unveiled at the 1922 Paris Salon and fitted to the CGS the next year was the new front brake system designed by Moyet with help from his fellow ex-Citroën colleagues Dubois and Cohen.

Four-wheel braking was a relatively new aid to drivers in the early 1920s, with many manufacturers coming up with their own answers to the problem of how to equalise braking effort across the front axle. Cable-operated brakes could be made to work with the inner cable pulling an actuating lever or cam with the outer cable casing anchored to, and swivelling with, the backing plate attached to the hub and spindle. These were probably better than nothing but only just, the effort required at the pedal was considerable and as cables would stretch with use they could never be adjusted exactly for equal braking at all four corners.

Hydraulic brakes were still a fairly new concept and yet to be proved to be as reliable as a fully mechanical system. Some had been experimenting as far back as the previous century, but Malcolm Loughead (who later changed his name to Lockheed) patented hydraulic brakes in 1917. Duesenberg had already been using them on their racing cars and was the first car manufacturer credited with fitting them to a production car in 1921. Amilcar's four-shoe arrangement for rear brakes as fitted to the C4 was a clever design that can still be made to work effectively and these came in for much praise from road test reports in car magazines of the day (see Chapter 15). Certainly, their capability was enhanced as the Amilcars were relatively light weight compared to the average passenger car, but increasing speeds and the large number of cars on the road by this time meant hazards were everywhere and better braking was needed.

It has long been said 'racing improves the breed' and this was demonstrated by the victory of Chenard & Walcker at Le Mans in 1923. To race around that circuit for 24 hours requiring speed on the long straights and the ability to quickly reduce speeds to safely get round the corners, the combination of a powerful 3-litre engine and reliable four-wheel brakes was a winning formula. Even the humble Charles Montier who brought a modified Ford Model T home in 14th place noticed the difference and vowed to return with superior braking next year. This he achieved by fitting the new front brake system patented by Henri Perrot.

On leaving Brasier, Perrot had joined Argyll in Scotland and along with John Meredith Rubury had patented a cable-operated four-wheel braking system as far back as 1910. This used a system controlled by both the foot pedal and handbrake lever. Henri Perrot continued to refine his braking designs, and it was improved enough by the 1920s to be adopted by many manufacturers including Delage and Talbot and later Renault. The Perrot front brakes employed a small shaft with cardan joints at each end allowing the shaft to act on the cam that operated the movement of the brake shoes whatever the angle of the front wheel in relation to the chassis.

The Perrot brakes were manufactured by Établissement Piganeau & Cie of Clichy and marketed widely with period advertisements showing a complete front axle assembly presumably available in various sizes to suit different cars. These assemblies, and variations thereof, were used widely by Amilcar's competitors, including B.N.C., Lombard and Salmson. A meeting with Perrot and American industrialist Vincent Bendix led to the formation of the Bendix-Perrot Brake Co which became the Bendix Corporation when Bendix bought the patents in 1924.

All of this would not have been noticed by Moyet, who went to work on his own ideas for a system of front-wheel braking that cleverly used a rod that was fitted inside the kingpin, meaning whatever the angle of the steering the pressure to each front wheel would be equal. Actuated by the brake pedal, a thin metal strap was connected to a small lever, which in turn pulled a short arm that swivelled on a shaft that was mounted to the front axle. The other end of this arm pushed the lower end of the rod in the centre of the kingpin in an upward direction. The upper end of this rod, in turn, pushed against another rotating lever that was connected to the cam inside the brake drum which pushed the shoes against the drum. This description may not be easy to understand but when combined with the patent drawings, or better, the photos of the complete system, it should become clearer.

The patent was applied for by the Société Nouvelle pour l'Automobile (SNPA) on 2 October 1923 and granted on 16 May 1924. Moyet had already been granted a patent in Belgium in 1922, but given this new system was again patented a year later it may be that the earlier patent was for a different design or only part of what was eventually used. It appears historically that no other car company took up the patent, although Alfa Romeo did use a similar design in the 1920s.

Amilcar consequently used this system on all models from the E-Type of 1923 through to the M-Type of 1934, with the exception of the 1932 5CV, which had cable-operated brakes. The later Pégase and Compound models were fitted with Bendix brakes.

This was Amilcar's first attempt to move into the growing medium-size market sector to compete with Citroën, Mathis and Peugeot, but may have been a step too far for such a new marque best known so far for cyclecars, and the limited manufacturing capacity at Rue du Chemin-Vert would have been a handicap to competitive pricing compared to the big name manufacturers who could produce cars in much larger numbers. Curiously, at the same time this model was also built for and sold as a Le Zèbre 10CV 'License Amilcar'.

As if that was not enough to keep the factory busy, Moyet was working on another sports car, the CGS or 'Grand Sport'. Officially rated as a 7CV voiturette, first shown at the Paris Salon on 4 October 1923, this was to become one of the most popular of the sporting Amilcars, incorporating many improvements developed from the lessons learned in competition over the previous year. One major step was the adoption of the new brake system for the front wheels, which had already been seen on the E-Type.

Sales were going well with the CC still popular in the cyclecar class, but there was no let up with development of the existing models and work went ahead on improving the C4 and CS, which soon also became popular sellers. If we accept that the CC name meant Cyclecar, the C4 kept the C prefix but the 4 represented the seating for four. It is probable that the V in the CV name stood for Vitesse, French for speed, and the S of the CS was for Sport. Such is the mix of Amilcar nomenclature.

A very pretty *conduite intérieure* coupé on a C4 chassis.

1923 Amilcar C4 in a French museum. Note the neat way of mounting the spare wheel.

The author's complete rolling chassis on its way home to be built as a replica of a C4 with Grand Sport body.

A 1923 Amilcar CS now restored and attending rallies in France.

Always popular in Australia, this CS was on the centenary rally in Renmark, South Australia.

For the C4 the factory offered open or closed cars with two, three or four seats, panelled with metal, wood or fabric skins; some of these were made by Amilcar, many more by Duval, but by now more of the established independent coachbuilders were also catering for the new style of small voiturettes. There was even a small delivery van listed as the 'Petite Livraison'. The rear axle was redesigned with a banjo-type casing and spiral bevel gears but still no differential. The brakes were also improved with a four-shoe arrangement fitted inside larger finned drums. There were a pair of shoes each side for the foot pedal and another pair for the handbrake lever utilising a simple adjustment whereby a large wingnut equalised the tension on the connecting rods to each brake shoe actuating lever. This system was very effective on what was still a small light car.

The CS continued as the sportier choice and remained on the catalogue until 1925. One significant sale occurred when a young English customer visited Paris and took home a CS with the intention of competing at Brooklands. We will return to more about him later.

Another Australian Amilcar, this time a C4, also on the centenary rally.

A very nice rear end. Even in Australia *Amilcaristes* sometimes have to dress for cold weather.

An Amilcar C4 owned by Detlef Kayser in Germany.

The typical skiff body was built in the style of those made by La Phocéenne.

Front view shows the distinctive 'Papillon' wings.

The pointed tail is like the prow of a small timber boat known as a skiff.

This 1924 Amilcar CC was sold by Brightwell's Auctions.

The Amilcar CC shows off its pointed tail.

The narrow cockpit has a typically sparsely equipped early dashboard.

This 1924 CC has engine number 4886.

COMPETITION CONTINUES

Throughout 1923 Amilcars were seen competing across France, of which the major events were the following (there are more results listed in the Competition Results appendix).

The Paris-Nice race, officially titled 'Le Critérium International de Tourisme Paris-Nice', was a four-day event starting on 17 February followed by a 500-metre sprint on the Promenade des Anglais and a 500-metre hillclimb. Morel's win created more headlines for Amilcar, although this time Salmson had not entered.

The rivalry between Amilcar and Salmson was renewed on 25 March at the Concours d'Endurance de l'UMF at Malmaison near Paris and, although this time Morel was unlucky to crash out, Mestivier took joint victory with two Salmsons and a Sénéchal.

Fratissier ready for the Bol d'Or, 20 May 1923.

Morel and Mestivier also lined up for the Bol d'Or.

The team returned to the Bol d'Or on 20 May, this time held on a circuit in the forest of Saint-Germain. Three cars were entered for Fratissier, Mestivier and Morel. The cars were clothed in identical flat aluminium panelled bodywork proudly carrying the 'Champion France of Speed 1922' tricolor rosette. This time Salmson was also there with three cars so the battle was truly on. Unfortunately, it was not to be an Amilcar victory again, with Mestivier and Morel retiring with mechanical problems and after delays for repairs Fratissier could only manage fourth behind the Salmsons of Desvaux, Benoist and Casse.

The 1923 24 Hours of Le Mans, officially known as the *Grand Prix d'Endurance de 24 Heures*, took place a week later on 26–27 May 1923. Among an entry of 33 cars representing twenty manufacturers, eighteen of these came from France along with a pair of Belgian Excelsiors and a British Bentley. The race was made more difficult by heavy rain, hail and strong winds. Maurice Boutmy shared his Amilcar CV as a private entry with Jérôme Marcandanti to race in the 1100cc class against a pair of Salmsons and two of the air-cooled S.A.R.A.s. The apparent winners were René Léonard and André Lagache in a Chenard & Walcker, but as this was in fact the first round of a three-year series counting towards the Rudge-Whitworth Triennial Cup, the overall victor would not be known until 1925. Each class was given a target number of laps, but this proved to be a long way short of what most finishers achieved and the Salmson of Desvaux and Casse which managed 98 laps took the lead in the 1100cc class and was classified 12th with Boutmy and Marcandanti's Amilcar 18th.

There were a few more victories for Morel in regional hill-climb events, but meanwhile the factory was rushing to build a pair of new exciting racing models designed specifically for speed events and due to make their debut at the Grand Prix de Cyclecars at Montargis in the Loiret department south

THE LE MANS 24-HOUR RACE

This legendary event continues today for cars ranging from almost off-the-shelf production sports cars to no-expense-spared hi-tech prototypes designed just for this race driven by an assortment of top professionals and wealthy amateurs. But it was originally planned as a test of endurance for what at the time were standard road cars and during the period when Amilcars would have been eligible the rules were very different.

The victorious Chenard & Walcker team at the first Le Mans 24-hour race in 1923.

The endurance race was first run in May 1923 on a 17.26km (10.7 miles) course laid out on the public roads around the town. Organised by Charles Faroux and George Durand under the authority of the Automobile Club de l'Ouest it was intended as a trial of reliability of cars and components, especially the still new and fragile lighting systems. The final regulations for the event were not completed until February 1923.

The requirements in the early days for so-called 'touring cars' included some type of weather protection and the cars had to run, for a specified minimum time at least, with rudimentary folding tops, have mudguards, running boards, a horn, at least one door and of course, lights. These rules gradually changed over the years, but the cars entered in 1923 at least resembled something seen daily on the roads. Initially, all cars with engines over 1100cc had to have four seats, but by 1930 the limit for two-seaters was raised to 1.5 litres. Minimum distances were also specified according to engine size, and every car had to meet a certain ratio of their minimum distance at the six-, twelve- and eighteen-hour marks or face disqualification. The ratios were 80 per cent, 85 per cent and 90 per cent respectively. The minimum distance after 24 hours for the 1100cc class was a fairly lenient 920km (572 miles), which required an average speed of 38.33km/h (23.8mph).

The vehicle had to carry 60kg (132lb) lead ballast for each passenger space aside from the driver. A maximum of two drivers were allowed and they alone could replenish the fluids, petrol, oil and water. There were also rules about carrying tools and spares and many other small details were added down the years such that by 1939 the rule book had grown to 44 pages.

The organisers hoped manufacturers would commit to the race for three years so the sponsor, wheel company Rudge-Whitworth, put up a trophy for the manufacturer whose car had completed the furthest distance in 24 hours over three consecutive years, meaning there was not exactly a winner until 1925. An odd quirk of the 1923 event was that it was the weekend that France changed their clocks to 'Summer Time' and at 11 o'clock it instantly became midnight, so although the race started at 4pm on the Saturday it finished at 5pm the next day.

PIERRE BALIAN'S BOL D'OR CC REPLICA

Pierre Balian from Paris has restored one of the earliest CCs as a replica of the car that Morel raced in the Bol d'Or of 1923. The chassis was originally from a CS. With the build number 464 it was probably made early in 1922. The engine block casting does not have the later modification for the fitment of a starter motor but it has been bored out to 58mm with new pistons fitted. The body was constructed by Pierre on the balcony of his apartment in Paris with views of the Eiffel Tower. It was later fitted to the restored chassis in another workshop.

Pierre Balian's recreation of one of the 1923 Bol d'Or entries.

Pierre constructed the body frame on his balcony within sight of the Eiffel Tower.

The car nears completion in Pierre's workshop.

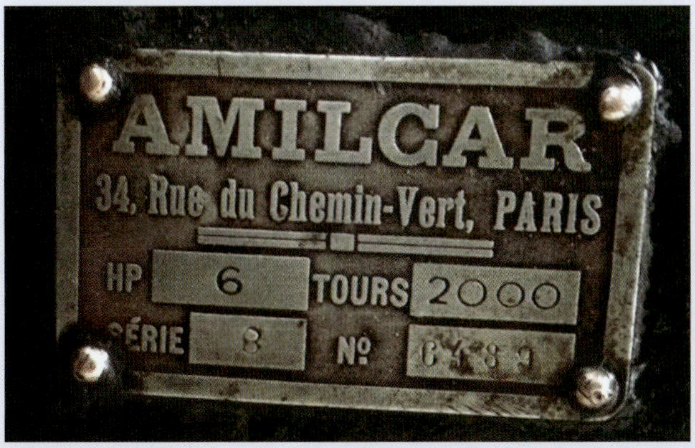

The engine plate has number 6489.

Pierre even got to drive it at a vintage meeting at Montlhéry.

of Paris. These prototypes were known as Tandems as the new narrow, and therefore aerodynamically more efficient, bodies positioned the riding mechanic behind the driver (see sidebar). This race did not have the hoped-for results and both Morel and Mestivier retired with mechanical problems, as did Fratissier in a regular touring model.

Returning to Mont Ventoux on 19 August, Morel discarded the bonnet and bodywork to save weight to set a new class record, this even after stopping to change the spark plugs! He had already broken two engines in practising and then had to rig up an extra water tank to allow his mechanic to operate a pump to replenish the boiling radiator while on the move. These men were certainly made of determination and guts.

At the same event a M. Riviera won the 1100cc Touring class, probably driving a CS.

On 30 September, Morel raced a modified CS in the Route Pavées to first in class at an average speed of 69km/h (42.8mph), which was very impressive over such rough roads.

The last outing for the year was the Gaillon hillclimb, where Mestivier took one of the Tandem racers to a class victory. Presumably to avoid competing against each other, Morel entered the 1000cc Touring class, where he finished second behind Sénéchal in one of his eponymous cars.

At the end of the year, the old rivals Salmson had regained the Speed Champion of France title, but the battle for supremacy would continue.

BRIAN CHISHOLM'S 1924 C4

This C4 dates from 1924 and is currently owned by Brian Chisholm of Sydney, New South Wales. His father Graham bought the car in 1978. The Australian Association of Motoring Clubs advise that the car was first registered on 20 December 1924 when sold new through Conn's Motor Engineering of 600, Elizabeth Street, Melbourne and was then sold again in 1956. Unfortunately, little else is known of the history, although it is believed that it spent a great deal of time in Baradine, New South Wales.

Since Graham bought it the ground-up restoration took almost ten years and was completed in February 1988. Upon removal of the body the chassis number was painted on the right-hand chassis rail, which matched the engine and gearbox number. Australian rules dictate a car has to have a chassis number, so the engine number was probably used by the original dealer when the car was first registered. During the restoration great effort was taken to ensure the car was how it would have been rolled out of the factory in 1924.

Brian Chisholm's C4 dates from 1924 and has been in the family since 1978.

Standard dashboard for a 1924 model.

Brian's car as his father found it all those years ago.

The engine and gearbox were rebuilt by Rob Rowe in Grafton. The radiator is the original finned tube. The only concessions to modernisation are brake lights and indicators.

The electrics are six-volt without a generator, so a deep cycle battery is used to run the lighting. Stone mesh guards have been fitted to protect the lights and radiator. The fitted magneto is a Bosch ZA4 with the original RB10/4 carried as a spare. There is a starter motor, which the owner tends not to use as the car is very easy to start on the crank; if she has not fired by the third swing, there is a problem to be tracked down.

With a few short runs to iron out any issues, Graham set out for a major rally in March of 1988. The car was driven from Armidale to Brisbane for the Brisbane to Canberra leg of the rally and upon completion of the rally she was driven back to Armidale; a total distance of 2,400km (1,491 miles). The car completed the run without any significant issues; the magneto was replaced at some point and a flat tyre changed at Gunnedah on the return to Armidale.

When Brian inherited the car, the suspension damper bushes required replacement and there were a few electrical gremlins to resolve before it could be registered again. In September of 2022 he took it to the centenary of Amilcar rally in Renmark, South Australia. It has since been on a couple of club events in the Sydney area.

Somewhere along the line she was christened 'Gigi', a name which he has retained. Gigi is a very pleasant and reliable car making her a joy to drive.

The body was restored as original, with rear-mounted spare.

THE AUTHOR'S 1925 AMILCAR CS

I already had a chassis and parts for a 1924 C4 that needed a lot of work and a new body, but with a lot of other repairs to do on our old house it stayed in the garage hidden under much furniture and junk and was not accessible to work on. This, along with writing two books and my role as President of The Australian Motorlife Museum, meant I was always busy and little was done for two years. When another apparently complete and restored car came up for sale in 2021 my lovely wife said to me: 'you have not got far with that one, why don't you buy a car that is complete that you can drive now?'. I did not need to be asked twice!

When this writer first saw this car it had been advertised as assembled as a CS with a C4 back axle and various parts correct for the time and described as 'fully restored' with a replica of the typical Duval Petit Sport bodywork. It looked nice in the photos and some people in the area who know about Amilcars told me it was a good one, so I bought it in November 2021.

Although it did indeed look very nice, mechanically it was a disaster. On my first attempt to drive it I found there were no brakes, but at least that was a fairly easy fix simply by adjusting the rods to the two pairs of brake shoes so that both the foot pedal and the handbrake

The author's Amilcar CS replica gets used for trips to the beach, weather permitting.

The body on the author's CS is an accurate replica of the Duval style made by Adrian Denman in Australia.

The 1004cc engine has been rebuilt and runs well.

worked fine. Next, I found the maximum speed was 50km/h (31mph), again an easy fix as the throttle was only opening halfway and again a quick adjustment of the actuating rod fixed it. But that threw up a much more serious problem. On the next drive I noticed an alarming vibration when I went past 60km/h (37mph). Investigation back at the workshop revealed someone had fitted a modern caged-type CV joint in place of the old style flexible coupling on the back of the gearbox and the retaining nut had come off turning the bearings inside to shrapnel. Again, a new flexible coupling from the Amilcar Register in the UK and some adjustments corrected that. Other problems were no wiring to the rear lights; when I asked why, the previous owner told me 'I never drove it at night'. Other problems included about 10 degrees of caster, fixed by shims between the front spring and axle, the starter motor seized up, which was replaced by a new one from AES in England, and the steering box had too much wear to adjust satisfactorily, so I replaced it with a better one from my other project car. The suspension was very stiff, so when I removed the Hartford friction shock absorbers, which were locked solid with plastic rather than wooden discs inside, I also found the leaf springs had been painted as one unit, sticking the leaves together. Once they were stripped and reassembled the ride was transformed. Meanwhile, I fitted an electric fan as we do sometimes get delayed in traffic on local roads and it can get quite hot here. I also found, bought, and fitted a second Marchal rear light to match the original one, helping with visibility on busy roads. Finally, I am having fun driving it and I now have enough confidence in the brakes and steering to deal with modern traffic but what appeared to be a bargain buy has cost a lot more in parts and time. Now I have to get back to the C4 project…

The Duval-style body looks just as good from behind.

Typical staggered seating has room for two, but it is a tight squeeze.

Dashboard holds just a clock, ammeter and not-too-reliable speedometer. The GPS was added for accuracy.

CHAPTER 5

1924–25 – GROWTH, A NEW FACTORY AND TRAGEDY

The new CGS was another step forward for Amilcar, although the C4 and the CS remained in the catalogue as cheaper alternatives and continued to sell. The CGS label referred to the C as in the previous models, although by now they were no longer legally cyclecars, and the GS was for Grand Sport. The CGS did cost more, but it had the performance to justify its price and was well put together with a chassis regarded as the best yet in the field, although the engine still gave a little away compared to the Salmson.

Once again, the bore of the 4-cylinder engine was increased, this time to 60mm, the capacity now was 1074cc, still fitting within the 1100cc class for competition and producing a respectable 30hp. The cylinder head was modified with enlarged water passages and improved combustion chambers following the design patented by the well-known English engineer Harry Ricardo and, after the first few were produced, a pressurised oil system was added. It was found that the increase in power combined with a nimble chassis resulted in higher cornering speeds, which in turn meant the splash-feed troughs carrying the oil to the crankshaft were emptied by the lateral forces and caused bearing failure.

The 2.425-metre wheelbase chassis was strengthened by reinforcing the front rails and the addition of dumb irons to carry the new semi-elliptic springs, which were needed to counter the braking forces on the front axle. These were mounted on brackets fixed to the outside of the chassis rails to aid stability. The brake drums were ribbed and larger at the front than the rear, 225mm and 210mm respectively, and the handling was much improved so even with a weight increase to 580kg (1,279lb) it had the performance to match its looks with a top speed of 115km/h (71mph). Some were again sold as bare chassis for customers to have clothed to their preference, but the standard Duval body for the Grand Sport was again a very neat design with the now fashionable pointed tail supplied with either the popular full-length gutter guards or the smaller cycle type, which may have saved a little weight. Of course, other styles were also offered from the Duval catalogue, including a very smart if somewhat claustrophobic coupé. Slightly different versions were made by licensed companies in Austria, Germany and Italy and bare chassis were shipped to other countries (see Chapter 12).

At a concours at the Parc des Princes in Paris, this CS owner looks pleased with himself.

The Dutch agent Peltenberg's stand at the 1924 Amsterdam Motor Show.

Another Amilcar at the Parc des Princes concours; this smiling owner appears to have a CS3.

At the Lisbon Motor Show of 1925, space was at a premium – as shown by Amilcars sharing space with Trojans.

A well-restored CGS on the Australian Amilcar centenary rally.

Another Australian Amilcar CGS. The so-called 'Centenary Rally' in 2022 was in fact a year late due to the COVID-19 pandemic.

Angus Mitchell's much-campaigned CGS wears its scars proudly.

An Amilcar CGS3, also at the Australian Amilcar rally in Renmark, South Australia

The CGS3 shows the third seat in the tail.

The CGS was an immediate success, quickly earning the nickname the 'Poor Man's Bugatti', although with a list price of 17,900 francs against the CS at only 12,700 francs one's definition of poor was surely a matter of interpretation of one's own financial situation.

The most common choice of bodies for the CGS was the Duval 'Grand Sport' type with the pointed tail and staggered seating for two. The early examples were fitted with the one-piece gutter-type mudguards and running boards but later models had the cycle type. Either style had two diagonal bars across the front of the radiator to brace the front mudguards. Of course, the racing versions dispensed with these in the interests of weight-saving. A side-by-side two-seater body was also offered. The radiator wore a more streamlined curved surround, a small change that gave a neater more modern appearance. By the time of the 1924 Paris Salon, which ran for ten days from 2 October, the CGS was joined by the CGS3. This was the same as the CGS using the same 2.425-metre wheelbase with an extension to the rear of the chassis frame carrying a crossmember to support a third passenger seat in the middle of the pointed tail. When bodied with the standard Duval offering the rear half was covered with leathercloth, but as usual some were supplied as bare chassis to have custom coachwork fitted elsewhere. It was highly praised in the

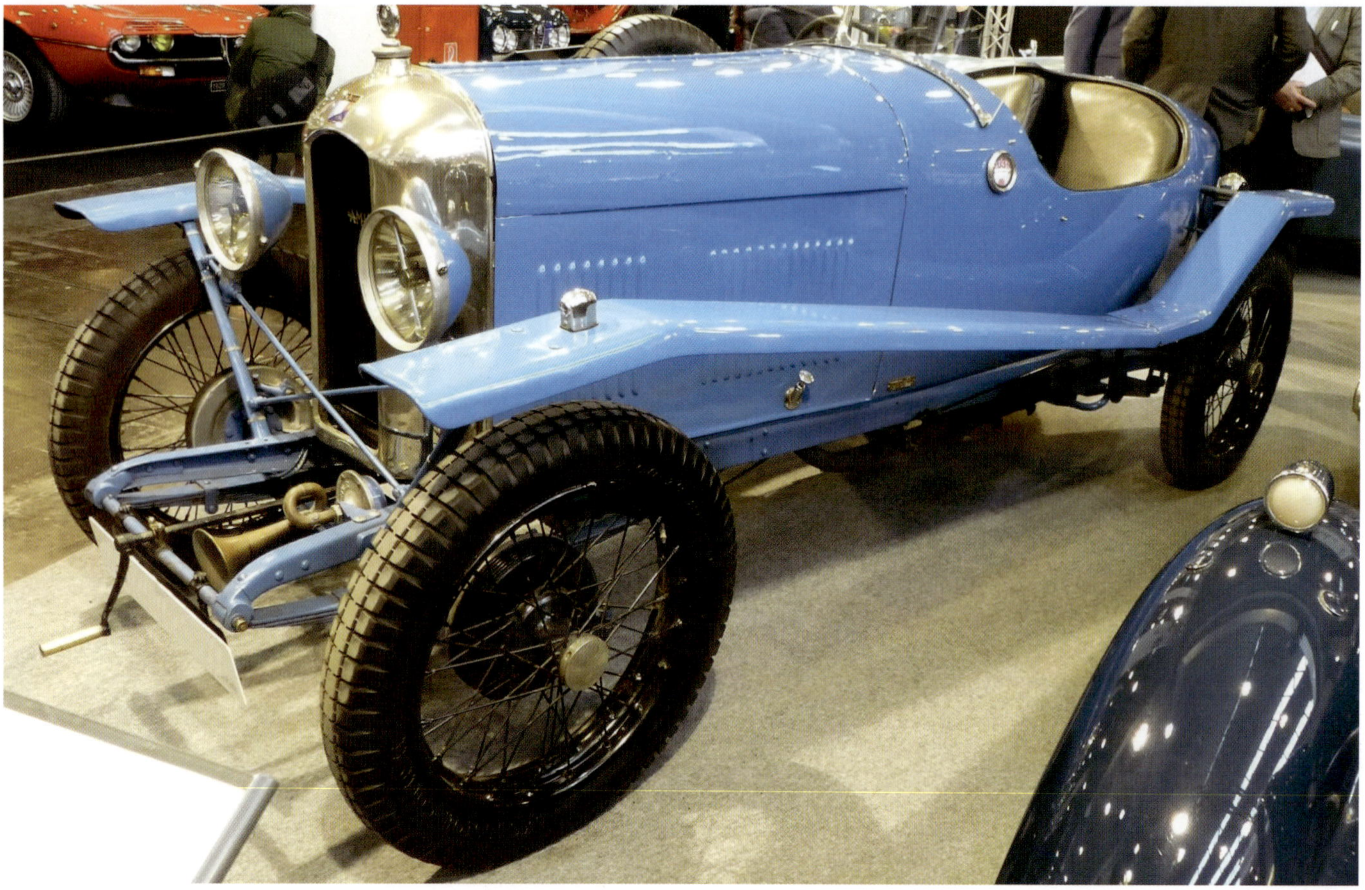

This CGS has the typical 'Gutter Guards' on a Duval Grand Sport body.

Another CGS with cycle-type guards.

press and sales took off. It became a popular option in Britain too, where the choices were somewhat limited between a cheap, basic Morgan or GN or a more expensive Frazer-Nash, although some were starting to get good performance out of modified Austin Sevens. It is thought about 500 of the 3,000 produced were sold there.

Another new model making its debut, in chassis form at least, was the G-Type, which was listed in the catalogue as available from May 1925. The slow selling E-Type was still available with the engine by now enlarged further for the 1924 Salon, the increased bore of 67mm taking it to 1572cc, increasing the power rating from 42hp to 46hp. The E-Type was not a great success if measured by sales; serial numbers indicate 400 of the first type were sold followed by another 100 with the larger 1572cc engine.

The cheaper CC was still in the catalogue and the CS continued to sell well, as did the C4, several of which also went across the English Channel imported by Brooklands racer Vernon Balls. After a brief time operating in Fulham, Balls had set up the official British Amilcar agency at 96, High Holborn, in London, and, strangely at the same time, Boon & Porter were selling C4s from their premises in Castelnau, Barnes, in south-west London, although there is no information about what happened to the previous arrangement with W.L. Stewart & Company of Mayfair. One report says that Boon & Porter were engaged to sell 'unsold' C4s – this could have been unsold stock from W.L. Stewart – and they continued selling them into 1926.

Since 1921, the staff at 34 Rue du Chemin-Vert had grown to 800 and as sales increased, Marcel Sée advised the partners that larger premises were needed. Late in the year, a site at 31 to 47 Rue de la Révolte in the northern suburb of St Denis was purchased. Previously used to make chassis for other firms, the factory was named '*Usine de la Fournaise*' (Factory of the Furnace). At the time of the move, it covered 30,000 square metres, but this was soon enlarged further. Additional investment in new machinery and tooling enabled production to step up to meet demand. As Rue de la Révolte had historically been the old road from Versailles to St Denis and Compiègne skirting the outside of Paris, it latterly acquired several names along its route, and on 26 November 1924 the part of the road where Amilcar was based was renamed Boulevard Anatole France, named after the famous writer who had died a few years previously.

Castings were bought-in from Aubert and Duval, a specialist steel company based in the Auvergne region (now part of the Airbus Group) and some other foundries to the north, but the

This Amilcar CGS3 is well looked after in France.

The CGS3 is either well preserved or restored as original.

new factory was well equipped for most tasks required; boring, turning and drilling and all final machining operations were now carried out in house. There were facilities for nitriding, a heat-treating process to harden the surface of various alloys, nickel plating and polishing. Finished chassis were checked in the running-in department, fitted with special carburettors to run the engines on town gas.

There were sub-assembly departments with staff responsible for building up engines, gearboxes and axles. These were then fitted to a chassis also assembled by an individual mechanic who worked at his own station. This was no Ford-style moving assembly line, but with less space, a choice of models and fewer sales the Amilcar partners probably never aimed for Ford's fast efficiency or envisaged a Citroën-sized ambition. Finished chassis were each road-tested by a test driver before the bodywork was fitted. These drivers carried a logbook to note any problems and on returning to the factory the chassis would be sent to a rectification department for any adjustment or repair.

With a staff of 800, soon to be increased further, the changeover must have been handled efficiently, as sales did not appear to suffer.

In 1925 Moyet was busy again working on several new models that are covered in the next few pages, but meanwhile the existing types were still being improved and updated to meet market demands. While the CC and CS models were phased out, the long-lasting C4 was now given a differential, possibly to standardise production as much as possible but probably needed anyway with the trend towards bigger and wider tyres. The E-Type was updated again and with a few changes the new version was renamed the J-Type. The engine was bored out further to 73mm, giving a capacity of 1878cc, and now had an oil pump for pressurised lubrication. The four-speed transmission was connected by a dry-plate clutch from Ferodo and the fuel tank was moved to the back of the chassis. This was linked to a Weymann Exhausteur feeding fuel to the carburettor by using engine vacuum from the inlet manifold to draw the petrol into a reservoir, which in turn drained to the carburettor. With the wheelbase extended from 2.97 metres to 3.0 metres and the track widened by 13mm to 1.273 metres, a bare chassis weighed in at 800kg. Typically around 1,200kg with a tourer body fitted, it was catalogued as a 10CV model, but the Ministry of Mines rated it at 11CV for tax payable. Amilcar had by now come a long way from their cyclecar origins, but that regulation to allow the lightweights of previous years to pay a lower tax was about to be scrapped anyway; it seemed the public no longer wanted those very basic machines and demanded more comfort and better performance.

THE TEST DRIVERS

When a chassis was completed at the factory it was sent out on the road for testing and troubleshooting before any bodywork was fitted. Covering a fixed route of 100km (62 miles), the test driver carried a logbook to note any faults or adjustments needed, which would then be corrected in a dedicated workshop back at the factory. Pierre Chan was one of the test drivers and he recalled later that there were usually ten taken out each day on test. The chassis carried a crude wooden frame with a cushion for a seat and they made quite a noise with open exhausts. The original route from the Rue du Chemin-Vert headed south through Paris to the Porte d'Italie and then on to Fontainebleu. The drivers, it was said, looked forward to lunch at a favourite restaurant before returning to the factory. Later, after the works had moved to Saint-Denis the test route headed north to Chantilly. The ride was even harsher than it would have been with a complete car, the chassis being much lighter without any bodywork. It would not have been the aim to run the cars to destruction, but running the early splash-lubricated engines flat out on a long straight road at Magny en Vaxin along an alternate route going north-west from Paris may have ended in trouble. Another test driver, later to become another racer, Van Parys called the long stretch of road 'the cemetery of the big end bearings'.

The other new model for 1925, launched at the Paris Salon in October 1924, the G-Type was a more typical Amilcar product. While the E-Type had failed to make much impression in the 10CV sector, Amilcar were better known for their smaller 6 and 7CV light cars, so it made sense to try something in between the sporty cars and the larger tourers. Listed as a 7CV model it used the engine and gearbox of the CGS in a new chassis designed to carry larger touring or sedan bodies. The chassis consisted of two main longitudinal rails with four crossmembers, a wheelbase of 2.6 metres, a banjo rear axle with the now standard differential and a drop forged front axle and four-wheel brakes. A new, larger steering box, still of worm and sector type, was introduced, designed to give a better turning circle and a lighter steering effort. The G-Type was listed in the catalogue at the end of 1924 but did not go into production until midway through 1925, the delay due to the move to the new factory at St Denis. Offered with comfortable four-seat sedan or touring bodies made in house, this was the first model to benefit from the new bodyshop created by the acquisition of the Margyl coachbuilding company. This facility was sited at 41, Quai de Seine in the industrial suburb of Courbevoie. Marcel Sée obviously saw no conflict of interest in Amilcar buying the business he had set up with his cousin Gilbert Nataf, the latter now being appointed as the body shop manager. The closed four-door sedan had a square-lined, fabric-covered body using the licensed Weymann system and retailed at 30,500 francs and the four-door open tourer, with a sportier looking body, also fabric-covered, with windscreen and hood, was listed at 23,500 francs. For 1926, the sedan continued with minor changes, but the tourer received a similarly styled squarer body. Prices had risen by approximately 15 per cent. These two G-Type models were joined by a two-seater with a third passenger 'dickey' seat in the back and a commercial tourer; the latter had a fold-down tailgate and removable back seat. This was a common body type in France combining a regular car with the ability to be used for light delivery duties. Cleverly designed to combine proven mechanicals with a more robust chassis capable of carrying four passengers in comfort at reasonable speed, Amilcar claimed 'Maintenance is little trouble and the performance is equal to that of competing cars of greater capacity'. The G-Type succeeded where the E-Type had failed in establishing Amilcar as a manufacturer of useful family and touring cars, finally gaining a reputation outside of the cyclecar and small sports car sector it had specialised in thus far. The G-Type was discontinued at the end of 1927 after 2,500 had been produced. Other medium-sized models would follow this formula for years to come. As if that was not enough, in 1924 Moyet, and his team in the drawing office, started work on the new 6-cylinder model with which Amilcar hoped to defeat the Salmsons in competition. Testing continued through 1925 making its official debut in October (see Chapter 7).

By the end of 1925 with production in full flow at the new factory, staff numbers had grown to 1,100 with 3,700 cars sold in that year.

AMILCAR IN COMPETITION

For 1924, André Morel and his teammates continued to race and develop the Tandem cars and many private entrants took the new CGS model to the tracks and hillclimbs. The year started well, with Morel scoring class wins at the Allauch hillclimb in January, La Turbie in March and at Planfoy in June. Two weeks later he was back at Le Mans for the 24-hour race. A single CGS was entered by the works for André Morel and Marius Mestivier as the Tandem specials would not meet the requirements of the rules for what were supposed to be fully equipped 'Touring Cars'. The car only completed thirteen laps due to a split oil tank. A second entry for Boutmy and Marcandanti in a CS with a CC body including the necessary windscreen and hood was classified 14th, and last-placed finisher. Luck was not with the Amilcar drivers once again at Le Mans, but they still had a good year on the regular speed events around the country, as did several customers in private entries.

While not suited to the major Grand Prix events, Amilcar concentrated their works efforts on the hillclimbs and speed events that they now excelled at. This may not have made the daily headlines but ensured that their targeted customers,

THE TANDEM RACERS

By the middle of 1923 the cars that had been raced so far with various modifications were becoming tired and the Competition Department was hard at work building a pair of new cars designed purely for racing. Designed by Moyet with some input from Morel, these prototypes were known as the 'Tandem' racers. The narrow bodywork was designed to be more aerodynamically efficient with the driver seated in the centre straddling the gearbox and the mechanic was seated behind the driver with his legs stretched out either side. The chassis was only 50cm (20 inches) across at its widest point and the new front axle with brakes and semi-elliptical springs as soon to be introduced on the CGS and E-Type resulted in a significant improvement in handling.

A faired-in headrest and a smooth underbody covering made the most of the power from the tuned 1100cc engine – a tuned version of that to be fitted to the upcoming CGS. This had been reworked extensively, including a balanced crankshaft with larger journals running in roller bearings, tubular steel connecting rods, a lighter steel flywheel and pressurised oil supplied by an oil pump with a reserve tank to compensate for the increased consumption. Water pumps were also tried. The heads were cast in bronze and aluminium – presumably both were tested – with a higher compression ratio and the ports reworked for better gas flow with larger staggered valves operated by a new camshaft. Running at up to 5,000rpm achieving 47hp, the cars were timed at up to 147km/h (91mph) in testing. Various changes were made to run either as light as possible for speed events and hillclimbs while cars destined for endurance races were designed for reliability over outright speed. Two cars were raced until the next year by Morel and Mestivier, with the first appearance at the Grand Prix de Cyclecars at Montargis blighted by unreliability due to the rushed preparations. Better results would follow at the speed events it was eligible for; at Mont Ventoux in August, Morel set a new class record and Mesitiver won at Gaillon.

In 1924 these special racing versions were further modified. Known as the 'False Tandems', they now had slightly wider bodies allowing the two seats to be almost side by side but slightly staggered to allow the riding mechanic more leg room. Again, with highly-tuned engines they underwent various minor changes through 1924 and 1925, the two almost identical cars differing only in minor details; Mestivier's wearing a smooth panelled bonnet while Morel's had large air vents.

Frontal aspect shows how narrow the 'Tandem' racers were in the interest of streamlining.

It was certainly a tight fit for two in the 'Tandem' cars.

Domenico Gamboni put up a good show at the 1924 Targa Florio around the roads of Sicily.

the amateurs that populated these competitions, would come knocking on the door. During 1924, Amilcar scored 102 first place victories and five world speed records including the flying kilometre at 147.42km/h (91.6mph), some of these in the modified 'False Tandem' racers. Meanwhile, the ambitious Morel did enter a few of the Grands Prix in Delage and Voisin cars when his commitments allowed.

1925 ON THE TRACKS

By 1925, Vernon Balls, along with several other drivers – presumably many of whom were his customers – were getting good results at Brooklands in England. It is likely many of the other amateurs, in France and elsewhere in Europe, who feature in the competition results appendix, were driving a CGS. For the first half of the year, it was business as usual for Morel. Driving the so-called 'False Tandem' racers he won his class, as by now was his habit, in many of the hillclimbs in the south that started the season. The team entered the Bol d'Or with three specially prepared CGS chassis clothed with a light-weight aluminium body. The three cars were painted in a patriotic salute to the French tricolor, red for Mestivier, white for Morel and blue for Chanu, Morel's former riding mechanic. Morel was declared the joint victor by winning the 1100cc Racing class with Doré in a Sénéchal winning the 1100cc Sports class. This was backed up by Chanu in second with Mestivier having retired due to an oil leak after having set a new lap record. Marius Mestivier won in two classes at Château-Thierry in April but an unfortunate tragedy befell the team in June. The Amilcar works only entered one car for the Le Mans 24-hour race this year. The racing department under Moyet had been rushing to develop a variant of the new 6-cylinder racer that was undergoing testing. The Le Mans car would of course have had to have suitable bodywork, two

Joseph Lamy, Emile Akar and André Morel seem to be celebrating another victory.

One of France's female drivers who was often competing in Amilcars was Madame Dupéchez, here posing with her CGS Coupé on the Paris to La Baule rally.

seats, folding hood, lights, mudguards and so on, as required by the regulations, but delays in tuning the engine to run well enough meant this project was shelved. A hurriedly built CGS modified with a CC body including a windscreen and hood was built instead, for Morel and Mestivier.

Disaster struck around eight on the Saturday evening when Mestivier crashed on the Mulsanne straight at full speed. He had hit a kerb and the car turned over, crushing the unfortunate driver. He was killed instantly. First reports blamed a blown tyre or a locked brake causing him to swerve off the road; other sources later claimed that he was struck by a bird, knocking him out, or another theory was that he was operating a hand pump linked to an auxiliary oil tank used to keep the engine topped up, which may have distracted him enough to lose control. This was to be the last time Amilcar entered the Le Mans endurance race.

In July, Morel entered the Grand Prix of Belgium at Spa, which was another 24-hour race, accompanied by the Belgian Charles Libovitch. Driving a CGS, which was one of the Bol d'Or cars with modifications, they were forced to retire. Undeterred, by August he was back to his winning ways at Mont Ventoux and victorious again in October at Gaillon, which was the first outing for the new 6-cylinder CO, which became the most successful of the works racers (see Chapter 7). Many Amilcars were in the hands of various drivers in other countries, notably scoring victories at hillclimbs in Austria, Belgium, Czechoslovakia and Germany. Despite the family tragedy, Maurice Mestivier, brother of the late Marius, was now made head of the competition department.

Meanwhile, pilot, engineer and Land Speed Record breaker, Ernest Eldridge had bought one of the 'Tandem' Amilcar racers and had it rebodied by Duval as a single-seater to race at Montlhéry and elsewhere. A keen advocate of streamlining, he added a faired-in headrest, smooth wheel discs and devised what became known as the 'Eldridge' cowl at the front, which displayed a distinctive narrow opening. This latter part was later offered as an extra from the Duval catalogue, tempting for any would-be 'boy-racer', even though its effect on cooling was questionable. In search of more power than the Amilcar unit could offer, he installed a 1500cc Anzani engine. His first outing at Montlhéry for the Grand Prix d'Ouverture in May 1925 resulted in a tyre failure, but not before he had been timed at 204km/h (127mph). He later raced at Arpajon and set more records at Montlhéry in this car.

A Record Year

The earlier models, the CC, C4 and CS, continued to sell although this would be the last year for the CC. Along with the popular new CGS and the G-Type sales increased again and, despite the interruption of the move to the new factory in 1925, Amilcar's production was some 3,700 cars.

A 1925 Amilcar C4 with aluminium pointed tail bodywork.

The pointed tail was a fashion in the 1920s that could be a problem to reverse-park today.

1925 AMILCAR G-TYPE TOURER

The G-Type utilised a chassis similar to the E-Type, while the engine was a detuned version of that found in the sporting CGS. Many of the G-Type Amilcars sold in Europe wore Weymann fabric coachwork, but cars exported to markets like England (where it was marketed as the 9hp under the RAC rating system) and Australia were often bodied locally, usually as tourers or saloons. The Model G became Amilcar's most popular touring model of the period and a number found their way to Australia when new, sold through local agents like T. D. Chapman of Sydney. This example was sold by Shannons Auctions in Sydney, Australia in 2022.

A handsome G-Type Tourer, one of many that went to Australia.

The G-Type Tourer has generous seating for four.

The G-Type with the hood up looks fairly weather resistant.

1925 G-TYPE SPECIAL

It seems quite a lot of the E- and G-type Amilcars were shipped to Australia and a few still survive. This charming G-Type was given chassis number 70532, as stamped on the front axle. The Australian authorities require a chassis number to enable it to be registered and, as Amilcar did not number the frames, it was normal to identify it by the axle or engine. Found as a bare chassis only in the early 1970s, it was then fitted with a replacement fabric-over-timber-frame sports body. It was later displayed with the collection at the famous Gilltrap's Auto Museum on the Gold Coast in Queensland, and then was sold on to a collector in the area. It was bought by the current owner, Ted Cross, at an auction in 2017. Although not original to the car the bodywork, with grey fabric covering and black mudguards and bonnet over a red frame, certainly looks the part. Previously wearing beaded-edge tyres, it now has a set of new Rudge wire wheels and well-based tyres and with a side-by-side two-seater configuration that fits the G-Type frame well it has an additional third 'Dickey' seat in the rear. Aero screens, a full complement of gauges and a Moto-Meter complete the sporty look for a practical driveable classic.

This G-Type was another Australian import.

A purposeful-looking sporty G-Type roadster in profile.

The fabric-covered body is not original and was rebuilt in a suitable sleek roadster style.

The G-Type used the same engine as the CGS.

A RARE CGS COUPÉ IS RESTORED

Probably a unique survivor, this coupé was made by the carrossier Duval.

One of the rarest versions of the CGS must be the Duval-bodied Coupé seen here. It is not known how many of this model were made, but this is the only known survivor. Of the approximately 3,000 CGS models built between 1924 and 1926 most of course wore the popular two-seat Duval 'Grand Sport' style open bodywork, many of which survive today. Duval also built this small, closed coupé, possibly as a one-off order. While Duval remained the supplier of standard bodies for Amilcars until 1926, the Duval catalogue also offered customers choices of other factory approved variations of mudguards and windscreens. There was also a taller squared off coupé supposedly built by Duval that is seen elsewhere with well-known Amilcar rallyiste Madame Dupéchez – again a rare, if not unique car. However, photos of the type featured here show more than one had been made: a period photo exists of one parked at Brooklands sometime in the 1920s, believed to have belonged to Vernon Balls. Another photo exists of one racing an Austin Seven in Bombay of all places, and *The Light Car & Cyclecar* magazine featured a road test of one in 1926.

The story of this one starts with Edita Morris, the Swedish wife of journalist Ira Victor Morris, who was the son of Ira Nelson Morris, an American diplomat at the embassy in Stockholm. Edita was also a writer best known for 'The Flowers of Hiroshima', a story based on their son's wartime experiences. The couple had a chateau at Nesles-la-Gilberde 60km east of Paris. Ira died in 1972 and Edita in 1988 and it was sometime in between the car was discovered and passed on to a car dealer. The car was eventually advertised for sale in 1995 in *La Vie de l'Auto*, the French weekly magazine. The car did not sell quickly and, thinking the unusual body may have been the reason why, the dealer created a replica open two-seater to replace it, but still wanted to sell the whole lot together.

Detlef Kayser of Berlin had seen the advertisements and, having a bare CGS chassis already, he persuaded the dealer to sell him the coupé body alone. However, when word got out that such a rare car should not leave France, Detlef had to make an arrangement with a friend to buy it on his behalf. Original plates identified the original chassis as 19390 fitted with engine 5754, and it was complete with the Duval coachbuilder's plate and all accessories. However, at some point it had been modified with replacement mudguards, which were not to Detlef's liking, so he replaced them with a set of the correct style as shown in the Brooklands photo. Engine, gearbox, rear axle and brakes were sourced to complete the rolling chassis. The body was restored, with a carpenter making new parts to replace some rotten wood in the frame, and the aluminium panels and Eldridge cowl were straightened out and the body was painted in the colours as described in the *The Light Car & Cyclecar* test as 'dove grey and carnation'. Photos of the remains of the interior were used to recreate the upholstery in black and grey and, finding a standard Amilcar steering wheel would foul against the inside of the door, Detlef had to shorten the spokes and make a new rim of 38cm diameter, probably as it would have had when new. The restoration was finished by 2011 and a chance meeting with the man who had discovered it at the Morris' chateau 30 years before revealed it had been in fairly good running condition at that time. The interior is reportedly a bit cramped, even with the staggered seating common to most sporting CGS Amilcars of the time, and it is fortunate that the two-piece windscreen can be opened for ventilation as the heat from the engine can make it quite warm in there. Detlef, a serial Amilcar collector and restorer, continued driving the car to rallies all over Europe until finally deciding his other Amilcars were more comfortable to drive and passing it on to the Louwman Museum in the Netherlands.

The Duval coupé as it was in the 1980s. It was in quite a dilapidated condition.

By the time Detlef was able to buy it in 1995, the body had deteriorated further to this sad state.

The coupé was restored by Detlef Kayser in Germany. He reports that it is rather claustrophobic inside.

CHAPTER 6

1926–27 – MORE SUCCESS BUT AT A COST

One has to be impressed by Edmond Moyet's continuing efforts to improve the breed. Not one to rest on any laurels, as soon as the CGS showed itself to be a success both in the showroom and on track he started work on the next generation, which turned out to be the best of Amilcar's production models, the CGSs. The 's' was added to denote '*surbaissé*' meaning lowered. The prevailing trends for sports and racing cars were changing fast during this time and, while some ground clearance was desirable for road cars having often to deal with rough roads, there were advantages to be gained in competition by lowering the centre of gravity to improve handling. The example of Bugatti showed the way forward; the earlier, and very successful Types 13, 22 and 23 were starting to show their age, riding high on tall thin tyres, and were totally eclipsed by the all-new lower and wider Type 35 that debuted at the

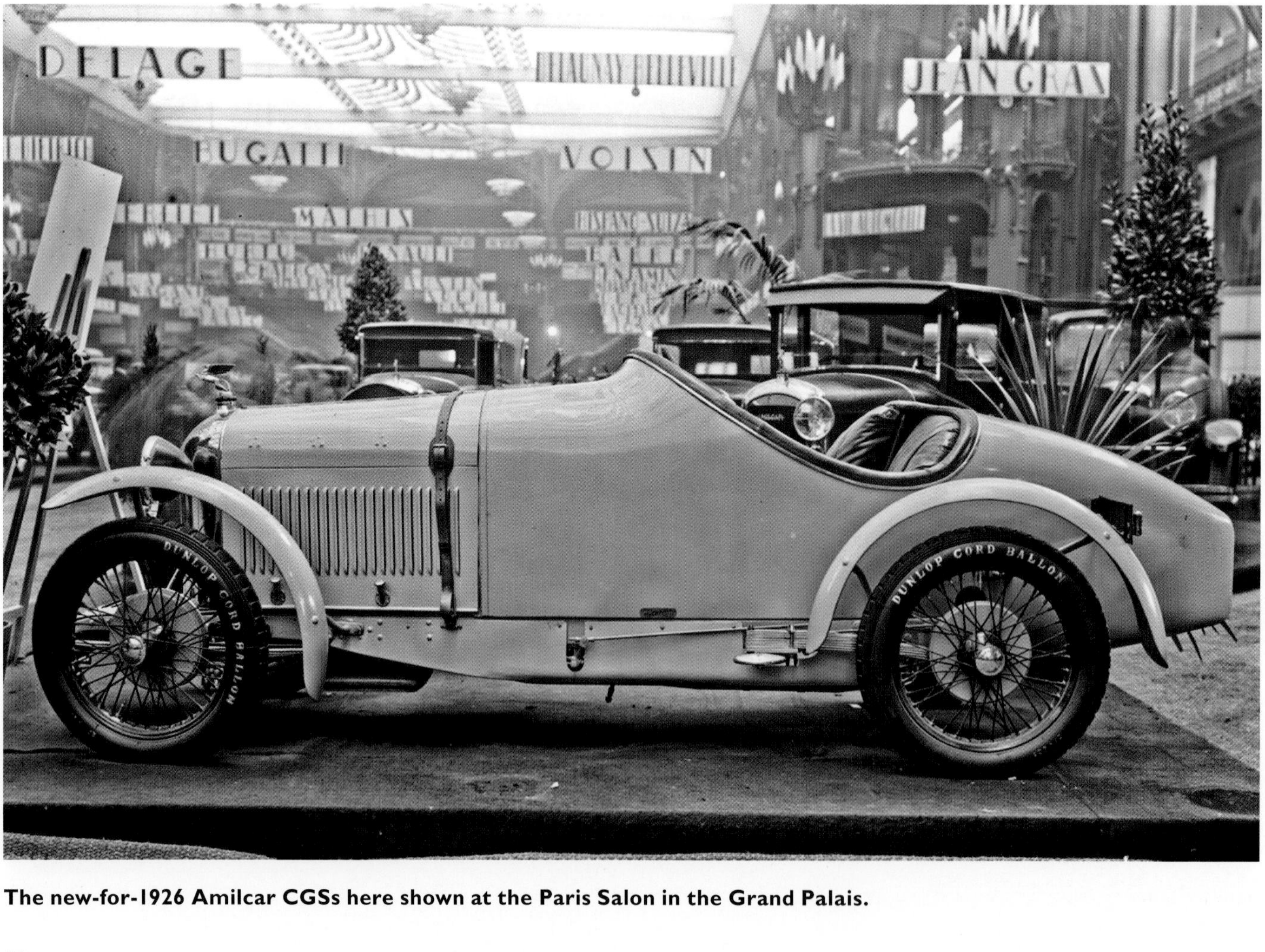

The new-for-1926 Amilcar CGSs here shown at the Paris Salon in the Grand Palais.

A fine Amilcar CGSs gets going at the rally in Australia to celebrate the centenary of Amilcar.

French Grand Prix in 1924. This model dominated its class for many years to come and, although priced well above any sporting Amilcars, must have had an influence on Moyet's thinking.

Unveiled in June 1926 to replace the CGS of which around 3,000 had been sold, the new CGSs used basically the same engine with a larger sump, the oil capacity up from 4 litres to 6, and an improved camshaft.

Now priced at 27,000 francs, the most significant changes were to lower the chassis, which was basically the same as the CGS. This was achieved by shortening the rear part of the chassis rails and the rear spring leaves, the shallower curve of the main leaf having the effect of lowering the rear axle. Thus, the wheelbase was reduced by 10cm to 2.323 metres. The front suspension remained the same but a new axle casting had a deeper drop in the centre. The new larger steering box as introduced on the G-Type was adopted. The radiator was also lowered and fitted with a shorter version of the distinctive rounded cowl introduced on the CGS, which combined with the shorter tapering tail created a sleeker, racy-looking profile. This look was accentuated further with the addition of a short upward curving wind deflector above the

This 1927 CGSs has the distinctive Eldridge cowl.

An anonymous lady poses for a photograph in her Amilcar CGSs.

dashboard in place of a conventional windscreen, although a small example of the latter would be added the following year. Curiously, the rear axle had no differential at first; this was later added with the change to larger tyres in 1928. Braking was improved further with larger drums, now 260mm front and rear. Although Amilcar now had its own in-house body facilities, this department was occupied with the tourer, so sedan offerings on the larger chassis and the CGSs were usually supplied with a Duval body as standard. For British customers, Boon and Porter labelled the new CGSs with its distinctive shorter tail their 'Manx' model; this had no connection with any road races on the Isle of Man, but simply a reference to the breed of cat with no tail.

As the CGSs was developed at a time when the competition department had been concentrating their efforts on the earlier Tandem specials, which in turn were replaced by the new 6-cylinder racers, this model was never used by the works racing team, but it was bought and raced by many amateurs, the ideal weekday road car and weekend racer. In total, 948 examples of the CGSs were produced between 1926 and 1929.

Amateur race driver M. Tamme seems happy with his CGSs.

The C4 continued to sell well and was subject to gradual improvements throughout its lifetime; for 1926 it received the new larger steering box introduced on the G-Type.

Total car production increased to 4,800 in 1926, with an income of over 80 million francs and the staff now totalled

This CGSs with polished aluminium bodywork dates from 1927.

1,200 people, but the recent capital expenditure would soon cause serious financial problems.

Morel, Martin and Balls Collect Trophies

With the new 6-cylinder racing machines well sorted, the year started with André Morel victorious again in his usual hillclimb events in southern France, now joined by former Bignan racer Charles Martin recruited to replace the late Marius Mestivier. The pair were later joined by another customer, Robert Jeuffrain, who would also appear frequently in the results listings. In August the Amilcar dealer for Le Havre, José Scaron, now armed with a C6, made a return to competition winning a sprint at La Baule; he would become another regular winner in the following years. That September Morel, Martin and Jeuffrain went well at the Montlhéry Speed Trials. In October Morel and Martin both won classes at Gaillon and Morel even managed two different class wins at the 17 Tournants hillclimb near Chevreuse, south-west of Paris. Joined by the experienced Belgian Arthur Duray, the works competition department was collecting a trophy somewhere nearly every weekend. Over in England, Vernon Balls and a few of his customers were doing the same at Brooklands while Arthur Legat scored a couple of wins in Belgium. In 1926 alone, Amilcar scored over 100 victories.

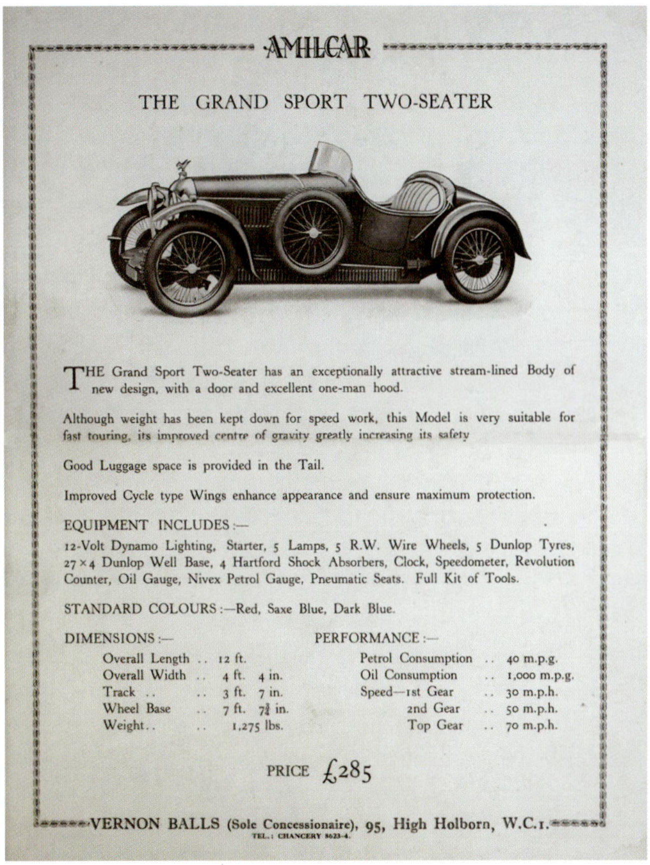

Vernon Balls advertised the CGSs fully equipped for £285.

THE DR OHV CYLINDER HEAD

Henri-Georges-Jean Renoult was Technical Director at Amilcar from the beginning. Having previously worked for Voisin on aero engines and a brief spell at Bugatti, his credentials were impressive. When the Salmson overhead-valve engine seemed to have the better of Amilcar in competition, Renoult proposed designing an overhead-valve head for the Amilcar four. Whether the management thought chasing more performance to equalise the gap to Salmson was not a priority or it was just that resources were needed elsewhere for the constant push for new models is not known, but his idea was shelved. As the timing coincided with Moyet starting work on the 6-cylinder racer, which was planned to give Amilcar a machine to beat all rivals anyway, there was no need to work on improving the four. Renoult took his design to Duval, who agreed a partnership deal to manufacture the cylinder head under the name *Ateliers de Mécanique DR*. The first test on a CGS occurred in late 1924 and the DR overhead-valve head was available to Amilcar owners who wanted to upgrade from the standard side-valve head, with an increase in power of 35 per cent advertised. The cast iron unit was a straight swap, with modifications needed to move the throttle control linkage as the carburettor was now sited on the right side of the engine, as were the spark plugs, the exhaust manifold on the left as before. Longer pushrods replaced the original items and there was an oil pipe added to lubricate the rocker assembly under an aluminium cover. Vernon Balls obtained one in 1925 for his entry in the Junior Car Club 200 at Brooklands in September, although it seems it did not start. Sales were minimal, however, and the DR heads today are very rare, only six examples known to the Amilcar clubs. There had also been mention of a Boon and Porter overhead-valve head, but this may have just been that company advertising the DR unit under their own name.

Renoult later joined another Amilcar design engineer, Edmond-Louis Delmer, and made a straight-8 sports car of their own design named the Robur 8 at Duval's workshop. Only one was built, to be sold to a Mr Alexis, who raced it before selling it in 1950 to Amilcar racer Clément Auguste Martin.

1927: AMILCAR GOES TO MONTE CARLO

Today a household name known as a tough competition, back in the 1920s the Monte Carlo Rally was a challenge for a mixed group of drivers from diverse backgrounds, seen as a test to prove strength and reliability as much as outright speed. In January 1927, with the option of starting from 24 different towns, Marcel Lefebvre-Despeaux, who was the managing director of tuning parts manufacturer Cozette, entered the sixth running of the rally across Europe. He set off from Koenigsberg, a Baltic port city in Prussia (now the Russian city of Kaliningrad) in a G-Type 7CV Amilcar, its 1100cc engine boosted by a Ricardo-designed cylinder head and one of his own company's superchargers. Carrying the registration 9053 X3 and four passengers to cover the 2,643 kilometres (1,642 miles) to Monte Carlo, he had to deal with icy roads in Poland, and heavy fog in the province of East Prussia. The team was further delayed on finally reaching the Mediterranean coast at Cannes, when he had to stop to help at the scene of an accident and go and find an ambulance. His total time for the distance was 74 hours and 10 minutes and the organisers who had devised the formulae for time and distance from each of the starting points thus declared Lefebvre-Despeaux the overall winner. Another outstanding result for Amilcar, which can only have enhanced their reputation for reliability on what was one of the toughest competitive events anywhere.

In a less stressful competition, a few weeks later in February, Lefebvre-Despeaux was invited to drive the car in a novelty scheme to publicise a new – and the first – multi-storey car park in Paris. The Garage de Banville was erected on the site of a former stables owned by the Paris Omnibus Company at the Rue Theodore de Banville in the 17th arrondissement. This was built up to five levels, with two more below street level, linked by a spiral ramp of 600 metres in length, which was used as an indoor hillclimb for the day. In a further coincidence, the new World Champion Robert Benoist, who had dominated the 1927 season

Marcel Lefebvre-Despeaux won the Monte Carlo Rally in this G-Type Weymann-bodied sedan in 1927.

Lefebvre-Despeaux and his crew celebrate the Monte win.

with Delage and was a former foe of the racing Amilcars when he won many races in a Salmson, was now unemployed due to Delage being forced to cancel their racing programme and took a job as sales manager for the new luxury garage business. He entered his Grand Prix Delage and called in several friends and rivals to have a go, including several Bugattis, and of course the Monte Carlo Rally-winning Amilcar of Lefebvre-Despeaux.

There was also a Chenard & Walcker tractor with a trailer carrying 25 people, half a dozen of whom fell off on one of the corners. In the end there was no 'winner' as in the name of safety it was decided no times would be recorded, but for the publicity gained the one and only Banville hillclimb was considered a great success, gaining valuable publicity for the garage and more exposure for the rally-winning Amilcar. The Banville Garage was closed down in 1986 and demolished to make way for an office block.

While many amateurs were still competing in the 4-cylinder cars, it was now the sixes that would dominate the 1100cc classes effectively ending once and for all the rivalry with Salmson.

Soon after the Monte Carlo rally, Lefebvre-Despeaux was invited to climb to the top of the Garage de Banville.

A couple of other Amilcars joined in the pretend hillclimb at the Garage de Banville.

This G-Type has a convertible two-seater body that appears to be in original condition. At the time of writing it was for sale in Italy.

Mounting the spare wheel on the back means there is room for doors on both sides.

What appeared to be a useful boot is instead a rather cramped 'dickey' seat.

A tight-fitting hood and wind-up windows would offer a rare degree of comfort for an early Amilcar.

A RARE CGSs IN THE USA

Not many Amilcars found their way to the USA and this one is one of the most desirable models: a well-restored CGSs, it would be welcome at any of the high-profile concours events that are so popular in America.

An immaculately restored CGSs sold by classic dealer Hymans in the USA.

Quite rare in America, this CGSs must be one of the best.

Staggered seating was intended to give both driver and passenger a bit more elbow room, but they still need to be good friends in this tight space.

The usual bare minimum of necessary equipment in this CGSs.

The left side of the engine shows the Solex carburettor.

The right side is less crowded and is as well presented as the rest of the car.

A purposeful front end, the nickel-plated radiator surround flanked by Marchal headlights.

It looks just as racy from the back, too.

A 1927 CGSs IN THE NETHERLANDS

This CGSs registered in the Netherlands AM-73-70 belongs to Henk Fortgens, who has discovered an interesting history. The original owner is not known and, although some old papers and names came with the car that show it was bought and sold around Sweden since 1927 and was recorded as CKD (completely knocked down) in 1955, it was only with paperwork from 1964-on that Henk has been able to verify a more complete history of ownership. At that time the parts of the dismantled car that came with the engine plate number 41481 were bought by someone else in Sweden for 300 Krona, including another engine 50541, but later the original engine, number 41481 and gearbox were found and bought from a boatyard in the Stockholm area. The still unrestored car was sold again, but once more it remained only as a collection of parts. Henk then bought the Amilcar project in 2005, after it was advertised on PreWarCar, and commenced the restoration. Certainly, various modifications to engine 41481 and its associated gearbox showed evidence of it having been converted for use as a boat engine. Five years later, in 2010, the restored CGSs made its first journey under its own power for at least 50 years, now looking as it should and running well, a credit to Henk and his efforts.

Another resident of the Netherlands is Henk Fortgen's CGSs.

This well-restored CGSs hides its complicated history well.

With engine number 41481, leading Amilcar expert Desmond Peacock dated this as produced around March 1927, and as Amilcars never had chassis numbers Dutch authorites applied car number 18309, stamped on the right dumb iron. The Amilcar Register has since confirmed the numbers are correct for that date. While much of the original beechwood body frame was kept some had to be renewed, and an outstanding repanelling job followed by Gary Pitney of Panelcraft in the UK. It retains all its original Jaeger instruments, Nivex petrol gauge and air pressure pump and Sifam ammeter. The original Ducellier dynamo has been rebuilt and converted to 12 volts and a Magneti Marelli SA4 magneto fires the plugs. A fine example of one of Amilcar's most sought-after models.

Plate has the number of the original engine now reunited with the car.

A well-stocked instrument panel tells Henk everything he needs to know.

One would not think engine number 41481 had a previous nautical career in Sweden.

RICHARD FEWSTER'S AMILCAR CGSs

Richard Fewster's Amilcar is one of the many survivors in South Australia. He first saw his Amilcar from a bus window in 1961, aged 16, when he was travelling from Renmark to Adelaide to stay with an aunt for a break after working on the harvest at the family apricot orchard. The Amilcar was parked on a used car lot and he and his younger brother persuaded his aunt to drive them back to the spot to have another look at this car that had captured his imagination. Finding out the next day the price was $240, Richard managed to arrange a family loan to add to his apricot picking earnings and the car was his. Coincidentally, while the car was being towed back to the aunt's house he was spotted by another Amilcar owner, who admired the car and gave him some details of contacts should he need any help or advice, which would prove useful later. Although looking quite smart, the blue smoke from the tailpipe suggested it was rather tired mechanically. After towing the Amilcar back to Renmark some 260km (162 miles) away, the boys drove it to school a few times before it threw a connecting rod when his mother borrowed it go to the shops, rendering the engine beyond repair. After a delay of a couple of years a replacement was found locally, which sufficed for a while, but as time went on the car spent a few more years in the shed until 1979, when Richard decided it was time for a complete rebuild, which took two years. Every mechanical part was reconditioned, even to the point of having new cogs made for the gearbox. It was apparent by now that the body also needed a professional restoration and the car was returned to the road in 1983. Richard also found out a lot about the history of the car, including the fact that it had been imported with one of the rare DR overhead-valve cylinder heads. He was lucky enough to be given one of the only six known to exist by Desmond Peacock, which is now on the car. The car has since been regularly used on the road and attending rallies in the area where there are many other active Amilcar owners.

Richard has had this car for over 60 years and still enjoys driving it.

This CGSs was one of the participants in the Australian Amilcar centenary rally in Renmark, South Australia.

South Australia registration 987 has been on the car since it was first imported in 1927.

Richard's CGSs has one of the very rare DR OHV cylinder heads.

A near-perfect CGSs looks good from any angle; the Eldridge cowl just adds to the style.

A LATE C4 WITH AN UNUSUAL BODY

This C4 was listed for sale as a 1929 model but with no front brakes, which were added late in 1928; its engine number 8104 is probably earlier. A rare survivor, it still has its original 'Touriste' style two-seater body. It was sold to a new owner in the Netherlands.

Not often seen on a C4 chassis, this one has a smart two-seater 'Touriste'-type body.

The style of the body is very similar to the G-Type shown earlier in this chapter and was probably made at Amilcar's own in-house body department.

A late C4 – though without front brakes, it is probably from before 1928.

It can still be enjoyed as an open two-seater in true Amilcar style when weather allows.

CHAPTER 7

THE 6-CYLINDER CARS

While the growing workforce at Saint-Denis were busy with new models, we have to back-track to another of Moyet's most spectacular designs, which was started in 1924.

Stung by too often coming second to the superiority of the Salmson engine and realising the little Amilcar 'four' had reached the end of any potential development, Akar and Lamy gave Morel the instruction to go ahead with designing a new engine from scratch that would dominate the 1100cc class. While the existing side-valve four was fine for use in the production cars destined for normal road use, the limitations of the two-bearing crankshaft meant the block would not be strong enough for any further increases in power.

Salmson were content to develop their 1087cc 4-cylinder engine. By 1925 the latest version, with a three-bearing crankshaft, twin overhead camshafts and twin-plug heads acquired the moniker 'San Sebastian', after Georges Casse won the Grand Prix of the same name at Lasarte. Although it was thought only 22 of this type of engine were made by Salmson – some for the works racers, some for customers – by no means were all the GSS and GSC Salmsons so equipped. This latest development was said to deliver 55hp, or even 80hp with the addition of a Cozette supercharger. There was also a modified version, some with roller bearing crankshafts used in the works racing GP cars too. All of which was beyond the capabilities of the existing Amilcar engine.

While the rivalry with Salmson continued in the popular 1100cc class, Moyet decided the only way to beat them was to design an all-new, 6-cylinder engine with twin overhead camshafts. Once the necessity of starting a new engine from scratch, primarily to gain the upper hand in competition, was agreed, it seemed logical to go all the way and design a complete racing car rather than try to continue modifying chassis that had been conceived for road use. Edmond Moyet was assisted in this project by Marcel Chinon and Pierre Chan after Maurice Dubois had left to set up his own machining business after a falling out with Moyet. While Chief Engineer Moyet remained in overall charge of the project with Chinon now named as his deputy, the latter took responsibility for the design of the engine, gearbox and supercharger. Chan was given the brief for the chassis, axles, suspension, steering and brakes, with other draughtsmen taking care of the finished drawings and minor details. Starting in the summer of 1924, progress was rapid and by the end of November Marcel Sée announced to the press that Amilcar were about to build six of the new racers aiming to be ready to compete in the summer of the 1925 season. There were hopes it would be ready to run in the Le Mans 24-hour race in mid-June, but this proved too ambitious a target caused by delays with various details, not least tuning the engine to run at full power, combined with the, to be expected, problems of moving to the new factory. A hybrid 'special' based on a CGS was hastily readied for the tragic Le Mans race, while testing of the new '6' continued at Montlhéry. The new CO chassis had 80mm deep curved side members with four riveted crossmembers carrying the suspension, steering and axles of the CGS and a wheelbase of 2.235m (7.3ft) with the front springs being hung outside the frame to lower the ride height. With the engine bolted in place, as was the scuttle-mounted fuel tank, the whole formed a rigid structure. The oil tank was mounted out front between the dumb irons to aid cooling. Testing soon revealed a lack of balance and the fuel tank was moved to above the rear axle to help weight distribution. The narrow aluminium bodywork was still a nominal two-seater, but it was a tight fit for the co-driver mechanic.

The engine was all new, designed specifically for racing with no regard to the mundane daily maintenance that the road cars required. The block and head were cast as one, the advantage being that it eliminated any possible head gasket problems. This 'fixed head' concept was fine for a racing engine with a dedicated team of mechanics to look after it, but it did make machining jobs such as cutting the valve seats more complicated. If a valve later needed replacing it required the complete dismantling of the internals, crankshaft, pistons and so on. In the first examples, the bore and stroke were 55 by 77mm, giving a capacity of 1098cc. The crankshaft had circular webbing and ran in seven bearings, the two end ones being ball-bearing types, the rest on rollers. The 33.5mm diameter valves with an included angle of 100 degrees controlled by concentric springs were driven by two overhead camshafts that were in turn driven by gears at the back of the block. The camshafts too ran in roller bearings. With lightweight connecting rods and aluminium pistons with a five-to-one compression ratio, the whole was designed for maximum revs. The castor oil lubrication was by a dry sump system with a two-stage geared driven pump fed by a 15-litre capacity oil tank located at the front at first, but this was later replaced by a larger 30-litre tank fitted inside the cockpit to the driver's left. Initially producing 75hp in unsupercharged form, further tests increased power to 90hp with an alcohol fuel mixture fed to a Solex side-draught carburettor by a mechanical pump and a Roots-type supercharger driven directly from the front of the crankshaft pressurised the inlet charge. Ignition was supplied by a magneto and the water cooling was fed to a honeycomb radiator by a centrifugal pump. Power was fed to a four-speed and reverse gearbox by a single dry-plate clutch. In the course of development and fine-tuning, different camshaft profiles were tried and the alcohol fuel mix was the subject of further experimentation. These engines produced up to 95hp according to fuel mix and supercharger pressure.

After some preliminary tests at Montlhéry, the car finally made its competition debut at the Gaillon hillclimb in October later that year. André Morel took the 1100cc class victory, beating Mestivier's record by 20km/h. While this put Amilcar ahead of the Salmsons again and of course created much interest, it was reported according to the *Light Car & Cyclecar* of 30 October as '...it is not the intention of its creators to market a 6-cylinder model at present'. This would change later with the introduction of the C6, but for now all efforts were concentrated on keeping ahead of the opposition on the circuits and hillclimbs. To this end, the so-called Racing Shop was renamed the Competition Department, which would take care of building and maintaining the CO and its subsequent variations.

Initially the team drivers were Morel and Charles Martin, later joined by Arthur Duray, who left the works team at the end of 1927, although he would later race privately-entered Amilcars in the 1930s, notably partnered by Jean de Gavardie. Duray was in turn replaced by ex-Talbot driver Jules Moriceau in 1928.

Through 1926 Amilcar dominated the 1100cc class, with Morel first at the Grand Prix de Provence at Miramas signalling a strong season to come. Just 31km (19 miles) south of Paris, a straight and flat, four-and-a-half mile section of the Route Nationale 20 at Arpajon was chosen by the Automobile Club de France as a site suitable for speed trials. In May of that year Morel and Martin shared a CO to take three world records reaching speeds close to 200km/h (124mph). *Cyclecars, Motos*

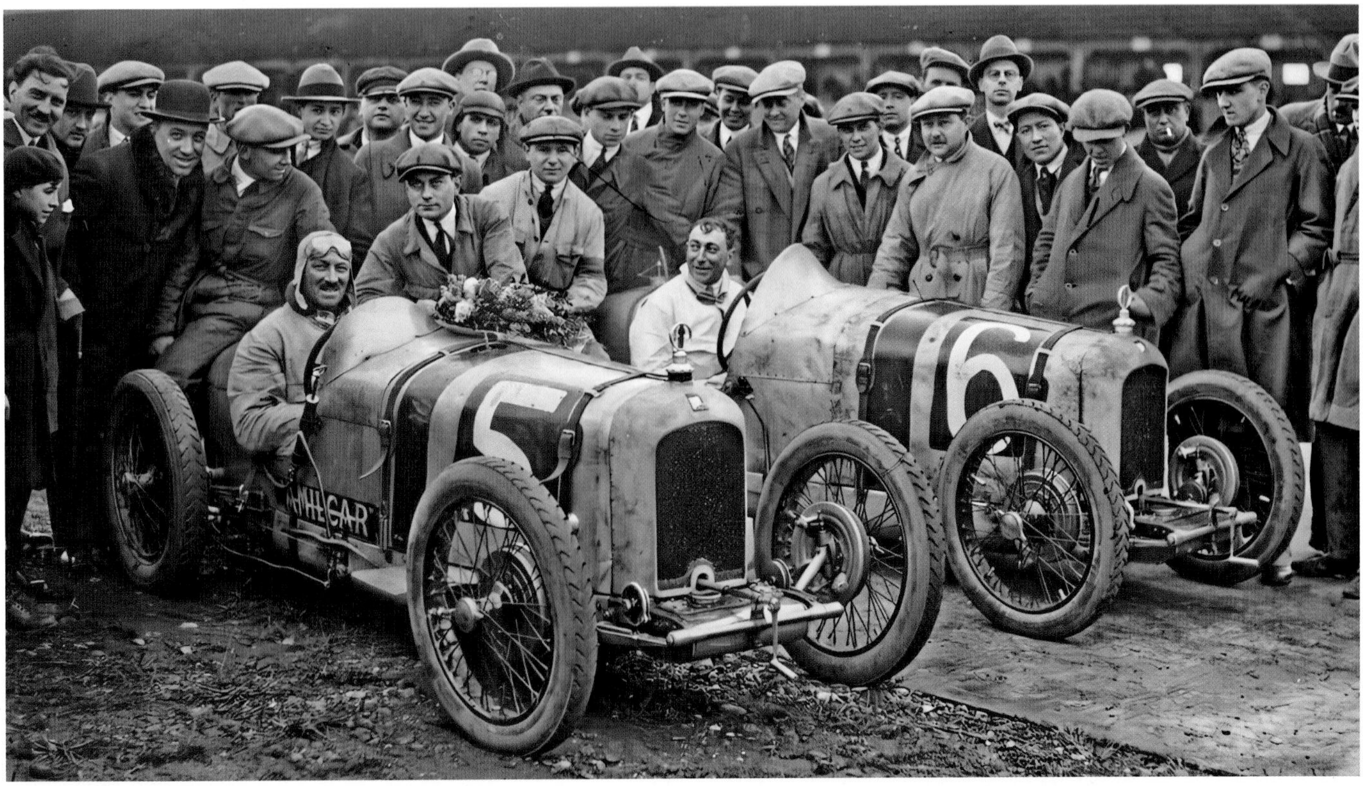

André Morel and Charles Martin finished first and second at the Grand Prix de Provence at the Miramas circuit in March 1926.

In August 1926 Morel took his CO to a class victory at the Klausen hillclimb in Switzerland.

André Morel in his CO again, this time at Montlhéry.

et Voiturettes magazine wrote of the occasion: 'Never in the world have similar speeds been achieved by an 1100cc car, which is all to the honour of Amilcar.' Returning to Miramas the next month, a CO modified into a short wheelbase racer was entered in the GP de l'ACF for Duray alongside two COs for Martin and Morel, but all three succumbed to valve spring failure unable to sustain the 6,500rpm engine speeds required. This problem was soon resolved by fitting springs from a different supplier and Morel took victory at Monza in the Italian Voiturette Grand Prix with Duray coming second. Three weeks later saw Martin victorious at the Junior Car Club's 200 Mile race at Brooklands, followed home by Duray and Morel.

If the Competition Department was not busy enough in 1926, they also turned out a short-lived single seater with a narrow, streamlined body. To save weight, no front brakes were fitted and the driver sat low straddling the gearbox and driveline. The stiff rear springs needed to allow the driveshaft to clear the floor made for a very stiff ride and it jumped around over bumps, which affected the handling. When Morel expressed a dislike to it at a test at Montlhéry, the experimental machine was dismantled and the parts reused in other cars.

When in 1927 the rule requiring a riding mechanic was cancelled, the design team set about designing the offset CO. A new narrower chassis was created with deeper side members, modified front suspension and a wheelbase of 2.19 metres, which had the driver seated to the right with the engine offset to the left so that the gearbox and driveshaft passed the driver's legs on the left allowing a lower seating position. The rear axle was also offset to meet the repositioned driveshaft above which sat the oil tank. The whole was clothed in riveted

Charles Martin also enjoyed success in his CO.

Morel at Montlhéry in April 1927, when he won the Tourist Trophy.

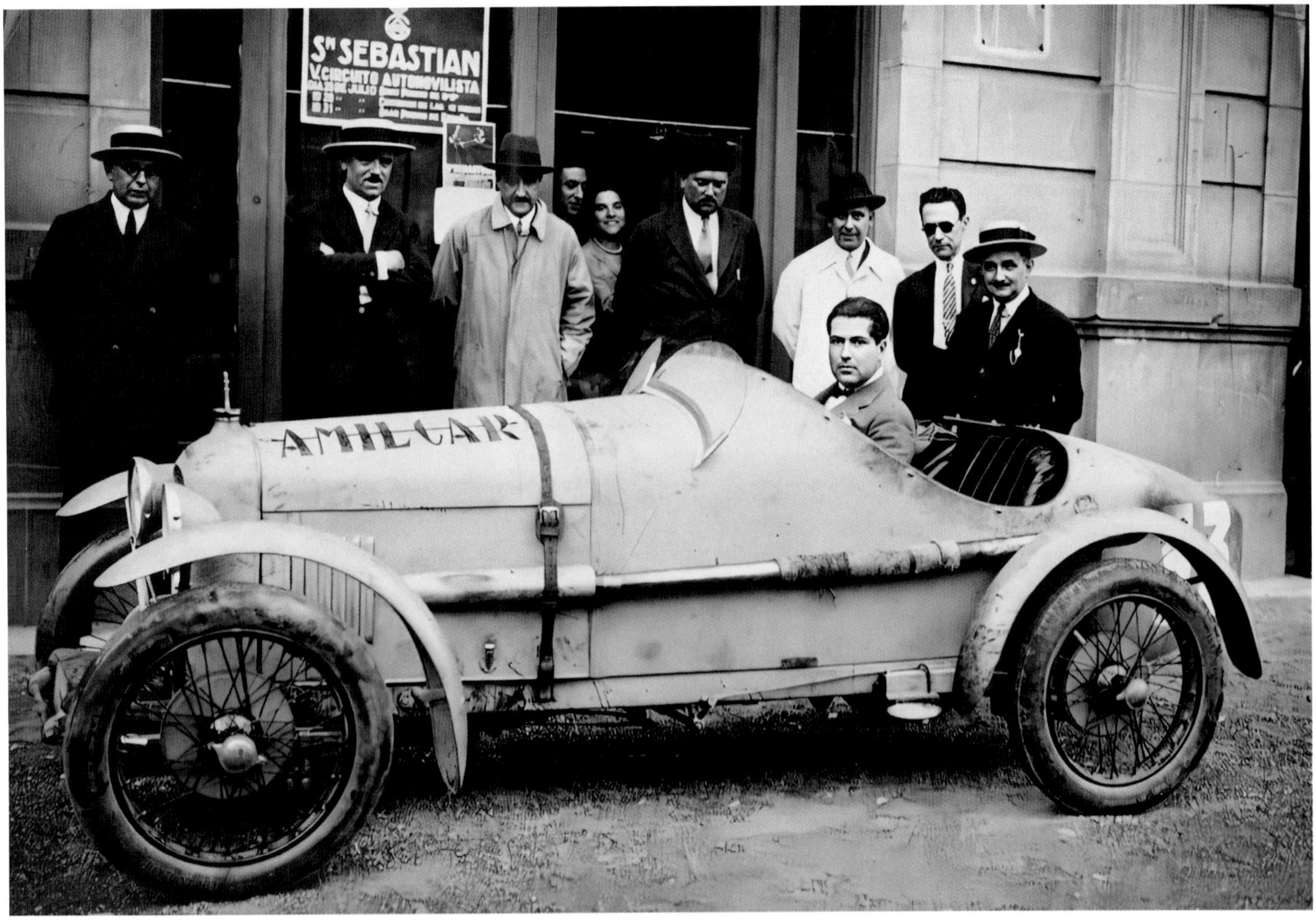

An unidentified Spanish driver in a CGSs at the San Sebastian Grand Prix in July 1927.

Maurice Mestivier chats to Morel in his CO at Brooklands.

Vincent Tersen in his CGSs at Montlhéry in 1928. Some drivers were still racing the old 4-cylinder cars, too.

aluminium bodywork, two cars were fitted with the standard radiator surround and one more was built with a streamlined cowling. These new racers also had a new engine with a shorter stroke, reduced from 77mm to 74mm, designed to allow increased revs, and the bore was upped from 55mm to 56 to maximise the 1100cc capacity limit. The supercharger was now of a horizontal configuration, the rotors side by side rather than stacked vertically, the earlier installation having had some mixture problems. The carburettor and inlet manifold were also moved from the left side of the block to the right and maximum power was now up to 105hp at 6,500rpm.

To hedge his bets, Morel took the first of the new cars to a Bordeaux hillclimb event in May along with his original CO, with the offset car just edging the CO to set the second- and third-best times behind Chiron's supercharged 2.3 litre Bugatti T35 and winning the 1100cc class. In July, King Alfonso XIII of Spain who was a keen enthusiast and Amilcar owner himself congratulated Marcel Sée personally on Charles Martin's class victory in the San Sebastian Grand Prix in a second offset CO (Morel had retired due to wheel bearing failure). More successes followed for Duray, Martin and Morel at Boulogne, Brooklands, Gaillon and Montlhéry to cap a successful year. Martin continued his winning streak into 1928 at Geneva with a new car before he went to Argenteuil and took the spoils in the 1500cc class with one of the offset chassis fitted with a new larger version of the Amilcar 'Six'. This engine had been produced specifically to allow Amilcar to challenge their upmarket rivals in the 1500cc class, Bugatti included. Boring the block to 57mm, the maximum possible within the existing casting, and fitting a new 83mm long-stroke crankshaft, gave a capacity of 1270cc. Whether this was intended as a serious possibility for future development or just an experiment to relieve the boredom of their dominance in the 1100cc class is not known, but it is believed very few of these engines were built, possibly only one or two if a spare was deemed necessary. The chassis was unchanged except for fitting larger front brakes. In April, Morel took the 1270cc car to the Grand Prix of Antibes joined by Martin and Moriceau (who had replaced Duray) in 1100cc models, but after Morel and Martin both retired Moriceau was left to pick up fourth place behind a trio of Bugattis. Later that month, Morel again triumphed with a 1500cc class win at the 17 Tournants hillclimb. In the final race for the offset CO with an 1100cc engine, Morel won the Rome Grand Prix in June.

The next improved version of this series was the MCO, which had first appeared with Martin at the Geneva Speed Trials in March. This was the final iteration of the racing

Morel in the offset CO at the Grand Prix d'Antibes in 1928.

'6s' – narrower, shorter, lower and lighter. Everything had been done to save weight – drilling bolts, lighter-gauge steel chassis rails with the radiator moved ahead of the front axle and covered with a sloping cowl. With minor differences in the bodywork, especially the cooling vents and streamlined headrests, one was built with the 1100cc engine, and another with the larger 1500cc class unit. After an initial test at Montlhéry, its first appearance was Martin's run at Geneva in March. Morel showed it to be a winner in July at the La Baraque hillclimb at Clermont Ferrand, then set a record at Troyes before heading to the speed trials at Arpajon, where the MCO became the first car in the 1100cc class to exceed 200km/h and switching between cars Morel took records in both the 1500cc and 1100cc classes. The cost of all of this had however taken its toll back at Saint-Denis and the racing programme was curtailed due to a lack of funds. Charles Martin was laid off, although Morel still managed to win at Gaillon and Morlaas (near Pau) and again in January 1929 at Marseille and at Geneva in March, with the last official outing for any works Amilcar racers.

In May 1929 an MCO was shipped out to America for Jules Moriceau to make a brave attempt at the Indianapolis 500. Moriceau had previous experience of the race, as he had attended the 1919 event as riding mechanic in Louis Wagner's Ballot, which had retired after 44 laps (*not* finishing fourth, as reported elsewhere).

Although *The Indianapolis News* reported the Amilcar as 'The smallest car in the race, of only 1100cc…', and in a later interview Moriceau recalled '…the capacity of the car was 1200cc…', most sources confirm it was one of the so-called MCO 1500 racers that had the 1270cc engine fitted but were referred to as a 1500, as in Europe that was the class they raced in.

Named the 'Thompson Products Special', as was the way of American race cars carrying the name of a (usually) automotive company paying to have their name on a car, it was sponsored by engine component manufacturer Thompson Products. Company president Charles E. Thompson was a friend of Marcel Sée, who had ambitions of getting Amilcar established in the American market, so accompanied by his mechanic Louis Roberjot, Moriceau and the MCO sailed across the Atlantic in April. After a stop at Thompson's Cleveland, Ohio headquarters, where the car was painted yellow and black, they arrived at Indianapolis on 7 May. The traditional format for the great race entailed much testing and practice through the month of May, leading up to the big event. In modern times the race takes place on the Sunday before the Memorial Day holiday, usually the last weekend in May, but in 1929 it was held on Thursday, 30 May. Once testing started, Moriceau immediately recognised he would be outclassed by the speed of the American Millers and Duesenbergs, but he plugged away slowly improving his lap times. With only 33 of the 43 cars entered forming the starting grid of eleven rows of three cars each, he

The new MCO fitted with the 1270cc engine for Morel's record run at Montlhéry.

Jules Moriceau in the CO before the Indianapolis 500.

As would be expected in the lead up to the Indy 500, there would be some publicity shots. We do not know who the ladies were, but that Packard Roadster certainly shows the small scale of the Amilcar racer.

did well to qualify on the fifth row with what was certainly the smallest capacity engine entered, recording an average speed of 170km/h (106mph) over four laps. Unfortunately, after grazing the wall four times, he was forced to retire with damaged steering, although with the generous cash prizes awarded by complicated formulae based on laps covered and the car's race position on each lap, he still sailed home with a $414 prize. The 500 was won by Ray Keech in the Simplex Piston Ring Special.

As this was Amilcar's last official race entry and the Competition Department now no longer existed, the MCO was put away and Moriceau gave up racing to take a job managing a garage in Paris.

As was common with racing programmes of the time, cars were continually improved and modified and often some were dismantled and stripped of parts to use in updated versions. It is not known how many of the racing CO and MCO were actually built, it is thought between nine and twelve of all versions in total and maybe a few extra spare engines, so not much was left of the CO series when the racing department was shut down.

At the end of 1929, Clément Auguste Martin (no relation to former works driver Charles Martin), who was the Amilcar agent for La Garenne, a suburb of Paris, bought seven of the now redundant CO and MCO racers including the Indianapolis MCO and set up his own racing operation, which he named 'Equipe de L'Ours Martin' (translated as Team Bear Martin). The sale included many, possibly all, of the spare parts, including some of the 6-cylinder engines. However, due to the complicated service regimes required, many of the cars were substituted with 4-cylinder engines, which were modified by Martin's workshop for improved performance and reliability with new camshafts, crankshaft bearings, water and oil pumps. There was at least one fitted with a 6-cylinder engine without supercharger to contest 1100cc classes. Martin's plan was to use these for endurance races rather than pure speed events. Among the drivers he recruited to the team between 1930 and 1935 were Auguste Bodoignet, Georges Boursin, Arthur Duray, Jean and Henri de Gavardie, Jean Nadeau, Camille Poiré, Fernand Pousse and Gaston Robail. The cars were usually recorded as the Amilcar CO Spéciale Martin. José Scaron, the Amilcar agent for Le Havre who had been racing with some success with his C6, acquired an MCO in 1930 from the factory stocks. Ex-works chief racing mechanic Maurice Mestivier had also been competing in a C6 and later, in 1933, bought an MCO.

Notable successes for the Martin Bears team in the 1930s included C.A. Martin's victories in the Bol d'Or in 1931 and 1932 followed by Jean de Gavardie's win in 1933. At the Le Mans 24-hour race in 1932, Martin with Auguste Bodoignet finished fourth in the 1500cc class, eighth overall. At the Circuit d'Orleans in May 1933, Martin, Fernand Pousse and Jean Nadeau scored second, third and fourth in the 1100cc class and at Le Mans in June, Jean and Henri de Gavardie were classified 12th overall. July saw Jean de Gavardie win the 1100cc class at the Spa 24-hour race accompanied this time by Arthur Duray, the same pair finishing the Le Mans race the following year in 14th place with Martin and Pousse in 20th and Camille Poiré and Gaston Robail in 22nd. There were records set at Montlhéry and at some point Scaron had also obtained an MCO to replace his hitherto successful C6 and carried on winning hillclimbs and speed events.

Amilcar MCO-001, the original MCO racer.

This MCO was used by André Morel in 1928 for record runs at Arpajon, Geneva and Montlhéry before it was sold to José Scaron, who continued to race it into the 1930s.

This MCO was restored by AutoRestorations Ltd in New Zealand.

THE C6

While the original plan for the 6-cylinder project was to build a few cars for the race team, there was no intention to produce and sell cars for sale to the general public. However, as soon as the first CO started collecting trophies in late 1925, there were enough enquiries from customers who were prepared to pay for copies that a production model was given the green light; and pay they did, as this was to be no bargain-priced cyclecar. It was André Morel who suggested that, as there was a demand, sales of the C6 would at least help offset the cost of building the CO racing cars.

Given the complications and high-maintenance nature of the 'fixed head' six, the decision was made to offer the public, who would not have had the facilities of the works racing department, a similar chassis fitted with a more serviceable engine.

The main difference from the works CO racers was the use of a detachable cylinder head and replacing the roller bearings of the camshaft, crankshaft and connecting rods with plain white-metal bearings. With a compression ratio of 6.6:1 fed by a single 40mm Solex carburettor and a Roots-type supercharger, the seven-bearing crankshaft enabled it to reach 6,500rpm developing upwards of 65hp. The C6 used the same chassis as the 2.195-metre short-wheelbase CO, with cable-operated 200mm drum brakes all round and a four-speed gearbox. There was a 100-litre fuel tank in the tail positioned over the rear axle in the interests of weight distribution. It was clothed in sheet steel panels riveted to the frame with a complete weight of 550kg, not including the optional lights and mudguards offered for those who wanted to drive them on the road.

The C6 chassis was first shown to the public at the Paris Salon of October 1926, displayed alongside a CO racer, but there were delays and after initial tests at Montlhéry in December, the first cars were delivered the following year. Guaranteed by the factory to have been tested at 165km/h (103mph) and

A rather battle-scarred C6 on display at Rétromobile, Paris, in 2017.

Another C6 seen from the driver's office.

selling at an impressive price of 75,000 francs, Amilcar were indeed entering a new market. With a projected production of 60 units, the price was gradually reduced to 60,000 francs at a time when a Bugatti T37 cost only 54,000, but by 1929 it was listed at 80,000 francs and as sales dropped off it was discontinued with various sources claiming a total of between 40 and 50 C6s sold. Most were sold in France, a few in other European countries and the results Vernon Balls racked up at Brooklands enabled him to import and sell six more in Great Britain. Balls, however, had competition for sales now that Boon and Porter had taken over the official UK agency for Amilcar and it was the latter who launched the C6 at the Earl's Court Motor Show in October 1926 (see Chapter 12). The C6 was superior in performance to the Bugatti T37 and more surprisingly, at £725, slightly higher in price, so the old cliché 'The Poor Man's Bugatti' hardly applied to this rather special sports car that was a step up from Amilcar's previous models.

While the works racers dominated the 1100cc class in France in the major events, customers racing the C6 were not far behind and when the works cars were absent, C6s

This C6 was in stock with a Munich classic car dealer.

driven by Robert Jeuffrain and José Scaron took the spoils at many hillclimbs and sprints. Guy Cloître and Emile Dupont took first and second at the Algerian Grand Prix in May 1928, a feat they repeated at the Tunis Grand Prix a month later, while Heinrich Joachim von Morgen and Walter Bartsch added to the tally in Germany.

Meanwhile, on the track Balls and some of his customers were scoring again at the many events at Brooklands with the C6. Balls had paid to have the CO racers brought over for the Brooklands Junior Car Club 200 Mile Race in 1926 and 1927, but to avoid such expense he decided to field a pair of C6s fitted with Cozette superchargers for the 1928 event, finishing first with W. B. Scott in second; another driven by Beris Harcourt-Wood finished in third place but was not classified due to not having covered enough distance. The latter car was then bought by W. E. Humphreys. Other Brooklands aces who campaigned Amilcar C6s included Harry Clayton, Goldie Gardner and Brian Twist. Clayton was also a regular competitor at both the Brighton and Lewes speed trials, while the Swedish driver, Henken Widengren, acquired a supercharged C6 sometime in 1932 and with continuing modifications gained several results at Brooklands, also setting a speed record at Montlhéry. The Humphreys and Widengren cars were maintained by the famous Brooklands tuner and mechanic Alec Francis and continued to impress through the remaining years of competition at Brooklands, which ended with the outbreak of war.

An Amilcar C6 today is the most sought-after of the marque and when one of the few do come up for sale they achieve high prices.

A.T.G. Goldie Gardner finished second in the 1930 Irish Grand Prix in his C6.

KLAUS BREMER'S C6

Klaus bought this C6 in 2011 and had it fully restored. It was bought from a previous owner in the UK who had in turn acquired it from a Mr Soederstroem, who ran a BMW agency and had a car collection in a museum in Sweden. He in turn had found it in Czechoslovakia in the early 1960s, although it was said to have not turned a wheel since the 1940s. Soederstroem had commenced a restoration but died before it was finished and the family sold it to the enthusiast in the UK. At that time, it had been fitted with a rebuilt radiator and a non-original supercharger, which were both replaced with the correct parts. It had the chassis number 11035 with matching gearbox and axles and engine number 90030 as originally supplied by the factory. The British restorer had many new parts made to build a new race-spec engine to protect the original engine rather than risk damaging it while racing. Klaus then completely overhauled the original engine 90030, installed it in the car and drove it in many rallies. C6 with the number 11035 is now back in the condition it left the factory.

Klaus Bremer's C6 chassis number 11035.

Engine number 90030 is now reunited with the chassis it powered when it first left Saint-Denis.

This C6 has travelled some distance since leaving France, with owners in Czechoslovakia, Sweden, the UK and now Germany.

Klaus's C6 lined up with five others at the Palais des Congrès at Vichy on an Amilcar rally.

AN AMILCAR C6 IN NEW ZEALAND

Probably the most sought-after Amilcar is the C6. Of the 50 built it is thought about twenty survive, so Peter White in New Zealand needed perseverance, some lucky contacts, the help of some specialists and clocked up quite a few airmiles to rebuild a fine example from spare parts. Probably the only C6 in the southern hemisphere, certainly the only one known in Australasia, it was an eight-year project from collecting parts from the UK and finishing the assembly in New Zealand. A keen Amilcarist in England had been collecting C6 parts for a future rebuild when he finally managed to acquire another C6 he had been chasing in Switzerland and consequently advertised the incomplete project on the PreWarCar website in 2015. Peter bought the lot and made plans to travel to England. He was then tipped off by the seller about a spare body that was available. Another C6 owner having had the body made as an accurate replica complete with upholstery and windshield had then found the remains of his car's original body and preferred to restore it to the chassis, thereby having a totally authentic car. A lucky find, Peter bought that too. He had already drawn up a set of suitable shipping pallets and made them on arrival in England using borrowed tools so he now had a safe means of shipping the car to the other side of the world. With an almost complete kit of parts including engine number 90042 and a body in excellent condition, he could then start assembly.

The chassis was an exact copy that had been made in France by a father-and-son team who had experience of making chassis for other Amilcars. The only parts missing were the oil tank, which was made later, and three oil-breather stacks to vent the block and sump and the oil and fuel caps. Peter drew the patterns for a pattern maker and had these parts made up by a local precision casting firm, even supplying copies of some of the rarer pieces for other C6 owners around the world. The friction shock absorbers were rebuilt and the wheels sourced from a well-known firm in Britain, as were some electrical parts, and the re-manufactured vanes for the supercharger, while the instruments were rebuilt in Ireland and a new crankshaft came from a specialist in Australia. Part-way through the rebuild Peter was unfortunately seriously injured in a cycling accident and consequently he was not able to complete the final assembly, so this was carried out by a business in Christchurch, New Zealand, which also made the oil tank from drawings supplied by Peter. The steering box was rebuilt, as were the gearbox and differential with new bearings and new pistons, and connecting rods were made and fitted. There were only minor jobs to finish on the body and the chassis was painted to match. Peter acknowledges help and advice from members of the Amilcar Salmson Register, who allocated the chassis number 99, and the finished car made its debut at a local car show in April 2023 and Peter is finally able to enjoy driving it. Another fine example of a rare model is now back on the road.

Peter White's completely rebuilt Amilcar C6.

Back on the road it looks every inch a real racing car.

In the workshop the chassis starts to come together.

The rebuilt engine back in the chassis, the front view is dominated by the supercharger.

The engine-turned dashboard has the full complement of gauges.

This is one of the finest Amilcar C6 restorations in the world.

Peter and the team at AutoRestorations can be proud of their work.

CHAPTER 8

1927–30 – THE C8 AND TROUBLE AHEAD

France fell into another economic crisis in 1927, with inflation causing the price of the raw materials Amilcar relied on to rise sharply, which, combined with the company having invested heavily in the new factory at Saint-Denis, led to a serious cash-flow shortfall. They were not alone; the French automobile business was struggling and it was the smaller companies that suffered the worst. Most of the cyclecar manufacturers had gone by 1927. De Dion Bouton, the oldest car company in France, was in liquidation, and others like Chenard & Walcker, Delahaye and Unic merged with a plan for the three brands to cover their own section of the market and not competing with each other. Another factor that could not have been foreseen was that there was now a trend towards closed cars in preference to the typically draughty and not exactly weatherproof tourers and open cars that had been the norm. The larger names were already producing closed cars in quantities sufficient to cover the costs – especially Citroën, who had already mastered the new methods of mass-producing all-steel bodies thanks to an agreement with the American Budd company. Amilcar were still able to sell small open sports cars within a shrinking market, but to stay in business they had to adapt to the changing fashions.

M.Benoit stands next to his M-Type sedan before the start of a road rally from Paris to Nice in March 1928. These rallies were run to a series of timed sections on public roads requiring a calculated average speed rather than real racing.

Although Amilcar sales had been good so far, the expenses of the move, the investment in tooling, and the cost of developing new models, all of which cannot have been helped by the outlay on the racing programme, left the firm in debt resulting in the liquidation of the Société Nouvelle pour l'Automobile (SNPA) in March 1927. Unable to raise any further finance, both Akar and Lamy were forced to relinquish their positions as directors, Akar being obliged to sell a few of his properties to pay some of the debt. With the capital value of the company now reduced from 11 million to 3.2 million francs, Marcel Sée brought in new investors to save Amilcar under the guise of a new company. The Société Anonyme Française d'Automobile (SAFA) was registered in July 1927, capitalised at 6 million francs with a board of directors headed by Albert Neubauer. An immediate reduction in prices across the Amilcar range of between 10 and 20 per cent helped boost sales and soon all appeared well: the racing programme continued; new models were introduced; and recovery was underway by the end of the year.

At the Paris Salon in October, the new L-Type was shown to replace the G-Type. Changes were few; the chassis was lengthened by 5cm and the stroke of the engine increased from 95mm to 105mm giving a capacity of 1190cc, which under the French system was rated at a taxable 8CV. Available as always as a bare chassis if required, the new body shop at Courbevoie offered three models: a four-door fabric-covered saloon and a fabric-bodied tourer, both built under Weymann licence, or a three-seater cabriolet, although other paint and luxury accessory options were offered. The L-Type only stayed in production for one year after about 1,500 had been sold. It was at this time that Amilcar adopted the winged Pegasus as a radiator mascot.

In January 1928, occasional Amilcar racer Fernand Pousse contested the Monte Carlo Rally in an L-Type accompanied by a M. Herteau, finishing in a respectable seventh place with a M. Desestre driving another Amilcar into tenth; the proof if needed that these were sturdy and reliable cars can only have helped sales. By May in the same year profits of 1,275,000 francs were paid to the new shareholders and with further investment SAFA was now valued at 10 million francs.

Of the existing models, the CGSs had been reduced in price at the 1927 Salon, now costing 23,900 francs, and continued to sell well. However, the price rose by 1,000 francs again in 1928 when it also gained a differential, 12 × 45 tyres and a 12-volt electrical system.

In 1927 the C4 had received larger 11 × 45 'Comfort' tyres and at the Salon in 1928 it was fitted with the larger CGS type 225mm brake drums on the front wheels, although the front axle remained suspended on quarter-elliptic springs. One would think this would cause problems with forces pulling the axle rearwards, but a reinforced lower leaf kept all in check and the system was said to work well enough. Aluminium back plates were fitted behind the kingpins and while the rear brakes were rod operated the fronts were controlled by cables with a compensating bar equalising the load. It was also now upgraded from 6 to 12 volt electrics. Trouble was brewing internally too; Moyet had suffered a fractured skull after a motorcycle accident when he was attending a record attempt at Montlhèry and, after a period of convalescence, he returned only to fall out with his assistant Maurice Dubois, accusing him of trying to take control, the result being Dubois leaving the company.

At the start of 1929 the price of the CGSs rose again to 25,900 francs and it now had a new redesigned body with two side by side seats, two small doors and the cycle-type mudguards were ribbed with stylish curved ends.

Sharing the Amilcar stand at the Paris Salon in October 1928, the last year for the C4 and CGSs, was a C6, the new M-Type to replace the L-Type and a prototype bare chassis fitted with a new 8-cylinder 1800cc engine to be named the C8 and hopefully move Amilcar into the luxury car sector.

An early M-Type, which was launched at the 1928 Paris Salon.

Mme Dupéchez again, with her Amilcar CGS Coupé at the start of the 1928 Paris to Nice rally.

The M-Type was broadly similar to the L-Type, carrying over much of the same bodies with the addition of new optional closed saloon, coupés, and open tourer and cabriolet designs. The main difference was that the engine was now enlarged to 1244cc thanks to an increase in stroke to 110mm, although due to a quirk of the French taxation system it was now rated as a 7CV, when its smaller-engined L-Type predecessor had been taxed as an 8CV. The M-Type was updated as the M2 in 1929 after 1,174 units had been sold, with the only difference being the three-speed gearbox was replaced by a four-speed. At the 1930 Salon the M2 received some new bodywork echoing the styles of the time; new close-fitting curved mudguards and a lack of running boards made for a modern, sportier look. Sales of the M2 totalled 2,650 units.

A four-door Amilcar M-Type with Swiss registration for the Geneva region.

As a consequence of the financial restructuring and the investment needed for the ambitious C8 programme, the decision was taken at the end of the 1928 season to close the Competition Department and cease all racing activities. Charles Martin was no longer required and although Morel did contest a couple more events in early 1929 at Marseille and Geneva, both resulting in class victories for the MCO, the last iteration of the works 6-cylinder racers, this was the end of Amilcar's involvement in competition in any official capacity. There was a plan to return to racing a year or so later as soon as finances and the new models permitted, especially with an aim to contest 24-hour races and endurance events, but this never happened. It was only the efforts of the private entrants that kept the Amilcar name alive in competition for some years after.

THE AMILCAR–DURANT ALLIANCE

More significantly the eight was the start of an ambitious new project that Marcel Sée had tasked Moyet with designing with the aim of getting into the lucrative American market, where buyers showed a preference for the more cylinders the better. The entry of a CO for Moriceau for the Indianapolis 500 race in 1929 was not just an optimistic gamble for the little French company to take on the might of the USA; Sée already had big plans and had been negotiating a deal with William Crapo Durant that would see the latter selling Amilcars through Durant's claimed 2,600 agents of his Durant Motor Company, while Amilcar would take on distribution of Durant and Star or Rugby models. Indeed, in October 1928 Durant had already confirmed an order for 350 of the new 8-cylinder Amilcar to be sold in the USA.

With the need to meet the expected demand for the new luxury car that was to be the saviour of the Amilcar brand, Sée once again invested heavily in more factory space and tooling to move manufacturing methods forward from the existing slow, handmade 'one at a time' processes thus far employed, to a more modern, mass production system. All of these distractions had already delayed the launch of the new C8, but Sée was still optimistic.

In March 1929, Sée embarked on a seven-week trip to Durant's headquarters in Lansing, Michigan, USA to finalise the details of the alliance between the two companies. Pushing his luck again, Durant, in an attempt to gain interest in his new imported car, had published a list of prospective customers, including many famous and influential names such as Herbert Hoover, then President of the United States, Louis B. Mayer, President of Metro Goldwyn Mayer, and many leading bankers and politicians.

An unfortunate series of events unfolded at the same time in America as the warnings that the rampant greed and optimism throughout the New York Stock Exchange was unsustainable continued to be ignored. On 25 March 1929, when the Federal Reserve warned of excessive speculation, the first, minor, crash occurred as investors finally listened and

MARCEL SÉE, 1893–1977

Marcel Jacques Sée was born 6 January 1893, at 9, Rue du Chateaudun in the 9th arrondissement of Paris, the son of an engineer. He started working for his diamond merchant father-in-law Samson van Moppes as a messenger. He was ambitious and must have come to the attention of Émile Akar, when he was recruited in 1921 as a deputy manager at the age of 28.

Sée and a family relation Gilbert Nataf had started a coachbuilding and upholstery business named Margyl, a contraction of their two first names, which they then sold to Amilcar in 1926.

By 1927 Sée had enough personal wealth, or at least the influence, to raise capital with help from Albert Neubauer to take control of Amilcar under the new company S.A.F.A. On being awarded the rank of *Chevalier de la Légion d'Honneur* in 1933, *La Vie Automobile* offered the opinion 'This man always knew what he wanted and how he wanted it'.

Ever more ambitious, Sée's investments in the St Denis factory and the planned merger with the American Durant Motor Company weakened his position enough that the following few years through to 1934 saw the company struggling once again. Even his restructuring another new company, S.O.F.I.A., and bringing in further backing only delayed the inevitable a few more years before the Hotchkiss takeover in 1937. He remained on the board until his resignation on 10 April 1940, when he went to London to join the French Resistance.

He returned to France after the war and started other businesses, but played no further part in the motor trade. Sée passed away in Paris on 18 May 1977, aged 84.

Marcel Sée.

W. C. DURANT, 1861–1947

William Crapo Durant was born in Boston, Massachusetts on 8 December 1861. In 1869 his family moved to Flint, Michigan and William dropped out of high school to work for his grandfather's timber business, then as a cigar salesman and then started up his own carriage-building company. He joined with Josiah Dort to form the Durant-Dort Carriage Company in 1886, which by the start of the twentieth century was the largest in the business. He claimed to not like the new-fangled automobile with various complaints, but this may have just been because he saw it as a threat to the horse-drawn carriage trade. However, he soon changed his tune and, using his new-found wealth, bought the Buick Motor Company in 1904, which he soon turned around to become the bestselling car in America by 1905. Durant then arranged a partnership with Canadian carriage-maker Samuel McLaughlin to build Buicks north of the border.

W.C. Durant.

In 1908, Durant founded General Motors Holding Company with McLaughlin a major shareholder and immediately bought the Oldsmobile company. With great ambitions for General Motors, he soon added Cadillac and Oakland as well as several parts and component suppliers, but this proved to be too much of a good thing and when he tried to buy Ford for $8 million in 1909, he found he had no backers. Suddenly finding itself with a cash shortage, the board of directors voted Durant out of the company he had founded only two years before.

Not to be discouraged, Durant and Dort then bought into the Chevrolet company and made it such a great success that by 1916 he was able to buy back control of General Motors with help from McLaughlin. They then formed the new General Motors Corporation in 1918, with Pierre du Pont in charge and McLaughlin as Vice President. With Chevrolet now part of the group, along with other acquisitions Fisher Body, Frigidaire and Republic trucks, business was again booming, but once again Durant was forced out in a takeover by the major shareholders McLaughlin and du Pont. Alfred P. Sloan of the Hyatt Roller Bearing Company was appointed president, and it was he who went on to lead General Motors as the world's largest car maker.

Still W. C. Durant was not finished, and in 1921 he started again with a new company, Durant Motors, with the Durant brand soon joined by Eagle, Flint and Star – although the latter would be sold as the Rugby in commonwealth territories where the British Star was already established. The acquisition of Locomobile gave Durant an upmarket brand to rival Cadillac and Packard. Curiously in 1928, in another of his extreme gestures, Durant had publicly offered $25,000 'for the best and most practicable plan to make the Eighteenth Amendment (prohibition) effective' at a time when his finances were once again shaky. Despite his wide range of products and a well-established dealer network, the financial problems arising from the Wall Street crash and the Great Depression of the early 1930s once again put an end to Durant's empire, not helped by his faith in pursuing investments on the stock exchange on Black Tuesday even when others were trying to get out, causing him to lose millions overnight. This would also put an end to any plans for the joint venture with Amilcar. As Durant's various business interests were wound down, any remaining assets and cash were not enough to prevent him from being declared bankrupt in 1936.

Again, Durant tried to bounce back by opening a bowling alley and restaurant in Flint, Michigan, followed by an attempt to get into mining and a hair tonic business. However, at the age of 80 he suffered a stroke and spent his remaining days in an apartment in New York until finally passing away on 18 March 1947.

rushed to sell off stocks as fast as they had been buying them. Immediately, investment in all industries slowed, retail businesses saw sales drop alarmingly, consumers whohad been encouraged to buy on credit found themselves in debt and consequently automobile sales suffered. A further slump in stock values saw another 'crash' in May, but still the warnings

THE FRENCH AUTOMOBILE INDUSTRY AND THE GREAT DEPRESSION

The Great Depression affected every industry in most countries and certainly France felt the pain. While the more conservative Peugeot and Renault carried on as before, Citroën appeared to be doing well, but soon the investment in developing the radical new 'Traction' model would send the company into the hands of their biggest creditor, Michelin, in 1935.

The Franco-Italian partnership SAFAF (Société Anonyme Française des Automobiles Fiat) began assembling Fiats in France in 1926. A new company was formed as Simca in 1935 and sales of the Balilla were enough to see it through until the introduction of the Simca Cinq, the French copy of the very successful Fiat 500 Topolino.

Mathis had been doing so well in the 1920s, with a high of more than 20,000 cars sold in 1927, that having outgrown their original Graffenstaden factory they invested heavily in a new facility at Strasbourg that could not be paid for from the suddenly reduced sales of the post-Wall Street Crash period. With a factory running at well under its potential capacity and Ford not able to keep up with the current demand for their Model A and the new Model B of 1932 at their Asnières-sur-Seine plant, it was convenient for both to merge to create Matford in 1934, whereby Mathis would produce Fords. From then on there were no true new Mathis models, but a compromise deal to rationalise the sales network meant that in territories where both Ford and Mathis dealers would be in competition with each other, some were to lose their franchise. At a time when people still held on to the old notion of brand loyalty, some customers were kept happy thinking they could still buy a Ford or a Mathis (according to preference) while for others the new name meant little. The Matford alliance ended with the outbreak of war in 1939 and Ford's French operations were taken over by Simca.

Bugatti somehow survived the expense of the design and manufacture of the Type 41 Royale, of which they were only able to sell three. Luckily, they were kept solvent by sales of 79 railcars powered by the Royale's huge straight-8 engines to the national SNCF rail company. Always a niche brand and never trying to grab a bigger slice of the car market, somehow they stayed afloat through the 1930s, catering to their small but loyal band of customers.

By 1932 Delage was making some of the best cars of the period in the luxurious and sporting D8 and D6 models, but could not sell enough and was in a bad enough financial situation to force Louis Delage into taking out a 25 million-franc loan to try to save the company. Even later selling his palatial home in the Champs-Élysées was not enough to prevent the marque being taken over by Delahaye. Somehow the latter continued to make expensive cars through the 1930s and survived until the eventual takeover by Hotchkiss, propped up by sales of military and commercial vehicles.

Hotchkiss themselves weathered the hard times with their AM and later sixes and could always rely on military contracts through both world wars to keep in the black. Hotchkiss, of course, would play a part in Amilcar's later years.

Panhard et Levassor powered exclusively by Knight sleeve-valve engines were by the 1930s concentrating on upmarket models and continued to trail a cloud of blue smoke around French streets. Their fortunes, as with Delahaye, were bolstered by sales of trucks and military vehicles. By 1936, the drivers of the ultra-Art-Deco Dynamic models must have felt smug about making such a fashion statement while cruising the fashionable boulevards.

Another French marque that had been producing quality cars in the 1920s and achieved some success with the A-22 racer in 1923 was Rolland-Pilain made in Tours (Indre-et-Loire). Attempting to go upmarket in 1929 with American made 6- and 8-cylinder Continental engines brought the company down and it closed in 1931.

Rosengart had started in the 1920s, building the Austin Seven under licence to be sold as a 5CV. While sales were strong enough the profits were small and by 1936 the investment in the slow-selling Supertraction model forced a restructuring of the company. The brand survived the war – just – but never regained enough sales to last beyond a few more years.

Ballot fell into the hands of Hispano-Suiza in 1931 and disappeared a year later. Berliet stuck to the commercial bus and truck lines, as eventually did Unic. Chenard & Walcker was bankrupt by 1936. Even one of the great pioneers of the 'horseless carriage', De Dion Bouton, stopped car production in 1932.

Of Amilcar's direct rivals, while Salmson struggled on, BNC, Derby, SARA and Sénéchal all went the way of the dinosaur.

While it may have been unrealistic to expect France to be able to sustain so many car manufacturers beyond the first few decades, certainly the Great Depression had serious consequences for the French automobile industry.

were ignored as the market saw a rise again in June; but it could not last. Durant was one of those particularly exposed and found himself over-stretched and cash-poor again. The Federal Reserve had clamped down on credit and security, meaning it was impossible to borrow against assets that were worth nothing more than a dubious paper value. Durant even tried to persuade President Hoover to reverse this restriction, which the President wisely refused to do, and Durant could only watch on as his empire crashed as spectacularly as the New York Stock Exchange did that October.

So, before it had even got off the ground, the planned Amilcar–Durant trans-Atlantic alliance was abandoned, leaving the French half of the partnership deep in debt again and the American company about to go under.

Committed as they were, the management at Saint-Denis had to concentrate on getting the C8 to market, which would be hampered further by the effect the Wall Street Crash had on the French economy.

As a curious footnote, Pierre Delage, son of Louis Delage of the Delage car company, joined the board of directors in 1929, although he did not remain there long. He was not to know at the time, but later when his father's company failed in 1935, the Delage name was taken over by Delahaye, who in turn would have a connection with Amilcar later on.

THE C8 AND CS8

When the J-Type failed to set any sales records, as had the E-Type before, Marcel Sée decided what Amilcar needed to crack the market for more luxurious touring cars to appeal to the middle-classes was something larger again with a bigger engine of more than four cylinders. After the success of the sixes and tempted by the lure of W. C. Durant's promise of US dollars, he asked Moyet to come up with an all-new 8-cylinder engine in a low chassis that would be clothed in modern fashionable coachwork befitting its underpinnings. Given Moyet's proven track record of getting adequate power from small capacity cylinders, it was decided to make the new eight follow tradition and be of a modest size. The first iteration was of 1.8 litres from a bore and stroke of 62 × 75mm with an overhead camshaft mated to a four-speed gearbox, which would be taxable as a 10CV. After a handful of this specification engine had been tested, the power output was deemed insufficient and Moyet and his team went back to the drawing board to come up with something better. By the time of the Paris Salon of October 1929, Amilcar launched two versions of the new eight; the 2.0 litre C8 with a bore and stroke of 63 x 80mm rated at 11CV and the 13CV 2.3 CS8 once again bored and stroked further to 66 × 85mm. The new chassis was suspended by semi-elliptic springs mounted outside and parallel to the side rails, giving a low 18cm ride height and braking by four large drums actuated by cables. Other accessories included a thermostatically controlled fan and a centralised Alcyl Lubrication system that applied grease to various chassis by the operation of a hand pump on the dashboard. Three body styles were offered: a four-door, four-seater saloon, a four-seater, two-door faux cabriolet and a two-seat tourer. Priced at double the cost of the 30,000 franc M-Type, the CS8 was competitive with the equivalent Delage DR and a lot cheaper than a 3.0 litre Bugatti T44, but considerably more than the nearest 6-cylinder 2.4-litre Citroën C6. Maximum power was claimed to be 58hp at 4,000rpm. The top speed was quoted at 120km/h (75mph), but that would have been dependent on the type of coachwork fitted. As usual, the C8 and CS8 were also sold in rolling chassis form for bodying by independent coachbuilders. It would be a gamble to see if Amilcar had done their sums right. Sée must have been an optimist, but given he had already committed his over-stretched finances to the design and tooling for the new model he had no choice but to press ahead. The Wall Street Crash of course affected the French economy harshly and with the collapse of the Durant deal the hoped-for US sales evaporated immediately, so inevitably sales were sluggish even though press reports were very complimentary. By the time of the 1930 Salon the C8 had been discontinued, but the CS8 was now in competition with most of the local marques offering a straight-8. As the factory followed a long process of testing every engine for twelve hours on the test bench followed by a 100km (62 mile) drive of the complete running chassis and a further 100km after the body was fitted, one has to wonder if they had enough staff to keep that up if they had been able to sell more cars. Never really a top performer, the CS8 was generally praised by the press for its light, accurate steering, fine ride and precise roadholding, but this was still not enough to stimulate sufficient sales and it did soon gain a reputation for unreliability blamed on insufficient lubrication.

A new four-seater open cabriolet was added to the range, running boards were now deleted giving a more modern sleeker look, and the smart Milord cabriolet stood out for

An Amilcar C8 13CV sedan.

A catalogue illustration of a 1932 Amilcar CS8 with Faux Cabriolet coachwork.

A catalogue illustration of a four-door sedan body on a CS8 chassis.

An Amilcar CS8 open four-door tourer in less than perfect condition.

its elegant two-tone paint scheme. Sales were still slow, and by the time of the 1931 Salon there were no major changes to the range offered. For the next year, apart from minor mechanical improvements – steel conrods replaced the hitherto fragile alloy parts – the bodies offered by the factory were rationalised to just the two, a saloon and a tourer with minor cosmetic changes. Production of the largest-engined Amilcar was stopped in 1933 and unfortunately its most significant impact on the Amilcar brand was to once again lead the company into a financial meltdown. A total of fewer than 800 8-cylinder Amilcars were believed built and very few survive today, although a couple of rough 'barn-find' cases have recently been sold through auctions in France, which will hopefully be restored by their new owners.

This CS8 Roadster is owned by Han Brouwers in the Netherlands.

Han Brouwer's CS8 was originally sold to an owner in Belgium who later had the rear bodywork altered.

Mlle Parera stands by her Amilcar CS8 Coupé at Neuilly before the start of the Paris to Saint Raphael rally for female drivers in February 1933. Such events for ladies only were popular at the time.

A RARE CS8 IN AUSTRALIA

The story of how this CS8 was saved goes back quite a long way, starting with a French student writing to Bryan Goodman in 1962 to tell him of an 8-cylinder Amilcar resting in a breaker's yard in Frejus on the southern coast of France. Having an interest in Amilcars, Bryan had thought he would have little chance of finding a CS8, so was immediately interested and bought it 'sight unseen' for £30. In 1959 a dam nearby had collapsed causing a flood that killed many and it is supposed the Amilcar had been under water for some time, leaving it even worse for wear.

On getting the car home to England, Bryan started on the restoration. The front wings and some panels were salvageable, as were the instruments and radiator. However, the magneto was not, so after hunting around an 8-cylinder Scintilla was found in an old shop in Paddington. He decided to build a new body copying the Weymann style fabric-bodied tourer Amilcar 8 road-tested by *The Autocar* in 1929. Finding he still preferred to drive his CGS, in 1968 Bryan sold the eight to David Johnson, then president of the Amilcar Register. David later advertised it for sale in *Motor Sport* magazine in June 1971. The car was purchased by Graham Steinfort, well known in the Vintage Sports Car Club, and shipped to Melbourne in 1971. In transit the bodywork was damaged by a forklift tine on the docks and was recovered under insurance in new fabric. During Graham's ownership it appeared in *Automobile Quarterly* Volume 18 #1. The engine developed a misfire (the result of a broken duralumin connecting rod) and Graham sold the CS8 in 1980 to Richard Creed, a member of the VSCC at the time. Richard sold it on to his father-in-law, Austin Tope, sometime during the 1980s, when another restoration was started. Panels and mudguards were repainted, the differential was rebuilt using a Rover crown wheel and pinion. The engine rebuild was started using modified Mitsubishi Galant connecting rods but not completed.

Ted Geerman's CS8 is one of the few survivors.

The Weymann style fabric-bodied tourer was built in England in the 1960s as a replica of the car tested in period by *The Autocar*.

The sad remains of the CS8 as it was found in a breaker's yard in Frejus in 1962.

Eight – yes, count 'em – eight spark plugs, more than any other Amilcar.

The left side of the engine looks a bit more crowded.

The CS8 was advertised for sale again in 2008 and Ted Geermans found the chance to purchase an 8-cylinder Amilcar too good to miss; however, the missing engine parts were a problem. A friend made the missing gears to drive a Subaru oil pump and contrived fittings for an external oil filter. Much more work was needed: the cylinder head was rebuilt with new valves; Peugeot 403 valve springs, new camshaft, timing gears and the water inlet housings were recast. The gearbox was rebuilt with new bearings.

As the interior trim had been removed new seats were needed that would allow passengers access to the rear; this was resolved with a modified pair of Peugeot 404 front seats, and the car was sent away to a motor trimmer and returned with new carpet, leather trim, new hood and tonneau cover.

Since the first trip to the Collingrove hillclimb in 2017, the car has attended many rallies around Australia. Whilst there is still some way to go before all the bugs have been attended to, the Eight is proving to be a terrific touring vintage car.

The CS8 also took part in the Australian Amilcar centenary rally in Renmark, South Australia.

A decent folding hood offers some protection when storms threaten.

CHAPTER 9

1931–34 – THE M2, M3 AND THE NEW 5CV

By 1931 it was obvious the 8-cylinder models were not going to save the company and once again the decision was made to revert to concentrating on what Amilcar was better known for – small capacity light cars. But the days of cyclecars were long gone and no more little sporty models would be in the catalogue again. There followed a confusing list of models for the next three years. The 7CV M2 was updated again as the M3 and launched at the October Salon alongside the last attempt to sell the CS8. This time the new M-Type was subject to more changes underneath and with more modern, stylish, bodywork. The engine and transmission remained from the M2 but with a new lower chassis replacing that which had served since the G-Type. The side rails were fitted with six crossmembers in a trapezoidal configuration with the semi-elliptic springs hung on the outside giving a lower ride height. This in turn allowed the body styling to be more in line with prevailing fashions. The complete bare chassis weighed 500kg with an all-up weight of around 1,000kg according to the type of coachwork fitted. The factory offered two- and four-door saloons, a two-door fixed head coupé, a convertible coupé

The 1930 Amilcar M2 faux cabriolet.

A profile view of the 1930 Amilcar M2 faux cabriolet. Note the square styling that was typical of the time.

1932 Amilcar M3 sedan has a bit more curve to the front mudguards and slanted louvres.

1932 Amilcar M3 cabriolet showing styling changes.

The same 1932 Amilcar M3 cabriolet in profile has a more modern look compared to the 1930 model.

A 1933 Amilcar M3 Roadster.

A 1932 M3 7CV Amilcar; the curved line at the scuttle adds flair.

and a torpedo roadster. The new-look horizontal bonnet louvres gave a sleek streamlined appearance and a lack of running boards on the open cars added to the modern look. This model continued to sell well but was not enough to keep the company afloat for much longer.

For the 1932 Salon, Moyet was once again given instructions to get busy with his drawing office team and come up with a new small car that would sell for a lower price in the 5CV category. Given a brief to come up with an affordable small car capable of carrying two passengers and their luggage with a top speed of 90km/h (56mph), the new model was called the C Type 5CV. Moyet had learned well from the earlier models and managed to come up with a small car that stood 1.4 metres tall, had a wheelbase of 2.15 metres and weighed 400kg. It was powered by a side-valve 4-cylinder engine with a bore and stroke of 58 × 80mm giving a capacity of 845cc providing 22hp. Moyet had once again met all of the targets set by Sée. It was also the cheapest 5CV car at the Salon that year at 11,950 francs for the two-seater in either cabriolet or sport tourer configuration, undercutting the nearest rivals from Mathis and Rosengart by 3,000 francs. The C Type was often referred to as the *'5CV License Moyet'* as this identification had been cast into the cylinder head. With the CS8 no longer in the catalogue, and the steady-selling, but not spectacularly so, M3 the only other model listed, the 5CV carried the responsibility of being the saviour of Amilcar.

Unlike its big brother the CS8, the 5CV at least was cheap to buy and to run and was reliable in daily use. It also had a charming style about it that gave it an edge in the small car market. Sales were good and in any other circumstance it would have been a commercial success.

For the next few years, the C-Type would receive some cosmetic changes to keep up with prevailing fashions. The C3 was introduced at the October 1933 Salon with a larger 877cc engine, a 10cm-longer chassis allowing the addition of a third seat on the Cabriolet Luxe and Coupé Luxe, the Grande Luxe Tourer remaining a two-seater, and the styling was updated with new longer swept-back front mudguards.

While the M3 continued as before, 1933 also saw another new Amilcar introduced – the M4. Using the same chassis as the M3, its main difference was an engine of a totally new design, probably intended to be the basis of future models, but it soon proved to be a wasted effort. The 1628cc engine with a bore and stroke of 72 × 100mm had a cast iron block and crankcase, a cast iron side-valve head, a three-bearing crankshaft and a sheet metal sump pan producing 37hp and the new M-Type was now rated for tax as a 9CV. The M4 shared the same bodywork as the M3. With a list price of 4,000 francs more than the M3, serial numbering suggests only 70 units were built.

Continuing to sell well as the C3, another new variant of the C Type, the C5, was announced in July 1934. With another increase in engine capacity to 929cc but still taxable as a 5CV, the C5 gained another 12cm added to the wheelbase enabling four-seater bodies and the top speed increased a little to 95km/h. Amilcar adopted the Aerodynamic name to highlight the new styling featuring a raked-back radiator, a sloping streamlined rear end copying the recently introduced M3 'Aerodynamic' with similar, but larger, bodywork introduced at the 1934 Salon. Another addition to the 5CV range was a light van offered with either the old-style front end or the new inclined radiator. Records suggest that about 2,456 of all C-Types including no more than 200 of the Aerodynamic were produced between 1932 and 1934. It is not known how many of the vans were sold, as they were only in the catalogue for a brief period. Finally, an Aerodynamic version of the M4 was announced for 1935; however, it seems this probably did not get beyond the prototype stage. All of the Aerodynamic models were in fact a dead end, as they never went into production due to further financial problems.

The other newcomer shown at the 1934 Salon was a prototype chassis for the Pégase. This was destined to be Amilcar's only offering from 1935 (see Chapter 10), although efforts continued to sell remaining stocks of the 5, 7 and 9CV models.

Without the existing financial difficulties hanging over them, the sales of the C-Type and the M-Type may have been enough to see them through these difficult times. The M-Type sold 1,174 units, the M2 a further 2,650 and the M3 production totalled 2,700; not enough to trouble the accountants at Citroën or Peugeot, this was still a success by Amilcar's standards.

Times were tough for everyone and while many of their rivals had, or were about to, go under, Amilcar needed to tighten a few metaphoric belts – this time calling for more drastic measures. In 1931, a business agreement saw André Briès and Marcel Sée acting as administrators of a company again on shaky ground financially. Amilcar stumbled on as best it could until late in 1933 Briès and Sée managed to raise further capital from friends and associates and took control setting up a new company, Société Financiere pour l'Automobile (SOFIA) at the beginning of 1934. Unable to sell enough cars to justify the existing overheads, major changes would be needed and Sée was not shy of doing whatever it took to keep the brand alive. However, as was becoming a habit with Amilcar, this reprieve proved to be once again short-lived.

In August 1934, the Saint-Denis factory was closed with many staff being laid off including Edmond Moyet, who returned to Citroën taking Marcel Chinon with him. One of the few who were retained was Maurice Mestivier, who was now responsible

1933 5CV advertisement, a bargain at 12,500 francs.

for managing the sales department. Sée had already established a smaller factory at 23–25, Rue de Bellevue, in the western suburb of Boulogne and this was set up to take on assembly of the next new model, the Pégase.

In competition there may have still been some remnants of reflected glory due to the efforts of C.A. Martin and his team of privateers still being competitive around the circuits of Europe. Another minor highlight came in early 1933. Occasional Amilcar racer Fernand Pousse had finished seventh in the 1928 Monte Carlo rally with an L-Type and decided to have another crack at the tough but high-profile event. This time using an M3 chassis, he constructed a light fabric-covered body and set off from Tallin in Estonia finishing twelfth overall and sixth in the under 1500cc class. Another Amilcar M-Type that also left from Tallin, driven by Roger Bravard, was listed as finishing sixth overall and second in the under 1500cc class. Not much is known about Bravard, but as he also went on to race Hudsons and Essex Terraplanes he may have had a connection with André Morel and Joseph Lamy, who were selling these brands by the mid-1930s.

Unfortunately, Amilcars would never again score enough results to keep the name alive in top level motorsport. In more modest company it would be up to the individual enthusiasts to keep them going in the post-war era in club events. Later still, by the 1960s, many sought them out when a new interest in historic racing gave many sporting Amilcars a second life.

The three body styles offered for the 1933 5CV C3.

1933 5CV C3 cabriolet, the pretty lady probably means this was photographed at a concours.

The 1933 M3 engine.

A 1933 5CV C3 cabriolet, again a concours pose.

A 1933 5CV C3 cabriolet with the sloping Aérodynamique radiator.

A 1934 5CV C5 convertible also an Aérodynamique model.

A 1934 7CV M3 Aérodynamique Roadster at the Concours d'élégance de Bagatelle.

A 1934 5CV C5 Coach, the last of the 5CV line.

Advertisement for the 1935 5CV C5 Aérodynamique.

A RARE M2 COUPÉ

J. Louis Limbourg's M2 is believed to date from 1929 or 1930 and still wears its original two-door coupé body with the curved trunk. Apart from having the interior trim recovered in the original colours and the engine cover panels repainted, it is otherwise as it left the factory. Another Amilcar with an appreciative owner in the Netherlands, it is the only known surviving example of this type.

J. Louis Limbourg's M2 is in original condition.

Amilcar only sold 2,650 examples of the M2, and this one is believed to be the sole survivor with this bodywork.

The interior has been retrimmed; note the fine veneers on the doors.

This profile view shows the 'bustle back' boot.

CHAPTER 10

ANOTHER MOVE – THE PÉGASE

First shown as a prototype at the 1934 Salon, the birth of the Pégase is the subject of some speculation and mystery. Also listed as the N7, it was a completely new departure from any previous Amilcar and with no common parts carried over there is no evidence that Edmond Moyet had any influence in the design. As the Salon opened that year on 4 October, and Moyet had only left the previous August, the first chassis, at least, must have been well underway by then and it is probable that as Chief Designer he must have been aware of the project. Even if Moyet and what was left of his team were still based at the Saint-Denis location, the new factory at Boulogne where the Pégase was being assembled cannot have been much of a secret. However, if Moyet really did have no input there is no record of who was behind the design of the car or the first body style shown at the Salon. Even by using a chassis and mechanical components bought in and the assembled whole clothed by outside coachbuilders, somebody in the Amilcar organisation must have had responsibility for the overall concept of the Pégase. One source claims Marcel Chinon had stayed on as Technical Director, this is doubtful, or certainly short-lived, as he was at Citroën with Moyet by 1935.[(4)] The Boulogne premises did not have any of the manufacturing facilities that Amilcar had previously enjoyed and the Pégase was assembled there from components bought in from various suppliers.

The chassis itself may have been all-new for Amilcar, but in fact it was just a copy of the Delahaye 134 frame and featured independent front suspension, with leaf-springs at the rear and had cable-operated Bendix patent brakes. With a 2.8-metre wheelbase the prototype as shown at the Salon sat on wire wheels. As with many French cars, it still retained right-hand drive, operating a worm and sector steering box. The four-speed gearbox too was from Delahaye with a single dry-plate clutch. The prototypes were fitted with an overhead-camshaft 2010cc 4-cylinder engine (bore and stroke 80 × 100mm) alternately reported as taxable as either 11 or 12CV, designed by the engineer Henri Grillot, not as stated elsewhere the work of Schmid.[(5)] Grillot had previously been best known for the straight-8 used in the Rolland-Pilain A22 racer that won the San Sebastian Grand Prix of 1923, driven by Albert Guyot. The new engines were not built by Amilcar as they no longer had the facilities and, like most other components, were bought in. These were supplied by Janvier, Sabin et Cie. This company was originally founded by Lucien Picker as Janvier-Picker in Châtillon-sur-Bagneux in 1912. It was, apart from briefly making cars under its own name, an independent machining shop that supplied engines to other small French manufacturers of long-forgotten car brands. The best-known of these was probably Tic-Tac, although they were even sold further afield as in the English KRC and Argentinian Anasagasti marques.

Sometime between the 1934 Salon and the Pégase reaching the market in 1935, the decision was made to abandon the Grillot engine in favour of the cheaper and readily available Delahaye four of similar capacity as fitted to the Delahaye 134N rated as a 12CV. The 2.15-litre overhead-valve push-rod engine had a bore and stroke of 80 × 107mm and was a smaller version of the 3.2-litre, straight-6 as used in the classic and sporty 135, which in turn had been based on a truck engine. Whatever its origins, it had proved reliable and effective and must have saved Amilcar from the risk of going with a more expensive – and unproven – engine from a small company. Power for the Delahaye was quoted as 50hp. By the time Amilcar were advertising the Pégase they were claiming 58hp; it is unlikely they any longer had the resources to work some tuning magic, more likely the modifications were also outsourced, later they also offered a twin carburettor version said to be good for 65hp. It is thought up to sixteen of the early cars were fitted with the Grillot engines; these were probably just test mules and any useable chassis would have had the engines replaced with Delahaye units before being finished and sold.

DELAHAYE

The Delahaye marque was started when Émile Delahaye developed his first, belt-driven car at the Brethon Foundry and Machine works in 1894 in Tours. Emile entered the 1896 Paris – Marseille – Paris race, followed by other long-distance road races, making a name for his cars. Later in partnership with George Morane and Morane's brother-in-law Leon Desmarais, the company was incorporated in 1898 with a move to Paris using a former hydraulic machinery plant owned by the Morane family. Desmarais and Morane took control of the company in 1901, when Émile Delahaye retired and factory manager Charles Weiffenbach replaced them in 1906, by which time the brand was one of the more prolific car makers in France. The early cars were single- and twin-cylinder chain-driven machines typical of the era and under Weiffenbach Delahaye soon expanded the range to include 4-cylinder cars, heavy commercials and fire trucks, some as a result of government contracts. There was even a marine engine for the water speed record-holder La Dubonnet. When peace returned after the 1914–18 war, Delahaye was mainly concerned with making trucks until a merger with Chenard & Walcker and Rosengart in 1927, a partnership that only lasted until 1931 when Delahaye was, like many others, in a precarious financial state. The decision was taken to concentrate resources on making powerful quality cars under chief designer Amédée Varlet. Delahaye recovered quickly with first the 134, the 18cCV Type 138, powered by a 3.2-litre 6-cylinder engine itself developed from their strong truck engines and the famous sportier 135, still recognised as a classic today. In 1935 the company took over the Delage brand too. There was also a new Competitions Department with which, in 1934, Delahaye set eighteen class records at Montlhéry and developed the 135 into a successful racer, scoring many successes in the late 1930s. A fifth place at Le Mans in 1935 was followed by second and third in 1937. In 1937, René Le Bègue and Julio Quinlin won the Monte Carlo Rally driving a Delahaye. Back at Le Mans in 1938, Delahaye celebrated a famous one-two finish with Eugène Chaboud and Jean Trémoulet sharing the winner and Gaston Serraud and Yves Giraud-Cabantous the runners up. Another famous Delahaye was the Type 145, powered by a 4.5-litre V12 which was driven by René Dreyfus to an average speed of 146.56km/h over 200km at Montlhéry in 1937. Dreyfus also scored a victory in the Type 145 at Pau in 1938, owned by American heiress Lucy O'Reilly Schell, who had funded the development of this winner and fielded a team of them under the Ecurie Bleue banner. With the coming of war again in France, Delahaye supplied some chassis to the French army until the German occupation put a stop to car production.

All French luxury car makers suffered in the post-war period due to economic restraints and punitive taxes on cars with engines larger than 2 litres and most of Delahaye's limited production was exported. The Philippe Charbonneaux-designed Type 175, 178 and 180 models were only sold in small numbers and they were discontinued in 1951. Until that time continued sales of trucks to the French army kept them afloat. Delahaye's last all-new model, the 2-litre Jeep copy known as Delahaye VLR (*Véhicule Léger de Reconnaissance Delahaye*) was launched in 1951 and in 1953 the last Delahaye passenger car, the 235, which was an updated 135 and of which only 84 were made, signalled the end of the line. Hotchkiss had a licence to build the Willys Jeep in France, and this was preferred by the military over the Delahaye VLR and led in 1954 to the takeover by Hotchkiss, which promptly shut down all Delahaye production. Shortly after, Hotchkiss was taken over by the Brandt corporation and by 1956 the name Delahaye, along with Delage, was consigned to the history books with Hotchkiss continuing to make military vehicles and some trucks until 1970.

Artwork for the Pégase Olympiade.

An early brochure cover shows the original plan for the headlights.

The first car at the Salon had a new streamlined look with an unusual front-end treatment with the headlights paired together high in the centre of the radiator grille. This feature did not appear on the production cars, although it does bear a similarity to the new-look Peugeot 402 first shown at the 1935 Salon: did Peugeot copy the idea from the Pégase prototype? One can at least guess they got the idea of the name from the Pegasus mascot.

By the time the Pégase was on sale in 1935, Amilcar advertised several attractive bodies to be made by outside contractors. There are suggestions that some, if not all, were designed by renowned artist Geo Ham, who is credited with illustrating the catalogue, so it is possible that the bodies were made to order based solely on these drawings. One can see a similarity between the sleek curves and the style of the cars he depicted in his art. The first catalogue showed ten drawings of saloon, coupé, cabriolet and roadster options. Of the four-door saloons, the Olympiade had a smooth streamlined sloping tail, with a note in the catalogue offering the same without the centre pillar as the Marathon, while the Saint-Hubert differed by having a larger luggage area which added a hump at the back.[(6)] The Stade was a two-door four-seater with a sloping tail carrying a covered spare tyre, the Polo a similar shape with an extended trunk carrying the spare. The Amazone was also a two-door four-seater but with a coupé style roof with no rear quarter windows, again with a spare wheel on the back. From the illustrations it is hard to tell the difference between the Amazone and the very similar Jockey that was also catalogued.

The Golf was a two-door two-seater coupé with room for two more in the dickey seat at the back, the Fleuret a two-door four-seat cabriolet and the Skiff a two-seat roadster with a windscreen that could be folded flat. The last offering was the Racer, listed as a two-seat Voiture Competition. The wire wheels of the prototype had been replaced by pressed steel rims with a perforated pattern and all were offered with the standard Delahaye engine, although later performance upgrades were advertised to include the Grillot engine at extra cost. The area around Boulogne certainly contained many skilled *carrossiers* but it is not recorded who made which bodies, or where, although Gilles Fournier did write that the Fleuret was the work of Dubos, a well-known coachbuilder situated in Neuilly-sur-Seine. It is also recorded that the Racer was clothed by Giuseppe (Joseph) Figoni, who had established

Artwork for the Pégase Amazone.

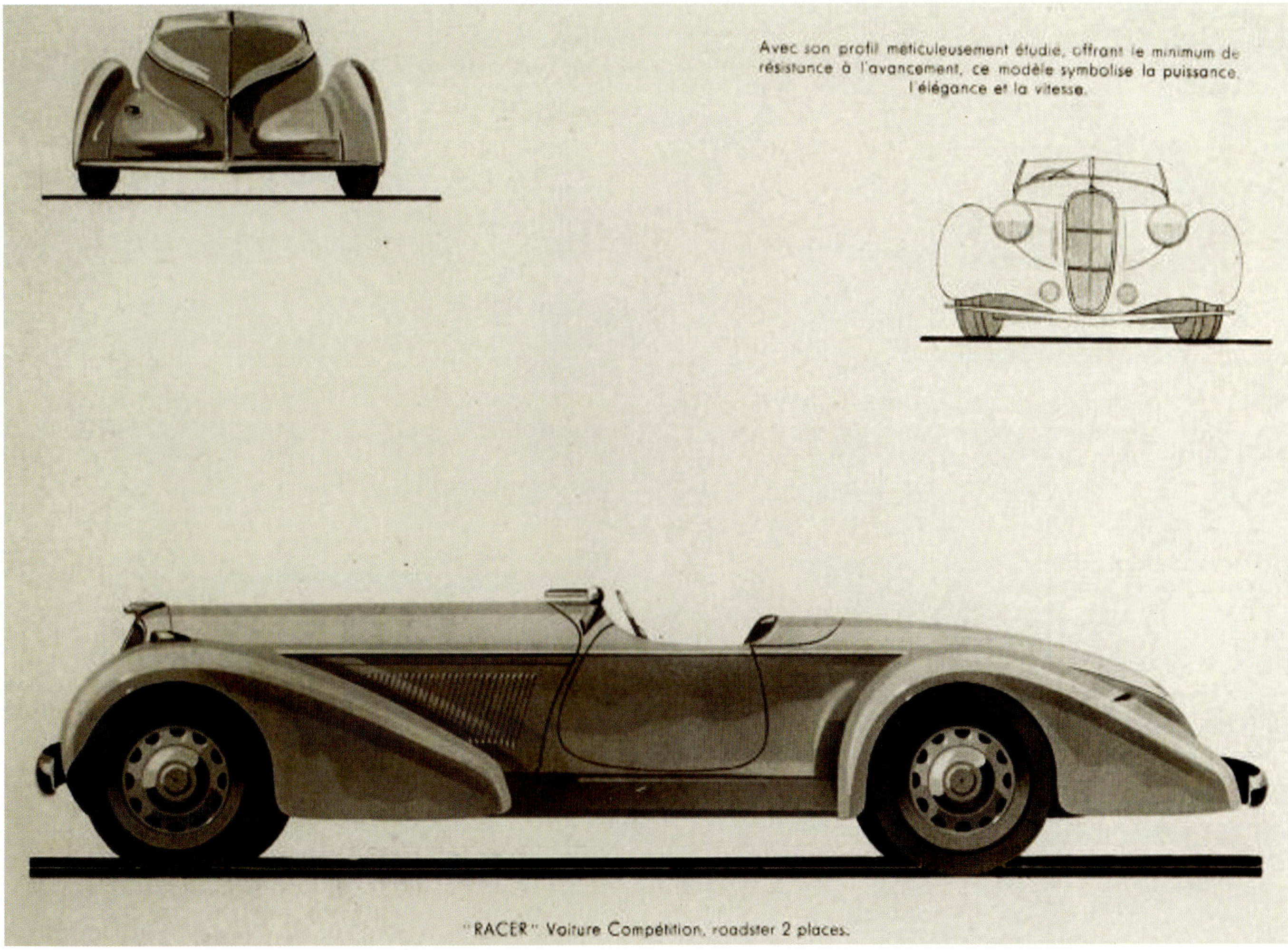

Artwork for the first version of the Pégase Racer.

Artwork for the Pégase Saint Hubert.

A Pégase cabriolet, possibly bodied by Dubos.

Another pretty lady at another concours with a 1935 Pégase cabriolet.

1935 Amilcar Pégase at the Reims Automobile Museum.

GEO HAM, 1900–1972

Georges Hamel was born on 18 September 1900 in Laval, Mayenne. Showing artistic ability from an early age his wealthy parents encouraged him and in 1918, he was accepted at the École Nationale Supérieure des Arts Décoratifs. Better known as Geo Ham, he is regarded as one of the world's finest automotive artists. He produced his first cover for *Omnia* magazine in 1920. After an early commission for a catalogue for Benjamin, he was very prolific producing illustrations for car companies including Amilcar, Rolls-Royce, Talbot, Delahaye and Chenard & Walcker. He worked in watercolours and gouache, often depicting the drivers of the day as caricatures. He also depicted aviation subjects and worked for *L'Illustration* magazine through to the 1940s. He is probably best known from the posters he produced for all of the major races in France, the most famous for the Le Mans 24-hour race and the Monaco Grand Prix, originals of which today are highly collectable. As modern photography started to take over in press and advertising Ham, like many commercial artists of his generation, found his commissions disappearing and he was no longer wanted. He was almost forgotten when he died in Paris on 30 June 1972. As well as designing the bodywork for the Amilcar Pégase Racer built by Figoni, he produced many advertising posters and artwork for the company.

Carrosserie Automobilie in Boulogne-sur-Seine in 1920 before forming the partnership with Ovidio Falaschi in 1935. The styling and details typical of his work can be clearly seen on a restored surviving example.

For 1935, Amilcar also offered a larger 'Sports' engine, again designed by Grillot based on his earlier design, a pushrod four of 2490cc giving 75hp. Featuring a modified cylinder head with larger valves, it was named the G36; one can assume this was G for Grillot and 36 for the following year. Primarily intended for the Racer the G36 engine may have found its way into other models at a 9,000 franc premium. For the Pégase Racer chassis, Amilcar replaced the cable-operated brakes with a hydraulic Lockheed system and fitted upgraded shock absorbers. A 12CV Pégase chassis was priced at 26,900 francs.

For the 1936 Salon later that year the range offered had been reduced to just four models: the Amazone two-door four-seater coupé, the Fleuret two-door four-seater cabriolet, the Saint-Hubert four-door four-seater saloon and

The Pégase chassis and running gear.

The Grillot-designed engine.

the Skiff two-seater roadster. A 12CV Pégase bare chassis was priced at 26,900 francs, the Amazone at 37,900 francs, the Saint-Hubert at 39,900 francs and the top of the line Fleuret or Skiff each cost 42,900 francs. All of these were expensive cars for where they fitted into the market at the time and were priced well above a comparable Citroën or Delahaye. No longer available for 1936, it is not known how many Figoni-styled Racers were produced; these are the most sought-after of the Pégase range. The engine options for these last models made was again the 12CV 'Normale' as standard fitment, with the 14CV Grand Sport an expensive 9,000-franc upgrade. The top speed of the various models would have depended on the type of body chosen, but Amilcar quoted a 130km/h (81mph) maximum.

Pégase production stopped some time in 1937 after the company was taken over by Hotchkiss, who had plans for the Amilcar name to continue on a new small model that would not compete with the existing Hotchkiss range.

There was however one last model to carry the Pégase name, this one a real racing car having little in common with the previous Racer model. Eight years on from when Amilcar last had their own racing team, and with no budget to start afresh, the works did somehow cobble together four new racing cars based on modified Pégase chassis. Intended to be raced in the high-profile endurance races at Le Mans and Montlhèry, the chassis was shortened by 30cm to 2.5 metres, with a wider track. It was covered in a lightweight streamlined body by Duval with removable wings and lights and a modified 80hp version of the 2.5 litre Grillot engine was installed, said to be good for 165km/h (103mph). Not officially for sale, one was shown at the 1936 Paris Salon, presumably to add interest to the Pégase range on show.

Three were sold to drivers Felix Boudot, Marcel Contet and Raoul Forestier, of whom Contet was the most successful. The fourth car was retained by Maurice Mestivier, probably as a private entry rather than a works car. At the first test of the new racer, the Grand Prix de la Marne at the famous high-speed Reims Gueux circuit, Mestivier raced into the lead before valve trouble forced his retirement. Contet could only manage fourteenth place but Mme Roux (who by now was Mestivier's wife) finished second in one of the Figoni Pégase Racers. Contet had better luck in September at the Grand Prix de France du MCF at Montlhéry, where he finished fourth behind Mme Roux who had taken over Mestivier's car.

Mme Fernande Roux and her Pégase at a concours.

A Pégase Racer on the Amilcar stand at the Paris Salon.

Marcel Contet must have lost patience with his Pégase, as in the next few years before the war he raced an Aston Martin, a Delahaye 135, a Peugeot Darl'Mat and a Riley Sprite in many races in France with better results. He later sold his Pégase to Emile Darl'Mat, who fitted a modified and tuned Darl'Mat Peugeot 402 engine and had some post-war success with Charles de Cortanze driving.

For the 1938 running of the Le Mans 24-hour race, Fernande Roux and Germaine Rouault started in Mestivier's racing car and were running in tenth place when they retired after 101 laps with a big-end failure. Mestivier and Roux had better luck the following September, when they finished first in their class and fifth overall at the Twelve-Hour race at Montlhéry. There are also reports of Charles Roch and a M. Fortier racing in Pégase models, but there are no significant results recorded.

Mme Roux also had some successes with her Amilcar Pégase Figoni Racer, particularly on the women-only Paris-Saint Raphael Féminin Rally, finishing third in the 2200–3000cc class and eighteenth overall in 1936 and first in class and tenth overall in 1938.

Very few examples of the Pégase appear to survive; a two-door sedan restoration project was sold by Bonhams in London a few years ago.

AMILCAR PÉGASE RACER

I make no apologies for including this car in this chapter as it is probably the best, possibly the only, example of a Racer model in existence – although it may have been better-placed in Chapter 16 with the 'Specials'. It was restored twenty or so years ago with a stunning example of the Figoni-made body covering a mix of non-original parts. The inappropriate chrome wire wheels are par for the course on the American concours circuit.

The only known surviving Figoni-bodied Pégase at an American concours event.

This one looks good from any angle, with echoes of the contemporary 'boat-tail' Auburn Speedsters.

The flying Pegasus mascot would contravene modern safety standards.

Simple but effective and comfortable cockpit.

Figoni's interpretation of Geo Ham's design is a masterpiece.

A G36 Pégase stripped of lights and mudguards for racing.

Mme Fernande Roux and Mme Germaine Rouault shared this Amilcar Pégase at Le Mans in 1938.

CHAPTER 11

HOTCHKISS AND THE COMPOUND – THE END OF AMILCAR

The last car that bore the Amilcar name could be said to be a Hotchkiss project that just borrowed the Amilcar badge for marketing purposes. As sales of the Pégase failed to cover the expenses of its design and tooling, as with the C8 before it, Marcel Sée once again found himself dealing with debts threatening the survival of Amilcar, which forced him to sell a majority of his shares in SOFIA, the company that now owned the Amilcar name. Harry Ainsworth, the boss at Hotchkiss, had in 1934 initiated a design for a projected small car for the Hotchkiss range. This was requested by dealers who were suffering a downturn in sales of the higher-priced cars during the depression years, but it was cancelled when he found out about the new small front-wheel-drive car that Jean-Albert Grégoire of the now defunct Tracta company was working on. Grégoire, firmly committed to the idea of front-wheel drive, had started designing what became the Compound in 1935 after sampling an Adler Trumpf.

J.A. GRÉGOIRE, 1899–1992

Jean-Albert Grégoire was born in Paris on 7 July 1899. Orphaned by the age of nine, he was brought up by a rich uncle who took an interest in the new automobile craze. Grégoire was enrolled in the Ecole Polytechnique and decided to study law rather than the technical studies. He graduated as a Doctor of Law, but with his inherited interest in cars he set up a workshop in Versailles with a wealthy friend, Pierre Fenaille, where they set out to produce their own car, with Fenaille favouring front-wheel drive. So, in 1926 the first Tracta was produced, driven by the patented Tracta joint. This was the first type of constant velocity joint, which became the standard fitment for early front-wheel-drive cars such as those from Adler and DKW and used in military vehicles made by Alvis, Daimler, Laffly and Panhard but most famously by Willys in the Jeep. Impéria in Belgium and Rosengart in France manufactured the Adler under licences.

With a move to a larger factory at Asnières, the Tracta cars produced between 1927 and 1934 employed S.C.A.P. engines for the smaller cars and Continental and Hotchkiss in the larger 6-cylinder models. Accompanied by Lucien Lemesle, Grégoire drove an 1100cc Tracta Gephi in the Le Mans 24-hour race in 1927 and finished in a respectable seventh place. Less fortunate in the next two years, in 1930 Grégoire partnered with Fernand Vallon drove a Type-A to eighth with another finishing ninth; at least they had proved the reliability of the front-wheel-drive concept. After some design work for Donnet and Chenard & Walcker, which came to nothing due to the effects of the depression sinking both firms, Grégoire designed the Amilcar Compound to be made by Hotchkiss. Although the German occupation supposedly put a stop to any new development in the French car industry, Aluminium Français commissioned Grégoire secretly working at his Asnières base to design a new cast aluminium prototype to be known as the Aluminium Français Grégoire or AFG. With an all-aluminium body, an air-cooled flat-twin engine and of course, front-wheel drive, this was to become the new Panhard Dyna, launched in 1950. Both Hartnett in Australia and Kaiser in the United States were interested in licensing the Dyna Panhard, but both deals came to nothing in their respective territories. His next new venture was the Hotchkiss Grégoire, a similar but larger model with a water-cooled 2-litre engine but, being too expensive to produce and sell, only 250 examples were made until it was cancelled in 1954. A couple of years later Grégoire produced a two-seat convertible with a 2.2-litre supercharged flat-four engine and bodies designed and built by Henri Chapron, only ten of which were made. Other projects had included an electric car and the experimental gas turbine-powered SOCEMA-Grégoire with a front-engined, rear-wheel-drive layout. Right until his death in Paris on 20 August 1992, aged 93, Grégoire continued to work with Aluminium Francais (today known as Pechiney) on research and development. A man of many talents, starting in 1949 he wrote and published many books on automobile history and engineering as well as writing novels and murder mysteries under the pen name Albert Gregory. He was also an acknowledged wine expert.

Amilcar Compound brochure for 1937.

Stripped Compound shows off J.A. Grégoire's alloy castings.

For his latest design Grégoire used a cast Alpax chassis frame for strength and light weight. Alpax is an alloy patented by American-Hungarian inventor Aladar Pacz, which has the advantage of not shrinking when cooling after casting but retains tensile strength. Grégoire came up with a design based around a central platform consisting of the front bulkhead bolted to deep section side rails all cast in the new wonder material. The idea for building a car around this enclosed 'tub'

Promotional artwork used the old advertising trick of drawing very small people to make the car look bigger than it was.

was said to have come to him in the bath. He still needed to prove his design would work and then find someone to make it. Concocting a hybrid by fitting his new chassis to the cut-up Adler Trumpf in which Grégoire covered 40,000km in troubleshooting tests, he then presented the proposal to Jean Dupin, the director of Aluminium Français. Dupin was impressed enough to assign engineer Jean-Jacques Baron to work with Grégoire to see what was feasible and to cost the whole project with the promise that Aluminium Français would cover the costs involved. The neat new body designed by Clément Vinciguerra would be made from light steel pressings and it was this combination of the alloy frame and steel body that coined the name Compound.

Grégoire was already known at Hotchkiss, having used their engines in the earlier Tracta, so Ainsworth and sales director Jacques Jacobsen saw an opportunity to use the radical new project. It would carry the Amilcar name, as it was a brand already known for such small economical cars, thus keeping the new car separate from and not damaging the reputation of the larger more powerful cars in the current Hotchkiss range. The potential clash of brands in the middle-class market sector was reason enough to drop the Pégase range as soon as Ainsworth and Jacobsen had taken control of the board of SOFIA.

Grégoire was assisted by engineer Maurice Moisy taking care of the mechanical components. With a wheelbase of 2.5 metres the running gear under the frame consisted of all independent suspension, by torsion bars at the rear, and rack and pinion steering with 1.75 turns lock to lock, which would have been adequate for a fairly small light car. Braking was by 20.5cm diameter drum brakes of the self-adjusting Bendix type on all four wheels, although the old-fashioned system of cable operation was by now out of date. Grégoire had been unable to persuade Ainsworth the added cost of using a hydraulic system was justified. Worse still, the prototype used the underpowered 929cc side-valve four of the earlier 5CV Amilcar C5. This was because Grégoire had been instructed to use this existing engine rather than incur the further expense and time delays needed to start afresh, as requested by Ainsworth, but the engine soon proved inadequate. The front-wheel-drive plan required the engine and gearbox to be fitted in reverse to its originally designed layout, which necessitated a cable-operated gearshift. For what was an otherwise very modern concept, this was also less than ideal. Once again compromises dictated by economic and time pressures would adversely affect what should have been a significant new model.

Compound had tidy and attractive lines typical of the late 1930s.

HOTCHKISS

Société Anonyme des Anciens Etablissements Hotchkiss et Compagnie was a French arms manufacturer first established by American Benjamin B. Hotchkiss at Viviez near Rodez in 1867, later moving to Saint-Denis near Paris in 1875. With extensive machine tools and staff, Hotchkiss started in the automobile business by making components for De Dion-Bouton and Panhard et Levassor, and in 1903 began making cars under their own name designed by Georges Terasse, who was poached from Mors. The first was a 17CV 4-cylinder model, and then the 20CV type C appeared based on the Mercedes Simplex. Models L, O and × were added and in 1910 the 2212cc Type-Z represented the Hotchkiss name in the small car market. With war coming in 1914, Hotchkiss switched the car factory back to armament supplies with another factory opened in Coventry, England, but resumed car production in 1919, initially using pre-war designs. The more up-to-date AM model that had been designed at Coventry arrived in 1923, but that factory was sold to Morris soon after, so Henry Mann Ainsworth and Alfred Herbert Wilde who had been in charge moved to Paris to become general manager and chief engineer of Automobiles Hotchkiss. While the AM sold well, Hotchkiss moved to a larger factory nearby still in Saint-Denis and in 1929 added the 6-cylinder AM73 and AM80 models. With Hotchkiss still regarded as a luxury car maker, the early 1930s models followed a new naming scheme; the 411 was an 11CV model with a 4-cylinder engine, the 413 a 13CV four and the 615, 617 and 620 were 6-cylinder models of 15, 17 and 20CV taxable rating. This was then changed in 1936 to a number of cylinders and the bore size, hence the 686 replaced the 620 and so on. Strong, powerful and reliable Hotchkiss cars won the Monte Carlo Rally in 1932, 1933, 1934, 1939, 1949 and 1950.

Of course, in 1937 Hotchkiss stepped in to take over Amilcar production, but that development is covered in Chapter 11. With the armament side of the business nationalised by the government in 1936, by the time war came again in 1939 the car factory was given over to manufacturing tanks for a short time. This was until the Germans occupied Paris in 1940, at which time the factory was requisitioned to work on repairs and maintenance of German military machinery. Ainsworth managed to escape to England and, as a result of a new Nazi Germany law that authorised the confiscation of businesses controlled by Jews, Peugeot was offered a controlling share in Hotchkiss. When peace returned, Peugeot relinquished its control of Hotchkiss and Henry Ainsworth returned to once again resume production of trucks and passenger vehicles in 1946. As with Delahaye and other luxury car makers, conditions in the post-war years were against them and only small numbers of cars were sold – although sales of the commercial and military vehicles, especially the M201 Jeep copy, saved the company. Ainsworth retired in 1949 and was succeeded as Managing Director by Maurice de Gary. The Anjou and Anthéor models appeared in 1950 and Hotchkiss had also bought the rights to the Grégoire front-wheel-drive car. The Hotchkiss Grégoire was introduced in 1951 but at a high price, double that of a comparable Citroën, and Hotchkiss lost money on every car sold. The unpopular model was dropped in 1952 after only 247 units had been sold. Sales of other models staggered on for a couple more years, but by 1955 when Citroën introduced the DS19 and Peugeot the 403, Hotchkiss were out-classed and even what export sales there might have been were limited by having stuck with the old tradition of right-hand-drive cars. Another possible saviour for Hotchkiss was a tractor. In 1951, Hotchkiss agreed a deal with the Standard Motor Company to manufacture the Ferguson TE20 tractor in the Saint-Denis plant. Until 1957, Standard-Hotchkiss built over 37,000 TE20 tractors there. In January 1957, the model was renamed the FF-30 and, when production ended in 1958, a further 29,000 had been built. Standard also considered buying the Hotchkiss plant to build the Triumph Herald in order to target local sales, but the deal fell through. As with Delahaye, the merger of 1954 led to nothing and both companies were taken over by Brandt soon after, leaving the Hotchkiss name to be used in a confusing mix of truck and military vehicles sometimes titled Hotchkiss-Brandt until all vehicle production ended in 1970.

Still, Grégoire worked fast and had the first prototype ready by mid-1937 for testing before its introduction as the new Amilcar Compound B38 at the Paris Salon in October that year. A bare chassis frame was on display showing the new construction methods of the cast bulkhead incorporating the windshield, the two cast longerons and front crossmember to which all of the mechanical components were fitted. This was accompanied by two saloons listed as the 'Normal' and 'Luxury' versions. The body design followed current trends, with an American influence. The old style of a shaped radiator grille apeing the even earlier standard practice of a separate radiator had been phased out with a curved cowling that flowed into the bonnet line with only some plated trim to outline the frontal aspect. While the front mudguards were still stand-alone pressings, they were smoothed into the sides of the bonnet and supported a pair of headlamps in the space between. The rear mudguards were narrower than before, almost absorbed into the rear quarter panels. There was no pretence at any remnants of running boards and all came with perforated steel wheels carrying a plated centre hubcap.

The overall appearance was a statement of sleek and clean modernity even for what was a modestly sized car. A roadster would also be offered when production got underway.

There was another delay when before production could even begin the decision was taken to replace the old C5 engine with a larger 1185cc side-valve four of 63 × 95mm bore and stroke. Ainsworth decided a copy of the existing Hillman engine would meet his needs, but rather than negotiate to buy them in he decided to copy the design and make the engine in house. Vincent Bertarione, who was Hotchkiss' engine specialist, was tasked with drawing this, something he thought was beneath him as he had previously designed racing engines for Fiat, Sunbeam and Talbot, but he got the job done. Ainsworth had already had form when it came to copying engine designs; in 1921 he had copied a Continental engine to be made by Hotchkiss, which was supplied in large numbers to Morris. With a power output now of 35hp the new 'Hillman' engine was ready for installation in the first cars delivered coupled to a new four-speed gearbox. The combination of light weight, around 750 to 800kg according to body type, and the improved engine allowed a claim of a top speed of 110km/h (68mph).

Ainsworth then persuaded famed motoring journalist William Fletcher Bradley – better known by his byline W. F. B. – as a regular contributor in *The Autocar* to undertake an extraordinary road trip in a Compound with the new 1185cc engine. Bradley was based in Paris and his reports were widely syndicated. This adventure took them from Paris to Marseille, boarding a ship to Algiers, and on through North Africa to Egypt and across the Suez Canal, driving on through the Sinai Desert to Jerusalem and then Baghdad. They continued to Palmyra, Damascus and Istanbul returning to Europe travelling through the Balkans, Belgrade, Vienna and Cologne. On returning to Paris the Compound was taken to the track at Montlhéry, where it covered 1,400km (870 miles) at an average speed of 104km/h (65mph). Bradley reported on this trip in successive weeks in *The Autocar*, all the while extolling the car's reliability. Of course, Ainsworth tried to make the most of the publicity, but delays, setbacks and possibly even the price would all count against much in the way of sales.

Production was said to have started in April 1938 after some delays with manufacturing processes for the steel panels, but progress was slow. With the cancellation of Pégase

Amilcar Compound 1938 cabriolet at the Musée National de L'Automobile in Mulhouse, France.

A B38 Compound in need of some restoration turned up at a London auction in recent years.

It looks quite solid, but one wonders if it sold well just for the use of the registration number?

production the existing Boulogne factory was closed in May 1938 and Amilcar's head office was relocated to the Hotchkiss premises at 71, Avenue des Ternes, just north of the Arc de Triomphe in the 17th arrondissement. While the assembly of the Compound was based at the Hotchkiss factory at Boulevard Orano in Saint-Denis, some components were outsourced to a Hotchkiss subsidiary, Nicole and Co of Montreuil, with Forges et Ateliers de Constructions Electriques de Jeumont a manufacturer of railway carriages supplying some bodywork parts. The all-important aluminium structural frame was cast by Léon Montupet at the Aluminium Français works. The Mines department responsible for such things granted approval for the new car on 3 May 1938, rated at a taxable 7CV. With hindsight it is obvious the planned production of 50 cars a week was too optimistic, but we have seen this unrealistic belief in the next new product being a winner so many times before it is surprising those in charge still hoped for the best. The larger and by now well-proven Citroën Traction Avant was selling at two-thirds of the asking price of the Compound. Still, from the launch at the Salon there appeared to be encouraging interest.

Even with a healthy order book, production at the factory never got up to the hoped for weekly output, one excuse being that the new Hotchkiss tank was now given priority with the belief that another European war was on the horizon. Indeed it was, but the Compound trickled out of the factory through the rest of year, while at the Salon that October Hotchkiss added a sunshine saloon to the range, basically a cabriolet by another name, differing from the roadster with fixed door and side window frames. As many 35 Compounds were made in the last quarter of 1938 and by early in 1939 output was up to a heady five cars a day, hardly enough to justify the investment. By the end of the year a further 576 examples had successfully left the factory gates. This was hardly cause for celebration, and with Germany threatening expansion in Europe and war looking even closer, it was logical that Hotchkiss concentrated on their military supply contracts, with even less interest in propping up what was by now a minor distraction.

Still, the little Compound stumbled on. Following comments that it could do with some more power, a new engine was designed. By taking the bore out to 97mm giving a capacity of 1340cc and fitting a new overhead-valve cylinder head output was up to 45hp with the taxable rating up to 8CV, the top speed was increased to 130km/h (81mph). This new model was first tested in July and labelled the Compound B67, to be launched at the October Salon, as was customary. Unfortunately, it was by now too little, too late and when France declared war with Germany in September, the Salon was cancelled and any further production of cars for sale was in doubt with a total of 671 Compounds made up to the end of the year. Very few of them, possibly only twenty, were the new B67. However, it was not until the occupation of Paris in May 1940 that all production of cars for civilian use ended, with a further 64 units turned out in those few months. Of the few that were exported the Compound was sold under the Hotchkiss brand. Shown at motor shows in Brussels and London and available in right-hand drive, the car was officially called the Hotchkiss-Amilcar Ten, even dropping the Amilcar name altogether in Britain, where it was advertised as just a Hotchkiss.

This B38 sedan was advertised for sale in France in 2024…

...like its London counterpart it looks like a simple restoration case.

Also, like the other one, it has lost its hubcaps; one wonders if they were prone to falling off?

Simple but functional interior, but that cable-operated gearchange was troublesome.

Hotchkiss also produced a few of the B67 engines which were supplied to truck maker Laffly, who installed them in prototypes of their V10R all-terrain vehicle.

The last of the old Amilcar team, Marcel Sée, resigned from the board of SOFIA on 10 April 1940 although this may have been in anticipation of the German occupation (Sée was Jewish) rather than any business decision.

We cannot know if Hotchkiss had any idea of using the Amilcar name after the war and from 1940 the ever-inventive Grégoire was already looking ahead to other projects including a design for a new car made from lightweight materials, possibly more Alpax again, for Simca, who until then had been making a licensed copy of the Fiat Topolino and would need something more modern for the future.

A smartly dressed lady and a handsome 1939 Compound roadster.

WARTIME PRODUCTION

It has been reported that two wheelbases of 250cm and 265cm were available, although the longer version may have been an adaptation for some war-time modifications. Between 1940 and 1942 Hotchkiss did produce 149 Compound-based estate cars, of which 50 were delivered to the postal service and 49 were delivered to the French Red Cross for use as ambulances. A further 50 seemed to have been sold to other customers. We can assume that as no cars were available for strictly civilian use, these may have been for other essential users – doctors, farmers and food producers – or for other essential supplies. These were all apparently built to the earlier B38 specification with the smaller engine, although there were also a few more Compounds made with the B67 engine with an adapted three-speed gearbox replacing the four-speed. Were these intended for some particular use? No factory records survive to explain their purpose.

AFTER THE WAR

With Grégoire otherwise occupied, the Hotchkiss design team was led by Marc Brosset and Clément Vinciguerra. There were no plans to continue any Amilcar production, but Vinciguerra did make one more prototype based on the Compound. Drawings were found for a planned 'Woody'-style station wagon dated from 1937 that Vinciguerra planned to go ahead with in 1946, but it seems that one was never built. More mysteriously, other drawings by Vinciguerra dating from 1941 referring to 'Project 704' showed an improved modernised design for a proposed post-war Compound using the B67 engine with mildly altered bodywork featuring an American look slatted front end. There may have been concern about the availability and cost of the previously used alloys, at least for this one-off prototype, so this project was built on a separate chassis frame. Whether the future hope was for it to be based on the original Grégoire cast frame or, in the interest of economy and from lessons learned from the costs of making the Compound it would have been of a more conventional body on chassis construction, we will never know. Surprisingly, during the war years, the design actually saw a prototype built, which was used as Vinciguerra's private car and survived for some time after the war, clocking up more than 200,000 kilometres before it was scrapped. Unfortunately, no photographs exist, so do we call this the last ever Amilcar or just another Hotchkiss project for a car that never was?

The remaining stock of B67 engines was sold, along with the tooling necessary for their production, to Impéria, who used them for a production run of about 1,000 of their own front-wheel-drive TA8 models.

THE PONS PLAN

The Provisional Government of the French Republic under General de Gaulle was tasked with rebuilding France and appointed Paul-Marie Pons to the Ministry of Industrial Production under the direction of the minister, Robert Lacoste. Directed to simultaneously reinvigorate and rationalise the motor industry, Pons had to draw up plans that would favour some of the 22 manufacturers of passenger cars and 28 manufacturers of trucks and appear to penalise others. The two largest and most powerful – Citroën and Renault – were both allowed to continue as they were. Peugeot were forced into an alliance with Hotchkiss, Latil and Saurer for commercial vehicle production and many of the smaller companies were forced into working in partnership with former rivals. Some of the pre-war prestige brands like Bugatti and Delahaye were not able to fit into any workable plan and never really recovered. In the passenger car sector, Citroën, with their existing Traction model, would occupy what would for now be considered the upper end of the market. Renault and Peugeot would produce mid-sized cars, and for the small car market Panhard and Simca were both tied into producing versions of the A.F.G. (Aluminium Français Grégoire), which was the latest front-wheel-drive aluminium-framed car from Jean-Albert Grégoire. So, there would be no need for Amilcar, who probably were not even on the list of post-war manufacturers. Government policy did not completely stop Hotchkiss from making passenger cars, but it did categorise the company's products as luxury cars and therefore critical materials could only be allocated for export sales. Under that definition there was no chance to relaunch the Amilcar Compound or any possible derivatives.

THE END

After the war, although Hotchkiss owned the name Amilcar and any remnants of the SOFIA company, the Hotchkiss company itself was bought and sold over the next few decades and the last traces of the SOFIA name only disappeared when the last iteration of Hotchkiss was absorbed into the Thompson Group in 1980. Some would say the true Amilcar story ended a long time before; one of the engineering staff, Pierre Chan, said in a later interview, 'For me, the Amilcar was dead after Saint-Denis.'

CHAPTER 12

THE AMILCAR AGENTS ABROAD

It did not take long for the Amilcar to gain a reputation around the world as an affordable sports car that was fun on the road and a winner on the track. The logistics of shipping cars around the world a hundred years ago must have meant some real demand justified the effort, but within a year or two they were available not just in the neighbouring European countries: Australia and the USA also had agencies established.

So popular was the Amilcar CGS that to meet local demand it was built under licence in Italy, Germany and Austria, where import tariffs and restrictions meant it was advantageous to assemble them locally.

AUSTRIA

Following a trade agreement between France and Austria in 1923, two businesses were established in Vienna to import Amilcars. Schlotterbeck & Kandl was a partnership between Carl Schlotterbeck-Simon, who also had the Swiss concession, and Bernhard Kandl from St Gilgen near Salzburg, both experienced competitors on the local hillclimbs. There was an import limit of 120 cars per year from France and this was soon found to be insufficient, as in this period there was an increase in the automobile market in general with French cars in general being in demand.

The radiator disguises the Grofri's Amilcar origins.

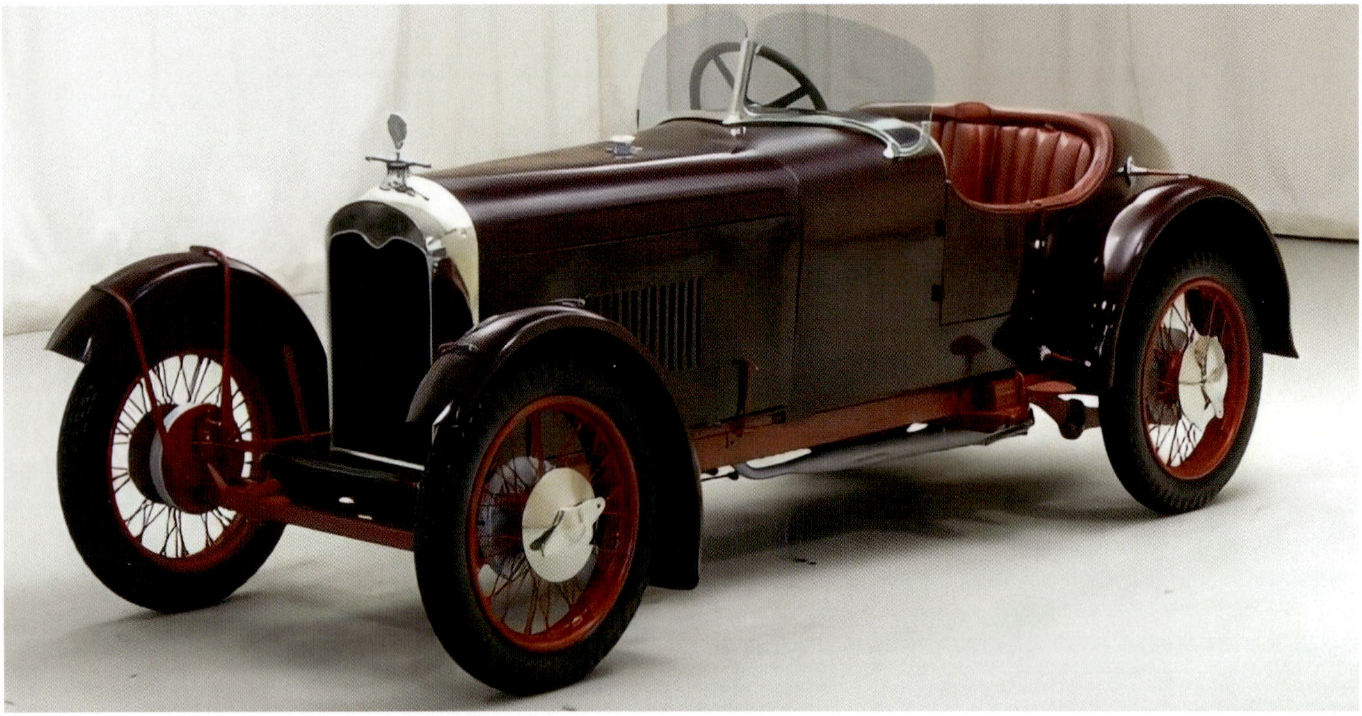

This Grofri was sold in the USA, apparently missing its headlights but otherwise in very good condition.

100 STÜCK À 200 KRONEN

100 AKTIEN

DER

№ 0078201 – 0078300

GROFRI-WERKE A.G.

MOTORFAHRZEUG- UND LANDWIRTSCHAFTLICHE MASCHINENFABRIK

JEDE ZU

ZWEIHUNDERT KRONEN 200 ZWEIHUNDERT KRONEN

durch welche dem Inhaber alle jene Rechte gewährt werden, welche jedem Inhaber von 100 Aktien der Grofri-Werke A.G. Motorfahrzeug- und landwirtschaftliche Maschinenfabrik nach den Gesellschaftsstatuten zustehen.

Atzgersdorf, am 31. Oktober 1923.
BEI WIEN

GROFRI-WERKE A.G.
Motorfahrzeug- und landwirtschaftliche Maschinenfabrik.

A share certificate for someone who invested 200 Kronen in Grofri-Werke A.G.

The Amilcar was proving itself a popular little sports car and was gaining a reputation in the many local hillclimb events, so with a limit on the numbers imported a new company, Österreichische Amilcar-Automobil AG, was established in Vienna to build Amilcars under licence. The company directors were Karl Pfeffer and Paul Wiesner who had ambitious plans for selling the locally-bodied Austro-Amilcar, starting in 1924. Despite, or maybe because of, all the talk of a busy production line assembling hundreds of cars, the money ran out within a year and Holdengräber & Schwarz, who were also the concessionaires for Voisin, took over their import quota. Another company, Gross & Friedmann based in Atzgersdorf near Vienna, acquired the licence to make Amilcars for the Austrian market under the name Grofri.

Robert Gross and Leopold Friedmann founded Grofri Werke AG in 1921, and built a large 6-cylinder Tourer before the agreement with Amilcar. They produced the GA I, a copy of the basic two-seater CC model but fitted with the 907cc, which had been used in the CV model in France. The GA II was a four-seater based on the C4 with the wheelbase stretched to 2.66 metres with the 1074cc engine of the CGS. There was also the GL II, a light commercial with the same chassis as the GA II but with the 1004cc C4 spec engine. The GS I used the standard 2.45-metre C4 frame with extended dumb irons at the front to carry the CGS-type braked front axle and had the 1074cc CGS engine with the option of a supercharger claimed to boost power to 40hp. Last was the GS II, a four-seater version of the GS I. All were built on a reinforced chassis to cope with the local roads. The neat front mudguards of the cycle type were mounted to the front hub backing plates, enabling them to turn with the wheels, which were fitted with larger 'balloon' tyres and some odd-looking large hubcaps. Purely cosmetically, to claim their own identity, there were minor changes to the shape of the radiator surround. Grofri also made farming equipment and closed its doors in 1931 because of financial problems. After 1927 when Grofri ran into difficulties and ceased making Amilcar clones, the concession to import Amilcars was held solely by Bernhard Kandl.

Some Grofris were fitted with Roots superchargers for competition use and achieved notable results in local hillclimbs. Opera singer Käthe Rantzau competed in one in hillclimbs and German Crown Prince Wilhelm in 1927 bought a silver Grofri Sport in Vienna, which had a Ricardo cylinder head for improved performance. Max Hoffmann, as he was then (he dropped the last 'n' after World War II) had been given an Amilcar by his father, with which he had some success, and he continued competing with a Grofri until 1936 even when Grofri was no longer in business. After emigrating to New York via Paris in 1941, Hoffman later became very successful as the importer of BMW, Jaguar, Mercedes-Benz, Porsche and VW for the American market.

GERMANY

The Automobilfabrik Zella-Mehlis GmbH was founded by Heinrich Ehrhardt in 1921 in Zella-Mehlis in the Thuringian Forest, 120km north-east of Frankfurt. He had made money from armaments in World War I and produced a range of cars and commercial vehicles. In 1922 Ehrhardt merged his company with Szabó and Wechselmann, a coachbuilder in Berlin, as Ehrhardt-Szawe Automobilwerke AG, but this did not last long as Erhardt was declared bankrupt soon after. He was still able to set up another new business as *Pluto-Vertriebs-Gesellschaft*, both to make large touring cars under the Pluto name as well as take on the Amilcar agency for Berlin. Encouraged by sales of the popular CC model, the company reached an agreement to manufacture Amilcar cars under licence with the Pluto name from 1924.

The C4 and CS were sold as the 4/20 PS with the 1004cc 20hp engine with a choice of two-seater roadsters either bodied in metal, a mahogany plank skiff style or as a smart brougham. From 1926 Pluto also offered a four-seat tourer and a light commercial based on the C4 chassis. The CGS was named the 5/30 PS, the 1074cc engine producing 30hp. Soon, the Pluto cars received 'improvements' at the German factory. There was the option of the CGS-type braked front axle and a supercharged racing version 5/30/65 PS, with a claimed output of 65hp. By 1927, with a new director Ernst Wolff, the company was renamed Pluto Automobilfabrik AG, but production ended later that same year. Voran-Automobilbau from Berlin used engines supplied by Pluto in the short-lived front-wheel-drive Voran. That company was taken over by AEG in 1930.

Pluto cars achieved some minor results with Hermann Friederich, Adolf Mederer, Paul Reich and Cord von Einem. Robert Gockenbach won the voiturette class in an Amilcar

This German Pluto wears a timber skiff body, as was fashionable in France at the time.

A Pluto offered with small sedan coachwork.

Stylish artwork for Pluto advertising.

at the Avus track near Berlin in 1924 and finished eighth in a Pluto at the high-profile Eiffelrennen race at the Nürburgring in 1927. In 1926, Cord von Einem set up a Pluto dealership at 29, Delitzscher Straße in Halle near Leipzig. At the same time Deutsche Amilcar Automobil Verkaufs *GmbH* were importing Amilcars from France, so there would have been a choice between both Amilcar and Pluto models in Germany.

ITALY

Eugenio Silvani had been importing Amilcars into Italy since 1922 through the Compagnia Generale Automobili based at Via Castro Pretorio 124, Rome before he acquired a licence to build the Amilcar Italiana in 1925. The cars based on the Amilcar CGS were built under the licence at a factory in Lecco, in the Como province. Amilcars were already attractive in Italy due to the tax advantages of the small-capacity engines and there was an added incentive to assemble cars from parts bought in as the import tariffs for parts rather than complete cars were cheaper.

By 1927, the Società Industriale Lombardo Veneta Automobili (SILVA) of Piazza Bra 26, Verona had taken over the licences from the CGA of Rome. In 1928 they introduced the 7 CV Gran Sport con Compressore, a supercharged CGSs. Sales had been healthy due to some successes in

This Amilcar Italiana is the only known survivor of its type.

local competition. The factory 6-cylinder cars had done well whenever they visited Monza for the Italian Grand Prix and again at the Tre Fontane circuit in Rome for the Royal Grand Prix, and Domenico Gamboni had shown well in the 1924 running of the Targa Florio against much more powerful opposition, finishing 19th in the overall classification and first in the under-1100cc class.

As seemed to be the pattern everywhere, the Italian market for luxuries such as cars took a dive in 1929 and assembly of the Amilcar Italiana ended in 1929. A total of 4,700 examples of the CGS and CGSs had left the Italian factories until they were no longer able to compete on price with the rival 509 model from Fiat, which in sporty 509S and SM guise was equal on performance.

AUSTRALIA

Australia is a big country, covering as much land area as the whole of Europe or the continental USA, but in 1922 it only had a population of five and a half million people. There was no home-grown car industry save for the coachbuilders that had sprung up since World War I. In 1916 the government had introduced a tariff scheme to limit the import of complete cars, the lower rate favouring rolling chassis with no bodywork. This was supposedly due to shipping restrictions during the war, but it also had the effect of giving work to the old carriage makers from the horse-drawn days who would become the new generation of coachbuilders. Some of these did good work, some not so good. There was at that time no organised network of official concessionaires controlling the importation of cars.

With some loyalty to the old ideas of being a British colony, there was a strong demand for the products of Austin, Morris, Rover and Vauxhall, but as these were not always suited to the local conditions the bigger and stronger American cars started to become more popular, particularly in the country areas where the driving conditions were much harder on the machinery. So, by the 1920s there was a collection of individual entrepreneurs – some smart, some decidedly dodgy – who set up as agents for whichever brand of car they could snare. Anyone, it seemed, could make an arrangement with a manufacturer to become an agent and relied on their own abilities as salesmen to make a go of it. This had the effect of finding some brands were selling in numbers in only one city or area, and with the distances between major cities meaning an agent for one brand might do well in their territory, that same brand was not seen in other parts of the country. Smaller manufacturers like Auburn, Bean, Jowett, Minerva or Rugby, for example, claimed a good share of the market against the better-known names in some states, and so it was with Amilcar.

The most successful Amilcar agents were in the south and south-east – Adelaide, Melbourne and Sydney. A few may have been sold through other dealers in more distant areas such as Northern Motors Pty Ltd of Launceston, Tasmania and Armstrong Cycle and Engine Agency in Perth, Western Australia, but there is no record of any agents in the northern state of Queensland, which by then was becoming quite populated around the city of Brisbane and along the east coast.

In South Australia the first reference to Automobiles Limited in *The News* on 29 July 1924, announced 'A new car in Adelaide'. *The Mail* newspaper of Adelaide wrote on 9 August 1924, that 'One of the best known light cars on the Continent is the Amilcar, the selling rights for which have been secured by Automobiles Limited, Grote Street, a new company formed to handle the car in this State'. One Hiram M. Drummond was the Managing Director, and by September the following year the business was trading as Drummond's Autos Limited, with added premises at Light Square. There had already been Amilcars registered in the state of South Australia as far back as 1923, so there must have been a way to import them even then. In fact, the earliest car in the state dates from 1921, complete with the early type of pressed steel front axle with the wood insert, but there is no certainty as to how it got there.

Australians had always been keen to set cross-country records, and in 1925 Drummond's service manager, Percy Pederson, set a new record time for the drive from Adelaide to Broken Hill in New South Wales, where Drummonds had also opened another agency – a distance of some 516 kilometres (321 miles). In 1926, Adelaide newspaper *The Register* reported on the New Year's Day Light Car Club Twenty Mile Handicap at Sellick's Beach. The race was won by H. H. Young with Percy Pederson second, both driving an Amilcar CGS. By this time Drummonds – who also sold Armstrong-Siddeley Flint, Moon, and Trojan cars – were claiming to sell one Amilcar per day and by then of course the stock included the CGS and E-Type tourers. It is recorded that more examples of the E-Type Amilcars ended up in South Australia than anywhere else in the world. In October that year H. M. Drummond started an Amilcar Owners Club, which was well attended by his happy customers. Drummond's sales staff were active not only in the city but made many sales in the surrounding country areas; one story was that they targeted sheep shearers as potential customers. The men who plied this trade travelled light and were paid by their productivity, so they needed to get from one sheep station to the next quickly, often across rough country roads, and the little Amilcar was just right for the job. Their light-handling and diminutive size also appealed to farmer's wives for taking drives from their more isolated locations to shopping in country townships.

Many of the imported Amilcar chassis sold in South Australia had bodies made by T. J. Richards and Sons in the Adelaide suburb of Keswick, a well-established firm who were known for quality coachwork on many brands of cars. As with many such car dealers, when times became tough in the late 1920s Drummonds went out of business; the last known advertising was dated 1928.

Meanwhile in Sydney, T.D. Chapman of 122, Castlereagh Street and 2, Flinders Street – who was also a Wolseley and Albion truck agent – was selling Amilcars at least as early as 1923. These usually had the bodies made by W. Green of 116, Parramatta Road in the Sydney suburb of Petersham. Thomas Dark Chapman and three of his four sons, Stewart, Owen and Robert, were regularly taking part in various road rallies and the long-distance reliability trials that became a regular occurrence around the country. Unfortunately, Robert lost his life when a prospective customer overturned the Amilcar he was driving near Orange. Stewart Chapman completed a drive in one of their Amilcars from Melbourne to Sydney in a record time of 14 hours and 38 minutes at a time when most of the main roads were still unsealed.

The Sydney Morning Herald reporting on the Royal Easter Show on 30 March wrote: 'T. D. Chapman makes an interesting exhibition of the Amilcar, a small French production, which recently established a lightweight car record from Melbourne to Sydney under exceptionally difficult conditions.'

A Six-Day Reliability Contest started on Saturday, 27 September 1924, from the RACA clubhouse in Sydney with 25 competitors. There were scores for time, fuel consumption, reliability and average speed checked over the course of what would be a gruelling drive around New South Wales from Sydney to Mount Kosciusko via Goulburn and back up the east coast. T. D. Chapman and one H. Chapman (possibly a typo or another of the sons) both entered in Amilcars. After a visit to a weighbridge and filling their tanks they all set off. By the complicated formula counting for all tests, the winner drove a Buick and the Chapman cars were classified twelfth and fourteenth, at least showing great reliability. Speedway racing had also become popular: Stewart Chapman raced his Amilcar at well-attended events at Penrith and Maroubra.

On Monday, 13 April 1925, *The Sydney Morning Herald* reporting on the Penrith Easter Meeting thus:

> *The race for the under two-litre class was won after a hotly contested race by A. V. Turner in his Bugatti. Turner and S. O. Chapman (Amilcar) fought the race out from the start to finish but in the last lap the Bugatti proved just a little too fast, and drew away to win by about 50 yards, at a speed of nearly 60 miles an hour.*

Sales in Melbourne and Sydney seemed to also boom, possibly outstripping Adelaide sales. Once the Grand Sport had arrived in late 1924, Drummond struggled to keep up supply with enough imports coming in and at one point asked T. D. Chapman in Sydney if he could supply him with some extra CGS cars. Chapman replied that they were selling all they could get and would be unable to let any go to other states. In many cases the cars were pre-ordered and sold before the boats even arrived with new stock.

Later, like many others, Chapman's business also suffered a downturn in the hard times of the Great Depression and closed for good. The service of Amilcars for the Sydney area was taken over in 1930 by a skilled mechanic, A. W. 'Bill' Anschutz of 11, Cambridge Street, Willoughby who continued to buy and sell Amilcars and advertise spares and servicing in *The Sydney Morning Herald*.

The Amilcar agent for Melbourne was Conn's Motors Pty Ltd of 600–608, Elizabeth Street. A report in *The Sydney Morning Herald* on a race at Aspendale Park on Sunday, 28 December 1924, mentioned the Handicap for Motor Cars up to 1100cc was won by a Gwynne with an Amilcar 7hp driven by a Conn in second place. This could well have been the dealer racing to demonstrate his faith in the Amilcar. There are to this day several Amilcars still driving around in Melbourne and while not much is known about Conn's Motors or who was Mr Conn, he appears to have been a good salesman. Once again, these cars were entered for trials to publicise their virtues and on 10 November 1926, *The Argus* of Melbourne reported:

> *Absolute Winner – In 623-mile light car reliability trials – The way of an Amilcar. The new 10/45hp Standard Touring Model Amilcar, on its first appearance in the only Reliability Trial held since its arrival, was the only car in any class to go through the Trial without losing a point. Full points were obtained for Dependability and one hundred points for each of the three sub-events, the Acceleration Test, Hillclimb, and the Flying Half-Mile. This is the first time that any car has ever gone through such a test without losing a point. Thus, the New Touring 10/45hp Standard Double-seater Model is a most worthy successor to the previous wonderful smaller AMILCAR models. They have been entered for every test held since the AMILCAR arrived here and have never failed to win a trophy. In addition, in the recent Trial ten first places were secured. Amilcar's present and past record for Dependability, Hillclimbing, Speed, and Acceleration is not even approachable by any other car on the road, whatever its class or price. This wonderful car Is awaiting your Inspection at Conn's Motors Pty. Ltd.,600–608 Elizabeth Street, Melbourne.*

Australians were already keen to race wherever they could, so by the time the Amilcar arrived there were competitive events all around the country. Many country towns already had a dirt oval track since the days when horses still ruled the roads and were raced by the locals at weekends. Later these tracks were taken over by local motorcycle clubs, so when light and fast little sports cars like the Amilcar came along it was only to be expected that enthusiasts keen to race joined in the fun. With such long distances separating towns and cities, many areas had their own dirt and speedway tracks and hillclimbs. Long-distance reliability trials and town-to-town records occupied other drivers. Racing in the red dust of the outback at Lake Perkolilli had been going since 1914 and beach races at Sellick's Beach in South Australia and at Gerringong in New South Wales saw Amilcars competing against Bugattis, Buicks and Vauxhalls across the sand. Thus was born the start of Australia's fascination with racing cars in all their forms.

Some 1,500 Amilcars were exported to Australia. Of course, the early CC, C4, CS and CGS models accounted for many sales and quite a few survive, but Australia received a lot of the larger models, especially the E-Type and G-Type tourers. It is pointless to guess how many Amilcars are still in Australia, but close to a hundred are known of and there will be many more neglected examples hidden away in sheds and barns waiting to be discovered.

BELGIUM

Marcel Rouleau was a successful racer and the Amilcar importer for Belgium based at Agence Générale: 9, Boulevard de Waterloo, Porte de Namur, Brussels. He later also had the Alfa Romeo agency for Belgium. His brother Roger Rouleau was also a racer and may have had a connection with the business.

NETHERLANDS

Appearing on stand 48 at the 1924 Amsterdam Motor Show, Leo Peltenburg was the first to import Amilcars to the Netherlands. From 1925, the busy years of the mid-1920s popularity of the sporty Amilcars, the concession passed to another importer, N.V.Automobiel-Maatschappij Telos of Amsterdam with agencies N.V.Automobiel-Maatschappij de Fremery & Greeve for the Hague, W.A. Janssens & Son for Rotterdam, N.V.Automobiel-Maatschappij J. Vermeulen & Co for Breda, N.V.Automobiel-Maatschappij for Arnhem and Firma H. Jansen at Apeldoorn.

At the 1926 Amsterdam Show Telos showed a Weymann-bodied G-Type alongside an open two-seater on the CS chassis, which for that country was advertised as the 7 PK Type. As sales of such light cars slowed down through 1927, Telos cancelled its Amilcar agency and Olanda Mij of Hilversum took it over until 1931. Later still imports of the Amilcar-Hotchkiss Compound, if there were any, were handled by Sieberg of Amsterdam.

Today the small sporty models that made Amilcar famous are still very popular in the Netherlands.

Advertising for Amsterdam dealer Telos.

SCANDINAVIA

I have not been able to find any record of who may have been an official importer in any of the Scandinavian countries, but there were certainly Amilcars competing there. Helmer Carlsson was the most successful driver, winning many Grands Prix, hillclimbs and ice races in Sweden and Finland in a C6 in the 1930s for the Västerås Racer Kompani team run by his brother Bertil with Karl-Emil Rolander as a teammate. There are also results showing victories for Per Nas and Börje Dahlin. In Denmark, Max Schreiner was another well-known local Amilcar racer. The best-known Amilcar racer from the area was Henk Widengren, the Norwegian who frequently raced at Brooklands and set records at Montlhéry. A local car website shows there are nine registered Amilcars in Sweden at the time of writing.

SPAIN

Jean Mauvais was the Amilcar agent in Madrid. Mauvais had finished second in a minor event near Madrid in 1924, the bigger headlines having been made by Oscar Leblanc, a former cycling champion and motorcycle racer and the visiting factory 6-cylinder racers. King Alfonso XIII bought a CGS for his son Jaime; however, none of this publicity seems to have stimulated many sales in the country.

SWITZERLAND

The Swiss had become aware of the new fashion for small lightweight cyclecar and voiturette cars in the early 1920s, so when the works team sent cars over for events like the Geneva speed trials and the hill (mountain) climb at Klausen, it can only have helped boost their market share. Carl Schlotterbeck-Simon of Basel and Zurich with another branch in Geneva had been operating as the Panhard et Levassor importer and was already known as a competitor in the early days of the local hillclimbs when he became the Swiss Amilcar agent from the early 1920s. He took a stand at the 1924 Geneva Salon, showing the C4, CS, CGS and E-Type models. Later, in 1926 with a C6 to impress the public, he also showed a stylish coupé with coachwork by the Geneva carrossier Brichet. Schlotterbeck had married into the Christe family of the famous coachbuilders Reinbolt & Christe in Basel and at one time shared premises with them, so it is possible some Swiss Amilcars were bodied by them. A Max Schlotterbeck won a couple of Swiss hillclimbs in Amilcars – presumably family, possibly Carl's son. For reasons not recorded the rights to the Amilcar agency were taken over in 1927 by Théo Sarbach at the Garage Metropolis in Geneva. Sarbach was killed in 1930 when his C6 caught a tramline and sent him off the road while contesting the Geneva kilometre speed trial. The next to take over as concessionaire was listed as Ernest Fankhausen in Bern, but that arrangement ended in 1932. Detailed records exist for all Swiss car registrations and by 1929 as many as 832 Amilcars had been imported, but as in every other market, sales tailed off soon after that. Switzerland had many of its own hillclimb events and Amilcars were popular with the local amateur drivers, Dr Hansen, Nyfeller and Rampinelli among them. It was the inevitable Morel and Martin with the works cars who made the headlines, Morel's outright win at the spectacular 21.5-km climb up the Klausen track in 1926 was a heroic victory. Charles Martin also starred at the Geneva Flying Kilometre event, winning outright in a CO in 1927 and setting the second fastest time in the MCO behind a 2.3 litre Bugatti in 1928, with the much travelled Benoit Falchetto winning the Grand Prix at Geneva in 1931. There is a healthily supported Club Amilcar Cyclecar Suisse catering for the owners and fans of these cars today, organising regular rallies and shows.

UK

Although W. L. Stewart & Company of Albemarle Street, London, had been appointed as Amilcar's UK concessionaires in late 1921, this arrangement did not last long. The Northern Ireland newspaper *The Northern Whig* on 4 November 1922, reporting on the British Motor Show at Olympia in London, mentions the display of Amilcars by W. L. Stewart & Co, on Stand 280. However, in May 1923 Vernon Balls was racing his Amilcar at Brooklands, so it must have been before then that he had paid his reported visit to Paris to place his order for himself. Why he did that rather than buy one from W.L. Stewart is not known, but as we find out later, he was certainly the entrepreneurial type and he soon became the importer and dealer for British customers, an agreement probably dating from a meeting in October at the 1923 Paris Salon. Balls had previously had an agency for Mors cars in Streatham, south-west London, but by 1924 he was the official Amilcar concessionaire based at 25, High Street, Fulham, London SW6.

This advertisement for Vernon Balls confirms he was still at the Fulham address in October 1925.

Balls would make a name for himself among the Brooklands set and attract attention to the abilities of the Amilcar by his performances on the banked Surrey racetrack. Then there was another strange twist to the story when he lost the rights as the official importer after upsetting the management at Amilcar by importing cars himself from local dealers rather than through the head office. It is not clear why he did this; possibly he got a better deal, or maybe it was just a question of the ready availability of stock. One story was that by buying through the Jersey agent he avoided paying import taxes.

In November 1925, Joseph Lamy had signed an agreement with Boon and Porter for exclusive representation for Amilcar for England, Scotland, Wales and Ireland. This contract would expire on 30 September 1926. There was a clause that said Boon and Porter had to sell at least 150 cars in that time with the option of renewing the contract on doing so. Boon and Porter of 159–163 Castelnau, Barnes, London SW13 had been around since the early days of motoring, having operated a Renault agency at the same address from 1909. They also sold a few Bentleys in the 1920s and even had a reputable coachbuilding sideline; at least one of those Bentleys survives today with Boon and Porter bodywork. Some Amilcars were also fitted with attractive bodies made in-house. Later they were selling Austin and Riley cars until the company was finally dissolved in 1953.

Boon and Porter had already been advertising Amilcars from their premises as early as 1924, and conversely, when they had taken the agency from Vernon Balls, he continued to sell Amilcars through 1925, so there was already a healthy rivalry between them, often taking out competing advertisements in the motoring press.

By 1925 Balls had traded up from his original CS to a CGS and continued to get results at Brooklands and was somehow the first to import the CGSs in June 1926. At the Olympia Motor Show that October it was Boon and Porter who took a stand showing the C6, which cost £725, still cheaper than a Bugatti T37, and for the Amilcar admirer who was less well-off there was a 4-cylinder chassis for £250 and a complete CGS for £285. It was at this time that Amilcar adopted the winged Pegasus as a radiator mascot, reportedly on the suggestion of Bob Porter after he had found a sculptor named Daret who designed mascots at the Paris Salon. Boon and Porter adopted the design and had the mascots cast to add a little extra flair to the cars they sold. This would later be taken up by the Amilcar works for fitting to the entire range, it was first seen on a G-Type at the Salon of 1926. Curiously, in an interview in 1972 with *Motor Sport* magazine editor Bill Boddy, Vernon Balls claimed it was he who had the idea to first use the Pegasus mascot, denying it came from Boon and Porter; even near half a century later their rivalry was still cause for argument.

The Boon & Porter premises at Castelnau, Barnes. One can only speculate why these Amilcars have numbers painted on the radiators.

Meanwhile, Vernon Balls managed to import seven of the new 6-cylinder model and proceeded to rack up more victories at Brooklands. Balls for his part financed the entry for three of the works CO racers at Brooklands in September 1926 at a cost to himself of £1,000, where Martin, Duray and Morel finished first, second and third in class and reinstating himself back in favour with the Amilcar management. It may be that Boon and Porter failed to sell enough cars as stipulated in their contract, or it may have been Balls' successes on track that swung the balance, but from 1927 he was again the sole concessionaire for the British market now trading as Amilcar (Great Britain) Ltd from new premises at 95 High Holborn, London WC1 with a service workshop at Chiswick in west London. To expand the range Balls offered fabric-bodied closed cars named the Carisbrooke Coupé and Balmoral and Sandringham saloons. When in a later interview he was asked how many Amilcars he had sold he replied, 'at least a couple of hundred'.

Just to add to the confusion, Vernon Balls had taken an agency for the French Derby voiturette, surely a close rival to the Amilcar CGSs, and these were renamed Vernon-Derby. It was probable that Balls had arranged this as a possible alternative in case Boon and Porter had renewed their contract with Amilcar in 1926, but any further conflict of interest was avoided when he passed the rights to Morgan Hastings Limited, of Berkeley Street, London, in 1928, although they continued to be sold under the Vernon-Derby name for another year.

Boon and Porter became a Riley agency and continued to sell unsold stocks of the Amilcar C4 for a while longer. Bob Porter must have still had a liking for the French marque as he co-drove a C6 with Brian Twist in the BARC 500-mile race at Brooklands in October 1930.

Other English dealers in the south-east included Ralph P. Warren of The Priory Garage, Hadlow Road, Tonbridge, Kent who claimed to be the Amilcar agents for that county. Wrynams of Winchester Road, Romsey were the preferred dealer in Hampshire and Moore of Preston Road, Brighton had the Sussex agency. In the 1930s Boon and Porter added an Austin franchise to their Riley sales and continued in business until 1953.

It is doubtful that many of the later models, particularly the Pégase, found their way across the channel and the Compound was advertised for the British market as a Hotchkiss Ten, eighteen of which were sold by H. M. Bentley of Mayfair, London.

USA

Amilcars were sold in the United States by the Maybach Motor Company of 253 West 57th Street, New York, who advertised themselves as sole agents for New York State and Florida. There is no record of how any Amilcars might have been imported or sold in any other state. Maybach must have bought any stocks through Hall & Collins of 10, Avenue Victor-Emmanuel III, Paris who were listed as the sole concessionaires for North America and Cuba. Presumably the latter business dealt with Amilcar's sales staff direct and then arranged for whatever Maybach Motors required to be shipped across the Atlantic. Further, Maybach were not offering cars from stock, they would be built to order and then shipped across the Atlantic, so incurring some considerable delay for any eager would-be 'Amilcariste'. Only the sporty models, the CS and CGS were listed, the latter priced at $1,850 as delivered dockside to one of the east coast ports. Given that a Model T Ford only cost $260 or a slightly sportier Chevrolet Superior Roadster listed at $480 at that time, it is hard to see who these little foreign cars were aimed at. The American market favoured much bigger and more comfortable cars with powerful engines; even the Ford T had a 4-cylinder engine of just under 3 litres and enough torque for any task. There was already by the mid-1920s a growing industry supplying tuning parts to give performance to the more mundane local machinery, which was the start of the American 'Hot Rod' craze. The taste for small European sports cars only really took off after 1946, when the returning military personnel brought with them the sporty MGs and the like that they had discovered could be fun. All of this would seem to indicate very few Amilcars would have made their way to the USA. We will never know if the failed deal with Durant Motors might have made the Amilcar brand better known. It is only in more recent times with a growing interest in vintage cars in general and an increase in awareness in historic racing circles that a few Amilcars have been seen in America, probably most of them imported privately many years after Amilcar had closed its doors.

CHAPTER 13

SALMSON AND THE OTHER RIVALS

It is relevant to mention the other marques making cyclecars, voiturettes and small sports cars through the period covering the years when Amilcar produced their more successful models until the late 1920s, and even after when there were still many competing into the 1930s. In Britain, of course, the cheaper Austin Seven and various Morgans were comparable in terms of performance and the smaller 990cc engine Fiats, 508 and 509 and particularly the S and SM versions, would have been popular in Italy. What follows is a brief description of Amilcar's French rivals in the cyclecar and voiturette market.

BÉDÉLIA

The Bédélia was manufactured by the Bourbeau et Devaux Cie. of Paris from 1910 to 1920 and designed by Robert Bourbeau. Borrowing from motorcycle practices as much as the then current automobiles, it featured tandem seating with the passenger in front and the driver seated behind. The front axle had a centre pivot supported on a coil spring with steering by bobbins and cable. The rear axle was mounted on elliptical leaf springs. Powered by single-cylinder or V-twin engines with a complicated two-speed transmission operated by pulleys, it has been suggested that the Bédélia was the origin of the term 'cyclecar'. Despite their odd design, they sold very well in both France and Britain.

On 13 July 1913, a Bédélia was classified as the winner of the 1913 Cyclecar Grand Prix at Amiens. A Morgan driven by Gordon McMinnies came in first but he was disqualified as the three-wheeler should have followed a different course as proscribed for the Sidecar class. Some still regarded this as a win for the Morgan and it was the publicity from this event that launched the British marque into the French market imported by Robert Darmont.

In 1920, a car dealer, M. Binet, obtained the manufacturing rights for the Bédélia and engaged Mahieux of Levallois-Perret to build an updated version with more conventional seating arrangements and three-speed gearbox along with a wider choice of engines. The timing coincided with an increase in the price of petrol and the introduction of the cyclecar tax reduction, so production continued for a few years but the business faded away with the rest of the cyclecar market in the mid-1920s. They may have been cheap to buy and run, but they would not have been much competition to the Amilcars in the local market and certainly not in speed events.

BENJAMIN

Maurice Jeanson began making cars named after his nephew Benjamin at Asnières-sur-Seine in 1921. The first car, the Type A, had a 4-cylinder engine of 750cc, weighed less than 350kg and was rated as a 5CV cyclecar.

In 1924, a new model designated AR (for arrière) was launched with a 2-cylinder, two-stroke engine of 525cc in the back. Covering their bets Benjamin also made two front-engined models; the P2 had a 2-cylinder, two-stroke engine of 750cc and the P3 had a 3-cylinder, two-stroke engine of 1125cc.

The next year the engine in the AR was increased to 636cc and the front-engined models received four-stroke engines, which by 1926 were supplied by Chapuis-Dornier. That same year a new company Benjamin Nova was set up to offer a twelve-month credit instalment plan to help sales, but financial risks hurt the parent company and in 1927 the name was changed to Benova (presumably the 'nova' part implying something new) and a new model with an 8-cylinder SCAP engine was offered. Bad timing heading into the recession at the end of the decade meant production ended in 1931.

Often scoring victories in the early 1920s, Benjamin had a fairly successful competition pedigree, although usually in the 750cc class, where there were no Amilcars or Salmsons. Class wins in the 1922 Paris-Les Pyrénées-Paris and the Circuit des Routes Pavées followed by the Bol d'Or and at Le Mans in 1923 kept the name in the headlines, as did Violette Morris when she won the Grand Prix de San-Sebastian and the Paris-Nice race in 1927.

BIGNAN

In 1918, Jacques Bignan who had already been making engines, set up the company Établissements Industriels J. Bignan in Courbevoie to make cars, initially making motors for Automobiles Grégoire for the British market before launching new models under his own name.

Taking a stand at the 1919 Paris Salon, Bignan's first model was an expensive car powered by a 4-cylinder engine of 2940cc rated at 25CV, initially available as a rolling chassis or as an open tourer.

A smaller 2-litre 11CV followed as well as a 1-litre Salmson AL3 built under licence. The competition version of the former featured desmodromic valve gear designed by Albert Guyot and Némorin Causan and produced 75hp. One of these was classified third at the inaugural Le Mans 24-hour race driven by Paul Gros and Baron de Tornaco with an unfortunate twist. Gros was seriously injured when hit by a Chenard & Walcker while crossing the track on foot. It was a fast car, scoring a class victory with Henri Springuel and Maurice Becquet at the 24-hour race at Spa-Francorchamps in 1924. Three smaller cars were entered in the 1920 Grand Prix de Voiturettes at Le Mans, with the cars of Nogue and Delauney finishing second and third behind a Bugatti Type 13. An 11CV saloon driven by Jacques Edouard Ledure won the 1924 Monte Carlo Rally.

The company foundered in 1926 and was taken over by the Société La Cigogne who failed to make any progress and it was sold again with cars named MOP-Bignan shown at the Paris Salon 1928, a continuation of the 2-litre 11CV model and a larger 14CV S.C.A.P. straight-eight 2.5-litre engined model. Neither sold in any numbers and the firm closed its doors in 1931.

B.N.C.

Bollack, Netter, et Cie, commonly abbreviated as B.N.C., was established at 39, Avenue de Paris in Levallois-Perret in January 1923. Lucien Bollack, an ex-Hispano-Suiza engineer, and financier René Netter were joined by technical director Jacques Muller who used the design of his previous J.M.K. cyclecar as their first product the DZ. Within a year they were offering three different chassis and three engines supplied by Ruby and S.C.A.P., with another from Chapuis-Dornier soon after, often boosted with a Cozette supercharger. Like many of their competitors they achieved some success on the tracks but little in the marketplace. They concentrated on sporting models similar in style to Amilcars. First shown in 1927 the B.N.C. Sport with overhead-valve engines from S.C.A.P. or Ruby and a distinctive inclined radiator is probably the model they are best remembered for and are popular today for vintage competition and touring. A lesser-known model came in 1928, the badly-timed Aigle. With a 5-litre 8-cylinder engine made by Lycoming, it was enough to weaken the company such that it was taken over by Charles de Ricou, who made a business of buying out struggling car companies (Lombard and Rolland-Pilain were next) and Bollack and Netter were forced out. Even de Ricou could not have foreseen the 1929 stock market crash and the ensuing depression. B.N.C. was closed down in 1931.

André Siréjols, who had made a name as a B.N.C. driver, bought out the remaining stock of parts and carried on making small numbers of cars under the name of B.N.C. Siréjols into the 1950s. The last of these had to make do with a humble 1172cc side-valve Ford engine, but B.N.C. deserve to be remembered for their stylish sports cars from the mid- to late 1920s. The victory that B.N.C. is best known for was another win for Violette Morris at the 1927 Bol d'Or at Fontainebleau, while a best result of seventh in 1927 from several attempts at Le Mans and a class win at the 24-hour race at Spa in 1930 does not do them justice.

BUGATTI

The Bugatti marque is well-known enough in its own right to need no introduction here; suffice to say the early Type 13 and Type 23 'Brescia' models were in competition with Amilcar in the early years. Based on the first true Bugatti, the Type 10, the T13 was first seen in 1910 with a 4-cylinder engine of 1368cc and a nimble handling chassis. A major advance was the four-valve head, which allowed it a healthy 30hp, enough to give the 300kg chassis impressive performance. It evolved through the Types 15, 17, 22 and 23 and put the Bugatti name in the forefront of all forms of motorsport. Bugatti Type 13s filled the top four places at the Brescia Grand Prix in 1921, and in honour of this victory, all subsequent four-valve Bugattis were given the Brescia name. These would certainly have been a major influence for anyone designing a light car with sporting intent at the time; surely Edmond Moyet must have noticed too when working on what became the Amilcar CC.

Later when the famous Type 35 variants were dominant they were already in a different class both in engineering terms and in price. The similar but smaller engined Type 37 is probably more relevant, as the Grand Prix formula was reduced to 1500cc from 1926 and it is believed that Bugatti sold 286 of this model, 76 of them the supercharged T37A. Although the specification was simpler than the Type 35 with wire wheels and drum brakes instead of the cast alloy wheels of the 35 and smaller 4-cylinder engine, these were still expensive cars at more than 50,000 francs. Intended to be used for racing many were also bought for road use by wealthier customers. Similar in performance to the Amilcar C6, the two would often meet on the track. Bugatti of course went on to become a legendary marque, but the rest of that story is not relevant here.

DARMONT

Many of the cyclecars that qualified under the new tax law in 1921 had only three wheels. Robert Darmont started importing Morgan three-wheelers from England before World War I and Gordon McMinnies' efforts at the 1913 Grand Prix at Amiens had already stirred interest and sales in France took off. When peace returned, he and his brother André set up a workshop at 27, Rue Jules-Ferry, Courbevoie, the suburb that was already a centre of motor manufacturers in the western part of Paris. The Morgans built under licence were sold as Darmont-Morgans, with air-cooled and water-cooled V-twin engines from Blackburne, JAP and M.A.G. with prices starting at 7,000 francs.

These were popular for speed events and quickly made a name for themselves with a win for Paul Houel in the Circuit de l'Eure in 1919 and at the many hillclimbs that became widespread in the early 1920s. André Darmont competed himself with some success, promoting the marque with their many class wins such as the prestigious Mont Ventoux event. Darmont also took the first three places in a road race from Paris to Nice in 1921, driven by Casse, Darmont and Sandford.

While they were initially sold as the Darmont-Morgan, at some point later Robert Darmont stopped paying the licence fee to Morgan and dropped the latter's name altogether, even making Darmont-branded copies of the British V-twin Blackburne engines.

The Darmont Spécial appeared in 1926 with twin magnetos, a Solex carburettor and double chain drive and a claimed top speed of 160km/h (100mph). More luxurious versions followed, the Étoile de France and the Aeroluxe, and in 1935 the Darmont V Junior was launched. The first and only four-wheeled Darmont, it was otherwise similar to the previous models with an 100cc V-twin and the, by then antiquated, hand throttle, but at least it now had a reverse gear. Not many were sold and as with many of the others who rode the cyclecar boom, Darmont closed due to bankruptcy in 1939 and would not return after the war.

Note: Some sources refer to a Roger Darmont instead of Robert, but I have gone with the majority and the more reliable references.

DERBY

Derby was another cyclecar maker based in Courbevoie, founded in 1921 by Bertrand Montet. The earliest models used American made V-twins, which were replaced by 900cc Chapuis-Dornier engines rated at 5CV in a two-seater resembling the small Citroën C-Type. As with Amilcar and others competing in speed events, Derby soon offered sporting models with either Ruby motors or in the case of the Spécial, an 1100cc S.C.A.P. with three valves per cylinder and the option of a Cozette supercharger. Sales peaked at 200 cars sold in 1925 but then declined, as did the demand for small voiturettes generally. These 1920s Derby sports cars featured in the usual events both sides of the English Channel, although even some success in junior classes at Brooklands did not stimulate many sales in England until Vernon Balls took on the agency, by which time the Vernon-Derby had four-wheel brakes and a four-speed gearbox.

Derby, like Amilcar and Salmson, attempted to move upmarket with larger 6-cylinder engined models with limited success. After Montet's death, British racer Douglas Hawkes took control in 1930 and, having bought an American front-drive Miller, he created the Derby-Miller racer that was usually driven by his future wife Gwenda Stewart who set various speed records at Montlhéry. This car influenced the design of the front-wheel-drive V8 Derbys that appeared in 1933. Mrs Stewart entered the Le Mans 24-hour race in 1934 and 1935 with no success. A Derby–Maserati racer with independent suspension front and rear appeared in 1935 followed by a prototype rear-drive Derby with a Meadows engine; neither accomplished much and the Derby factory closed its doors in 1936.

D'YRSAN

Raymond Siran de Cavanac, formerly an employee of Sandford, founded his own business in 1923 at Asnières-sur-Seine, making cyclecars under the D'Yrsan name, with three or four wheels. The three wheelers, like others, copied the Morgan design, with a 904cc Ruby side-valve engine in the Type A. A year later the BS model appeared at the Paris Salon with a new 972cc overhead-valve Ruby unit and the DS in 1925 produced 35hp from 1097cc, but production of three-wheelers ended in 1926 after 530 examples had been built.

The Grand Sport with four wheels and the 1098cc Ruby engine was announced in 1927, but it did not catch on and production ended in 1930 with only 50 sold.

Unlike the other marques listed here, D'Yrsan never had much success in competition and an entry in the 1929 Le Mans 24-hour race for Eugène Trillaud (standing in for Siran who was unwell) and Henri Lachner in a 749cc Ruby-powered Grand Sport came to nothing. It started badly with the D'Yrsan left at the line and the unlucky Trillaud lost seven minutes pushing the car up the road trying to get his engine fired. After failing to reach the minimum distance at the three hour check required by rules, the car was retired. This was doubly frustrating as, being the only car entered in the 750cc category, just reaching the finish would have bestowed the bragging rights that go with a class win.

LOMBARD

Automobiles Lombard was only in existence from 1927 to 1929. André Lombard worked as the Commercial Director for Salmson until 1923 and also drove Salmsons with some success until he left in 1923 (*see* Salmson below). He supposedly agreed to a five-year non-competition clause, but he set up Automobiles Lombard less than four years later taking a stand at the 1926 Paris Salon to show his new model for sale next year. He had raced GN and Salmson cyclecars in the early 1920s, winning the Grand Prix de l'U.M.F. Cyclecars at Le Mans in September 1921 in a Salmson AL. On Sunday, 21 May 1922, in a cyclecar race at Tarragona near Barcelona, Lombard was involved in a major accident when he hit several spectators and the car rolled over. Lombard escaped injury but his riding mechanic, Paul Honel, and three spectators were killed. He also raced regularly at Brooklands and around Europe but his ambition was to make cars under his own name.

In 1927, he demonstrated his first model, the Lombard AL1, at Montlhéry, accompanied by a pair of streamlined AL2s reminiscent of the contemporary Bugatti 'Tanks'. These were the prototypes that formed what became the Lombard AL3 that followed soon after and was Lombard's first serious production model. Designed by Edmond Vareille who had been Émile Petit's assistant at Salmson, the AL3 was powered by a 4-cylinder double-overhead-camshaft engine of 1083cc with an output of 49hp, the optional Cozette supercharger increased the output to 70hp. In 1928, another model, the AL4 with a 1500cc engine and hydraulic brakes was shown, but none were sold although these improvements did find their way on to some later AL3s. An entry at Le Mans in 1928 for Lucien Desvaux and Pierre Goutte could only manage to finish 13th, but there were some successes elsewhere including a fourth place in the 1928 Spanish GP and a victory in the 1929 Bol d'Or for Marcel Dhôme. Although most of the racing was in Europe, a customer, Bill Lowe, drove a Lombard AL3 in the 1929 Australian Grand Prix, finishing third outright and winning the 1100cc class.

This concentration of resources on the racing programme was hurting finances and, although there was a proposed 3-litre 8-cylinder model announced in 1929, it was too late to save the ailing company and Lombard was no more. The assets and remaining stocks were bought by B.N.C., who assembled a few more AL3s; it is thought a total of 94 Lombards were made.

MAJOLA

Jean Majola started his company in 1908 at Saint-Denis on the north side of Paris, initially for the production of automobile engines. By 1911 the company was building complete cars, the Type A designed by Maurice Doutre with a 1300c engine and the later 1000cc Type B, both with chain-driven overhead camshafts and hemispherical combustion chambers, which were very advanced for their day. The Type B returned after the war as the Type F, now with 1088cc. Majola had a reputation of being well made and fast cars, the 1390cc DT model of 1921 already had a four-speed transmission, but having outgrown their limited production facilities they were being built by Georges-Irat in Chatou. By the time of the Paris Salon in October 1926, Majola exhibited their 7hp and 10hp powered by the two 1088cc and 1390cc engines, and the last new Majola was a small cyclecar with air-cooled flat-twin motor designed by Vaslin who made aircraft engines. This model was introduced in 1927, but the company was taken over by Georges-Irat the following year and the Majola name disappeared.

While sporty enough for some amateur drivers, Majola did not claim any major race results. Jean Majola himself participated in the Le Mans 24-hour race in 1925, accompanied by Fernand Casellini, but the car retired after fourteen laps.

MATHIS

Émile Mathis was a successful dealer in Strasbourg in the Alsace region and early on he had collaborated with a young Ettore Bugatti who designed cars Mathis sold under the Hermes name. Bugatti went on to his own greater future while Mathis settled on making cars bearing his own name from 1910 with Stoewer engines, followed by a smaller model, the 1.1-litre Babylette appearing just before World War I, accompanied by a 1.3 Baby Mathis. While Alsace was still part of Germany, Mathis was able to travel to Switzerland during the war and then went to France. When peace returned Alsace became part of France again and, as with Bugatti, Mathis and his business were reunited as part of the French motor industry. Initially continuing with pre-war models, later in 1919 Mathis presented the 10CV SB model aimed at the new Citroën Type A, but it was not until 1921 that they were able to offer a cheaper smaller car, the 6CV type P. The 5CV type T was followed in 1923 by the 7CV type M. The 11CV type G of 1924 replaced the traditional Mathis side-valve engines with a new overhead valve design. There were also larger models that had no Amilcar equivalent and by the mid-1920s Mathis were turning out 100 cars a day and ranked fourth in sales of the French brands. At the 1926 Paris Salon the 8CV MY replaced all the previous models and became a popular seller with a 1200cc side-valve four. There were various other larger-engined six and eight-cylinder cars, which have no relevance to the Amilcar story, there was even an experiment with an overhead-camshaft 1700cc straight-nine, but for the most part they concentrated on the staple side-valve fours.

Mathis cars often featured in competitive events. Strangely, Émile Mathis himself entered the French Grand Prix at Le Mans in 1921, but with a 1.5-litre car when the new rules set a 3-litre formula, he never stood a chance. Things went better at the 1923 Touring Car Grand Prix de l'A.C.F. held on a road course at Tours with Lahms and Bocchi finishing first and second, a feat they repeated in 1924, this time with de Brémond coming in third in another Mathis. For 1925 Mathis tried to copy the now fashionable streamlining adopted previously by Bugatti and Voisin, but the odd result with what looked like a vintage car front bolted on to an upturned boat was not successful. Among the amateur drivers in local competitions, several Mathis entries appeared but none troubled the superior Amilcars and Salmsons in the results.

In 1930 there was a plan to merge with W. C. Durant for an attack on the American market, which came to nothing and Mathis merged with Ford to become Matford in 1934.

PEUGEOT QUADRILETTE

Peugeot had some success with the earlier Bébé designed by Ettore Bugatti, which was a direct rival to Le Zèbre, and after the war made a new model for the cyclecar market.

While it was not an obvious choice for any speed competitions, the little Quadrilette was a direct rival to Amilcars for road use. The Type 161 was first shown at the 1920 Brussels Motor Show, went on the market in 1921 and soon acquired the nickname Quadrilette. Aimed at the new cyclecar tax class the 4-cylinder water-cooled engine had a capacity of just 667cc, which was enough to move the little lightweight car around but no great performance was expected. The first models featured a narrow body with two seats in tandem, one behind the other, until the wider Type 161E with side by side (but slightly staggered) seats appeared later that year. At 9,900 francs fully equipped it was competitive with the first Amilcar although not as lively, with a top speed of just 60km/h. The Type 172 was launched in 1924 with a wider body allowing two-abreast seating but keeping the same engine. A BS Grand Sport model with a 720cc engine was available but one has to wonder exactly how 'sporty' it really was, especially when compared to the contemporary Amilcar CGS. Possibly aimed at the more conservative light car buyer or with an eye on the sales of the Citroën Type C, the Type 172 was also sold as the 5CV at the same time and subsequently the Quadrilette name was dropped after 1924. A total of over 12,000 sold in three years justified Peugeot's approach to the small car market of the time.

RALLY

Automobiles Rally was founded in 1921 by Eugène Affovard Asnière in Colombes, a suburb in the north-west of Paris close to many of the others in competition with Amilcar. The first car was a cyclecar with a 989cc Harley-Davidson V-twin engine and then, as was typical of the cyclecars that grew into small two-seater sports cars by 1922, they were buying in small 4-cylinder motors from the likes of Chapuis-Dornier, Ruby and S.C.A.P. that put them in the 1100cc class. Some early cars featured the same staggered seating as the more sporting Amilcars with the passenger (or riding mechanic) positioned slightly behind the driver allowing a narrower body.

A new model, the Grand Sport, was shown at the Paris Salon in 1926 with a supercharged 1093cc Chapuis-Dornier engine and a claimed top speed of 180km/h (112mph).

By 1927 the new Rally ABC was offered with a lowered chassis and a choice of 1093, 1170 or 1494cc engines with the option of superchargers and in turn, these were superseded in 1931 by the Rally N, which used the 1300cc Salmson S4 engine and a four-speed gearbox. Some carried the Salmson badge as well as that of Rally. Variants of this were the NC (C for *courte*, being French for short) and then the NCP (the P denoting *puissante* or powerful) and there was briefly a Model R offered with an 8-cylinder S.C.A.P. engine of 1480cc, but this was replaced in 1932 by the R15 with the Salmson 1466cc motor.

As with many of the other manufacturers in this field, Rally had concentrated finances on their competition efforts and this, combined with the effects of the depression, drove them out of business in 1933.

On track the Rally was popular with several amateur drivers but rarely scored major victories.

In the 24-hour race at Spa in 1931 Naden and de Turage won their class, a feat repeated by Danne and Gergaud in 1932. A couple of Le Mans and Mille Miglia entries in the early 1930s came to nought.

SALMSON

Salmson was Amilcar's closest rival both in car production and sales and on the track through the 1920s and into the 1930s, so it is worth telling a little of their story too. The company was founded by Émile Salmson in 1890 in Paris as Émile Salmson, Ing., making compressors and pumps for railway and military use. When two engineers, George Canton and Georg Unné, joined the company from Westinghouse in 1896, they began making petrol-powered motors as Emile Salmson & Cie. By the time of World War I, they were supplying aircraft engines in a factory at Billancourt followed by making complete aircraft at a factory at Villeurbanne near Lyon.

After the war and the death of Émile Salmson, the Billancourt premises turned to car production led by Émile Petit, initially building British GN cyclecars under licence. While previously employed at Société Rhône-et-Seine, Petit designed a new 4-cylinder overhead-valve engine with a clever use of one pushrod to actuate both inlet and exhaust valves by pulling on the former and on the next cycle pushing to open the latter. The Société Rhône-et-Seine factory at Levallois also made rear axles for the Sigma light cars, which is how Petit met André Lombard, who was a sales agent for that brand and consequently recommended Petit showed it to the management at Salmson. Originally designed as an air-cooled engine, Salmson asked Petit to modify it to water-cooling, as they had a distaste for air-cooled engines after their experience with the GN. It was first used in the AL model in 1921, which was similar in specification to the first Amilcar except for the overhead- valve engine.

André Lombard, who had joined Petit at Salmson as Commercial Director, took one to a six-day trial competition in Switzerland where he won a gold medal. Another twin-cam engine followed for the larger D-type soon after and with this engine fitted in the prototype racer another victory at the Grand Prix des Cyclecars at Le Mans and the title of Champion de France Vitesse (Speed Champion of France) put the marque on the sporting map. In 1922, the car company Société des Moteurs Salmson was set up as a separate entity from the aircraft business and the marque adopted a St Andrew's cross (in honour of André Lombard) on the radiator grille as their new identification in a market crowded with similar looking cyclecars and voiturettes. The AL model designation was also a reference to Lombard's initials. New models followed: the AL3 and VAL3 were popular sellers and many subsequent models approximately parallelled Amilcar's models through the 1920s. Meanwhile, Lombard and Petit had a falling out in 1923 resulting in the latter leaving the company, supposedly with a 'no competition' clause forbidding him to build any cars for five years.

While the two manufacturers were chasing a similar buyer, Amilcar had a reputation for a better-handling chassis, but the Salmson engine was the better performer in competition and often had the upper hand at the races and with drivers Benoist, Bueno, Casse and Desvaux, victories in 1923 included the Bol d'Or and Le Mans. Despite this success there was a lack of funding for the race team, and they missed most of the 1924 season, although by now many private entrants were getting results in France and at Brooklands in England.

Victory for Georges Casse at the Cyclecar Grand Prix at the Lasarte circuit in San Sebastian in 1925 in what became the next new model, the GCS with the braked Perrot-Piganeau front axle and dual ignition, gave Salmson new impetus and was promptly answered by Amilcar with the 6-cylinder Amilcar MO in the same year. The success of this supercharged racer in turn was followed by Salmson introducing the GS-GP 'Grand Sport/Grand Prix' in 1926 with a new chassis and the DOHC engine; some were sold to customers in 1927. Fitted with a Cozette n°8 supercharger they produced 85hp at 4,000rpm.

In 1926, Baconin Borzacchini drove one to victory in the Targa Florio, with Salmsons also second and fourth with Francesco Starrabba the best Amilcar in fifth. Borzacchini repeated the feat the following year and Starrabba retired with a broken engine. At Le Mans class victory for Casse and André Rousseau in 1926 was emulated in 1927 by André de Victor and Jean Hasley. The rivalry was at its peak, but both brands would soon scale back their racing programmes. Salmson had won 500 races between 1921 and 1928 and closed their racing department in 1929.

A 6-cylinder version of the DOHC four was shown in a new 9CV S-type model at the Paris Salon in October 1928, but it was not a success. The S4 launched in 1929 to replace the existing D-type, however, was a winner from the start and the competition between Amilcar and Salmson for sales of road cars continued into the 1930s. Early versions of this model fell into the 8CV tax bracket, but it soon evolved with ever more powerful engines that were classed as 10CV for tax purposes and it gained a reputation for excellent roadholding, a comfortable ride and stylish bodywork. As a competitor in the mid-size market, it featured superior engineering to the more common models from the likes of Peugeot and Renault and sold reasonably well to those who aspired to something a little more sophisticated. Because Salmson had started the S4 series with a sound design and it was continually improved, they fared much better through the 1930s than Amilcar, who by now were struggling with a mix of different models, none of which were as successful in sales. The Cotal Preselector transmission was optional from May 1934 for an extra 1,500 francs, and the range was available with Berline (saloon), Coupé or Cabriolet body styles or as a bare chassis to be clothed by one of the many independent coachbuilders still operating.

The factory was destroyed by British bombing raids in 1942, but production resumed in 1946 and later versions of the S4-E with a 2.3-litre engine continued until April 1952 alongside the similarly styled but cheaper 1730cc 10CV S4-61. However, post-war economic conditions in France meant sales were slow and the larger G-72 Randonnée luxury model introduced in 1951 fared even worse and only lasted a year. The poor economy and a government taxation policy that penalised cars with large engines were hurting many of the manufacturers and Salmson would soon go the way of other upmarket brands like Delahaye and Talbot-Lago. With the company already in administration thanks to the banks withdrawing support, the Salmson 2300 Sport was launched in 1953, although soon after the company was declared bankrupt and this last-gasp attempt to save the name only saw 227 produced over four years. It was a more modern-looking little coupé styled by Eugène Martin and using the latest 2.3-litre version of the DOHC engine that was first seen in 1922. While the chassis were made by Salmson most of the bodies – 188 of them – were made by Henri Chapron, the other 39 supplied by Carrosserie Esclasson. It should have been a success but the market was depressed, and although highly regarded by the few who bought them, it was not enough. Renault bought the Billancourt factory and assets in 1955 and the Salmson name, at least as far as car production was concerned, was last seen in 1957.

Salmson scored 550 race victories and set ten world records between 1921 and 1928 before, as Amilcar had before, closing their racing department in 1929.

There had also been a British Salmson subsidiary from 1934 that had been bought out by the management and, after car production ended in 1939, the now independent company moved into making printing machinery. The Salmson name continues to this day in what was its original guise making pumps with subsidiaries around the world.

SANDFORD

Malcolm Stuart Sandford, a motorcycle racer from Birmingham, opened a business in Paris after World War I selling military surplus motorcycles and imported Morgans. He had some success racing the Darmont-Morgan, but as his own Morgan sales suffered he decided to go it alone in direct competition with the Darmont and started making his own three-wheelers in 1923, moving to larger premises in Levallois-Perret in 1925. Powered by proprietary Ruby side-valve and overhead-valve engines, it was better equipped than the Darmont but was much more expensive. By 1924 the Sandford had front wheel brakes and a three-speed transmission and in 1927 the Super Sport was available with a 1098cc Ruby overhead-valve engine with an option of a supercharger. The polished aluminium pointed tail bodywork was made by Olivier-Lecanu-Deschamps in Levallois. Sandford stopped making his own cars in 1936, reverting to building Morgans under licence, but as an English subject Sandford was imprisoned during the war and the marque disappeared.

S.A.R.A.

The Society of Air-Cooled Automobiles started making cyclecars in Courbevoie in 1922, their main difference being that they used air-cooled 4-cylinder engines of 1100cc.

A clever development was the centrifugal blower, which forced cooling air into a jacket around the cylinders, but otherwise they followed the fashions of the time with shaft drive and no differential. Front wheel brakes were added in 1925 and the three-speed transmission later became a four-speed in 1927.

A later larger model had a 6-cylinder 1806cc engine in either saloon or coupé guise, but the S.A.R.A. was also gone by 1930.

They had a chequered career in competition: at Le Mans, for example, Erb and Battgliola were classified 30th and last in 1923; Marandet and Francois did better at 12th in 1924; Erb and Mottet 16th in 1925; and finally Marandet and Lecureul 11th and Duval and Armand 12th in 1926. Marandet and Lecureul achieved a remarkable 6th overall in 1927, including a 3rd in the Index of Performance. The later 1.8-litre version finished 15th with Duval and Mottet in 1928, but that was the end of the road for S.A.R.A. in front-line competition.

One of the toughest hillclimb events in Europe was the KlausenRennen up the 21.5km-long gravel road from Linthal via Urnerboden to the top of the Klausen pass, 1,300 metres higher. A test of any car, a Lausanne garage owner, Louis Ramuz, thought he could promote the S.A.R.A. by entering the gruelling race to the top in 1927. He won the 1100cc class. He also won a race against the Paris to Lausanne train.

SÉNÉCHAL

Sénéchal was a French automobile manufacturer between 1921 and 1929. Robert Sénéchal, a racing driver, aviator and businessman started his eponymous company in 1921, also based at Courbevoie. With previous experience with the forgotten Éclair brand of Anzani-powered cyclecars, the first cars bearing his name were also cyclecars equipped with V-twin engines, but as became common practice, these were soon replaced by the 900 and 972cc 4-cylinder units from Ruby mated to a three-speed gearbox in what became voiturettes. By 1924 the 900cc had gone the way of the V-twin and an 1100cc was offered. Unable to meet demand from the small workshop, some Sénéchals were built by Chenard & Walcker, who having no equivalent in the voiturette class saw no conflict in the market. They bought out the company in 1925. Small and sporty, the Chenard- Sénéchals continued in production with Chenard & Walcker engines until 1929.

SIMA-VIOLET

SIMA Violet was a late arrival in the cyclecar market; by the time the first car was launched in 1924 the demand was already falling, but they persisted with some sales success until 1929. Another company based in Courbevoie, SIMA was the acronym for Société Industrielle de Matériel Automobile and Marcel Violet was the owner of the business and the designer of the cars. He had a preference for two-stroke engines and the SIMA-Violet had a flat-twin engine of 497cc driving through a two-speed gearbox that was mounted on the rear axle, but due to lightweight construction this modest specification was good enough for anyone brave enough to get along at 110km/h (68mph).

The two-seater Torpedo was nearly half the price of an Amilcar at 4,950 francs, although some might say it was half the car too. A single-seat sports version was also offered. In a possible attempt to disguise the air-cooled origins, or maybe just following fashion, by the time of the 1928 Paris Salon it was displayed with a dummy radiator grille on the front, but it was too late to save the little machine and production ended in 1929.

The company continued as SIMA-Standard with a series of conventional 5CV models designed by Émile Dombret with 860cc 4-cylinder engines supplied by Citroën – although one source claims most of the rest of the parts were made by Amilcar. A change to new models with 1.3-litre engines was not enough to prevent the company disappearing from the market in 1932.

In competition on hill or track, their power-to-weight ratio often helped SIMA-Violets to class wins, usually in the 500 or 750cc classes so not in direct competition with Amilcar. Violet himself won a few minor hillclimb events, but of the major races, there is not much on record for the smaller classes. They did well in the 1926 Bol d'Or at the Forest of Saint-Germain with Treunet victorious in the 500cc Touring Class, Stanton winning the 500cc Racing Class and Violet himself taking the 750cc Racing Class win. The following year was even better with a record of three cars entered and three cars finished. A one-two in the 500c Racing Class for Treunet and Stanton, with Violet again winning the 750cc class. In 1928 Violet took the 750cc Touring honours while Dumoret won the 750cc Racing Class, a feat he repeated the next year.

There were surprisingly several entries for these little racers in the gruelling 6 Heures des Routes Pavées between 1926 and 1929, driven by such names as Mouissonnier, Pollet, de Villeneuve and Dumoret, although not so surprising is the fact that none seem to have arrived at the finish.

A 1.5-litre racing car was built with which Marcel Violet finished third in the Boulogne Grand Prix in 1926 and Violet then set up Huascar in 1929 and took a class win with an 1100cc Violet-Huascar racer in the Bol d'Or of 1932.

In 1923, an established motorcycle manufacturer named Alcyon also started production of cyclecars, using SIMA-Violet 500cc two-stroke flat-twin engines, but these only lasted until 1928.

SPIDOS

Aimé Vassiaux began producing Spidos cyclecars in Lyon in 1921 with a factory at Bron, 10 kilometres east of Lyon, and a sales office in the centre of the city.

The Spidos achieved great sporting success in the short time they existed. Its cars were equipped with Ruby 4-cylinder 1095cc engines. Vassiaux won the 1100cc class of the Grand Prix du Moto Club de Lyon in May 1922 (beating Morel's Amilcar into second place), and the Miribel hillclimb in September of the same year. Interestingly, a Madame Vassiaux won the 750cc class at the same event in a Spidos, so he must have made at least one with a smaller engine. The customer model was a two-seater with staggered seating that was listed at 8,400 francs in 1922, somewhat cheaper than the contemporary Amilcar CC. After 1923 Vassiaux stopped production and raced for the Italian Chiribiri marque and in 1925 he competed in the 24-hours of Le Mans partnered with Giulio Foresti and drove an OM to fifth place, while the Spidos cars disappeared from the racing scene.

CHAPTER 14

THE RACING DRIVERS

VERNON BALLS

Vernon Stuart Balls was born on 1 August 1887, in Clapham Park, London, the son of veterinary surgeon George Balls, whose father, also George, had run a successful coaching business in the southern counties during Victorian times. He regularly competed at Brooklands and at local hillclimbs and became known as the leading Amilcar racer in the country. Starting with the blue skiff-bodied CS he had travelled to Paris to buy, he graduated to a CGS by 1925. Always one to experiment, looking for an edge he added a streamlined body, this time painted dark blue. He was assisted by Lockert, a mechanic he had brought over from France and his foreman Inman as riding mechanic in the longer-distance races. He even credited a Mr Lawson of the Solex company as helping him with carburation. There was another version of the CGS that was clothed in a straight-sided streamlined body that had a distinctive 'Ace of Hearts' shaped radiator-opening at the front. Further efforts to boost performance saw Balls add a Cozette supercharger to a shortened chassis racer for 1926 before getting his hands on a 6-cylinder C6.

When a new speedway was opened at Greenford in west London in 1928, Balls also raced Amilcars at the half-mile circuit that the Junior Car Club claimed was to be 'Britain's first authorised dirt car racing track'. This novelty was taken seriously enough to attract some well-known Brooklands aces – Kaye Don, Brian Lewis and Archie Frazer-Nash – and Balls was later instrumental in the introduction of American-style midget racing at the same venue. Later in the 1930s he also raced an Ulster Austin Seven, a modified Crossley 10, known unsurprisingly as a Vernon-Crossley and an OM 665.

He took an official posting in World War II serving as Assistant Director of Tanks in the Ministry of Supply and continued competing in a Vernon-Crossley in later years. Vernon Balls died in Wimbledon on 25 January 1975.

Vernon Balls.

MAURICE BOUTMY

Maurice Alphonse Boutmy was born in Amiens in the Somme department on 8 May 1877 and by 1922 was the appointed Amilcar sales agent for the area around Amiens. He was recruited by Morel as a reserve driver for the racing team and scored class victories at the Pont-Réan hillclimb near Rennes in June and the Crochat hillclimb at Limoges in July the same year. This was followed at the end of July by the three-day events that made up the Grand Prix de Boulogne-sur-Mer. Starting on the Thursday with a sprint, a hillclimb and a 3km race all went well, with Boutmy classified third so far, but the headline event was the Voiturette Grand Prix de Boulogne on the Saturday in which Boutmy and his mechanic Crespel crashed on the fourth lap. Boutmy received cuts and bruises, but after a quick medical check he was allowed to return to his hotel; Crespel was the more seriously injured, although he did eventually recover. Boutmy's injuries may have been more serious than reported as he was replaced by Fratissier for the Grand Prix des Cyclecars at Le Mans the following September, as he was still not fit enough. He was however entered for the inaugural Le Mans 24-hour race in 1923 accompanied by Jérôme Marcandanti in an Amilcar C4 and they stayed the course finishing in 18th place at an average speed of 64km/h (40mph).

For 1924, the works team concentrated on running the two tandem cars for Morel and Mestivier and it was not until the

Le Mans race came around again in June that Boutmy returned to the track, this time in a CV model finishing 14th. As Boutmy was running his own agency in the north and was only ever a 'reserve' driver, it is not surprising he appears to not have raced again for Amilcar, although he did enter either a BNC with a SCAP engine or a Tracta (records vary) in the La Baule Grand Prix in August 1928 without much success. He died at Parigné-l'Evêque, Sarthe on 6 May 1934.

ARTHUR DURAY

Arthur Jules Joseph Duray was born in New York City on 9 February 1882 of Belgian parentage and later became a French citizen. An early advocate of aviation he held Flying Licence Number 3 in Belgium and started racing cars in 1902 with a Gobron-Brillié taking part in the infamous Paris-Madrid road race of 1903. Over the next few years he set several Land Speed Records and drove a De Dietrich for the French team in the Gordon Bennett Cup races, and in 1907 won the International Race from Moscow to St Petersburg in a Lorraine-Dietrich 60hp and in 1908 ventured as far as America to contest the inaugural American Grand Prize in another De Dietrich. His fame spread and he was asked to attempt the flying kilometre record on a Belgian road at the wheel of the mighty Fiat S76 owned by Prince Sukhanov, but fell just short at 220km/h (137mph), later managing 225km/h at Ostend.

He finished second in the 1914 running of the Indianapolis 500 driving a Peugeot and returned to France to fight in the French Foreign Legion in World War I. By 1924 he was at Brooklands at the wheel of a Hispano-Suiza-powered D'Aoust later finishing second in the same car in the Coupe de L'Autodrome at Miramas near Marseille and third at another Formula Libre race at Montlhéry.

He raced three times in the Le Mans 24-hour race for Aries, a marque for which he finished fourth in his last Grand Prix appearance in Belgium in 1930. By the time he started racing for Amilcar in the CO in 1926 he was already forty-three years old and a seasoned professional and went on to score many victories for the factory team, later racing for C.A. Martin's Équipe de l'Ours in the Le Mans and Spa 24-hour races. His final race was in 1934 at the age of 52, finishing 14th at Le Mans with Jean de Gavardie in an Amilcar CO Spéciale Martin. Duray took up French citizenship in 1933 and died on 11 February 1954, in Paris, France.

ERNEST ELDRIDGE

Ernest Arthur Douglas Eldridge was born on 18 July 1897 at Willesden in north-west London to a wealthy family. Educated at Harrow School he left while in the sixth form to join the British Red Cross Society as an ambulance driver in World War I. There are rumours he also served in the French Artillery. He married Marjorie Tooth in 1915 at Brentford in Middlesex; she later died in the 1930s but not before Eldridge, a bigamist, married a second time in 1925 to a French woman named Marie, while still married to Marjorie.

Used to high living on his father's wealth, he was happy to spend it all on gambling, flying and racing. In 1919 he purchased his first plane, a Sopwith Gnu. In 1922 he survived a plane crash at Brooklands in a B.E.2e and qualified for his pilots licence the following year at Hendon Aerodrome, and then sold the Gnu to replace it with a Sopwith or Grasshopper. He was said to have lost £60,000 in Monte Carlo, on the turn of one card, in 1922. Eldridge had started racing at Brooklands in 1921 with a chain-driven Isotta Fraschini with a Maybach engine in which he finished second in the Long Handicap with

H.T.H. Clayton at Brooklands.

Arthur Duray.

a lap time of 90.72mph on his second lap. This monster was even fitted with side lights so he could drive it on the road. Another of the aero-engined specials was his 21.7-litre Fiat-based 'Mephistopheles'. The ex-Navarro SB4 Fiat racer had been bought from John Duff who had blown up the 18-litre engine at Brooklands, so Eldridge replaced it with a 21714cc 6-cylinder A12 Fiat aero engine stretching the chassis to accommodate it. Eldridge took the flying kilometre World Land Speed Record on 12 July 1924 at Arpajon at 234.985km/h (146mph) with this car. He also raced a Gwynne at Brooklands that year, possibly having some financial involvement with the London manufacturer. On 12 October, he won a match race at Montlhéry with Mephistopheles beating the other aero-engined specials of Parry Thomas and Arthur Duray.

In 1925, he started racing with the Eldridge Special, based on an Amilcar chassis with an Anzani engine, competing in many of the Grands Prix into 1926. He also entered the Indianapolis 500 in 1926 and in December that year during a record attempt at Montlhéry the front axle collapsed leading to a spectacular crash with Eldridge receiving serious head injuries resulting in the loss of an eye. After more record attempts at Montlhéry in a Chrysler he then got involved with Captain G.E.T. Eyston helping in his speed record projects in a 750cc Ratier, the MG EX120 for which Eldridge worked on supercharging the engine, and then Eyston's Rolls-Royce diesel-engined 'Speed of the Wind' machine that Eldridge helped design. They went to the Bonneville salt flats for the record attempt and on returning Eldridge contracted the pneumonia that he subsequently died from in Kensington on 27 October 1935.

CHARLES MARTIN

Charles Martin was born in Gensac-Lapallue (Charente) on 30 August 1889, and began his racing career at Bignan, including three attempts at the Le Mans 24-hour race and wins at San Sebastian and Spa. André Morel recruited him to drive for Amilcar at the end of 1925 to replace Marius Mestivier as a works driver; they had been frequent rivals at racing and hillclimb events and Morel must have rated him highly.

Amilcar let him go at the end of 1928 due to the cutbacks in the racing programme. In those few short years he achieved many successes in the 6-cylinder cars and after that it seems that Martin left the motor industry with his departure from Amilcar. Some records list him as Jean Martin during his Bignan years and there is not much other information available about him, but he should not be confused with another Charles Martin, a Welsh driver who had much success in the 1930s with Alfa Romeo P3, Bugattis and ERAs, nor with Clément Auguste Martin, who raced Amilcars in the 1930s. Charles Martin died in Paris on 5 May 1946.

CLÉMENT-AUGUSTE MARTIN

Clément-Auguste Martin was born in Rueil-Malmaison, Paris, on 18 May 1902. By 1921 he was running a garage business in Rueil-Malmaison converting road cars into racing cars and became one of Amilcar's early sales agents. Later, when Amilcar closed their racing department in 1929, he bought most of the surviving equipment including seven of the CO and CO 'offset' models and some spares. He ran the Équipe de l'Ours (translation, Team of the Bears) also known as the Equipe Martin-Amilcar from 1930 to 1934, using 4-cylinder engines in many of the cars instead of the more complicated 6-cylinder ones. These were thought to be better suited to endurance races like the Bol d'Or and the 24-hour races at Spa and Le Mans. He started three times in the 1930s in the Le Mans 24-hour race with a best result of eighth overall with Auguste Bodoignet in 1932 and had a few other minor results in this period. However, his main contribution to the Amilcar story was preparing and entering these cars for other professional drivers, who continued to keep the Amilcar name in the results through the years after the factory had stopped racing.

Martin switched his allegiance to Simca in 1935 and the Martin-Amilcars were sold to continue racing in private hands. C.A. Martin passed away in Île-de-France on 25 January 1991.

Charles Martin.

MISS M. J. MACONOCHIE

Another lesser-known but noteworthy driver was Miss Margaret Jean Maconochie, who bought a C6 from Vernon Balls and competed in a few events at Brooklands. She had previously raced a Salmson and her brother Archibald Benn Maconochie also raced, sometimes driving the famous Chitty Chitty Bang Bang. Wealth can come from some strange sources: Margaret was born into the family that produced Maconchie's Irish Stew in Aberdeen, which fed the troops in World War I. There were other women drivers in that privileged set who referred to themselves as 'The right crowd and no crowding'. Interviewed by the press after winning the Ladies Handicap race at Brooklands on 6 August 1928, she said:

> *Oh it was simply ripping. I have always been a bit of a demon on the road. I love fast motoring. I am keen on many sports, particularly horse riding. I do not see why women should not make as good motorists as men.*

MARIUS MESTIVIER

Marius Georges Mestivier was born 5 July 1895, at Chouzy-sur-Cisse, Loire et Cher, the older brother of the later Amilcar driver Maurice Mestivier. A skilled mechanic, Marius Mestivier was chief chassis tester at Amilcar and then was promoted as Morel's deputy in charge of the racing department.

Marius Mestivier in the driving seat with mechanic Jérôme Marcandanti.

He then stepped up to driver for the works racing team alongside Morel in 1922, making his debut at the Concours d'Endurance de l'UMF at the Circuit de Marly in February. He scored a few good results in the typical French hillclimbs and started twice in the 24 Hours of Le Mans. Tragically, at the second attempt at Le Mans, Marius Mestivier was the first racing driver to die in a Le Mans race in 1925. On the 18th lap his car left the road on the Hunaudières straight at full speed, overturning and killing him instantly. Various reports claim a brake locked, a tyre punctured, he was distracted by manually pressurising his oil tank or even possibly he was hit by a bird. Whatever the cause, at about 8.15pm on Saturday 20 June 1925, not yet 30 years old, with a fractured skull Mestivier was gone. Despite this tragedy his brother Maurice took up racing later.

MAURICE MESTIVIER

Maurice Mestivier was born on 17 April 1902, at Saint-Pierre-des-Corps, Indre-et-Loire, and started working at Amilcar as a mechanic in 1921. His older brother Marius was chief test driver and the younger Mestivier also inherited the family gene for engineering ability and he became chief mechanic in the racing department after his brother's death. Mestivier started racing his own Amilcars in the 1930s with a privately entered MCO and later a Pégase and even sharing a Compound with his wife Fernande Roux, herself a successful racer, at the 12 Heures de Paris at Montlhéry in 1938. He remained with Amilcar employed as an assistant to the sales manager until the end in 1939.

After the war he was elected president of l'Association Générale des Amicales et Coureurs Indépendants (l'AGACI, the French Racing Drivers Association).

In 1950, he set up a tuning and parts business, Autobleu, with Roger Lepeytre who was secretary of the AGACI. Based in the 17th arrondissement of Paris and specialising initially in manifolds for Renaults, this venture became well known for tuning the best-selling Renault 4CV; at one time these were used by the police. Other applications included the Renault Dauphine and later the R16. After a single-seater based on Simca mechanicals, they also made a few custom sports cars based on the Renault 4CV through the 1950s, and made and sold Abarth parts under licence. The business continued very successfully until 1971. Maurice passed away on 13 October 1975, at Chouzy-sur-Cisse, Loire et Cher.

ANDRÉ MOREL

Morel was the first, the busiest, and the most successful of the works drivers. His role at Amilcar is covered elsewhere but his results on the tracks and hills deserve mentioning here. He competed in Amilcars in more events than anyone else; his record of Amilcar race results is listed in the Appendix.

André Morel.

When his Amilcar commitments allowed, he even found time to fit in the occasional race in a Delage or a Voisin. At Delage he teamed up with Robert Benoist, his erstwhile Salmson driving rival in the 1100cc class, scoring victory at the San Sebastian Grand Prix in 1925 and third in the French Grand Prix of 1927. The next year he entered the German Grand Prix in a Lombard but did not finish.

He was entered in the 1923 French Grand Prix in one of the legendary Voisin 'Laboritoire' racers and set many records for the marque at Montlhéry. After his run of success with Amilcar, Morel raced Hudson and Essex cars for his old ally Joseph Lamy, taking victory in the 1929 running of the Tour de France Auto. He followed this in 1930 with class victories on some stages in a Hudson and in 1931 with victory in the sports car class at the Mont Ventoux hillclimb. There followed a short spell at Minerva and in 1933 he was recruited by Talbot as a test driver and before long was back on the tracks competing, achieving more results in the Talbot 150C and later T26GS. Post-war he continued with the 4.5-litre Talbots at Le Mans with a DNF in 1949, finishing 13th in 1950, 17th in 1951 and ninth in his last race in 1952 at the age of 68. Wikipedia credits him with 58 wins and 43 world records, although there were probably a lot more class victories not counted in that total.

JULES MORICEAU

Jules Auguste Moriceau was born in Nantes, Loire-Atlantique, on 2 January 1887. He worked as a mechanic at Mors and Darracq and served as an ambulance driver in World War I. Moriceau sailed to America in 1919 to accompany Louis Wagner as his riding mechanic in a Ballot for the Indianapolis 500, in which they finished fourth. He joined Talbot in 1921 as a mechanic in the competition department working for Henry Seagrave and Albert Divo, again acting as riding mechanic at Brooklands and on the Targa Florio and later became a Talbot works driver himself before leaving to replace Duray at Amilcar at the end of 1927 when Talbot, like Delage and others found the economies of racing too difficult. His last major race was another attempt at the Indy 500 in the MCO with the 1270cc engine in 1929. Retiring with suspension damage on the 31st lap, he returned to France and gave up racing to manage a Paris garage. Moriceau died at the age of 90 in Garches, Hauts-de-Seine on 20 June 1977.

JOSÉ SCARON

Joseph Scaron, known as José Scaron, was born in Brussels on 19 April 1895 and later became a French citizen, signing up for the French Army in 1914 to fight in World War I. He was

Jules Moriceau.

A.B. Pemberton won the JCC Novices Handicap at Brooklands in April 1926.

appointed the Amilcar agent for Le Havre as soon as the first car was launched and started racing in 1922, in an Amilcar of course, crashing it in his first race. He then contested the Bol d'Or the same year but nothing more was heard of him in the sports pages for a few years. Once Scaron got his hands on a C6 he became a regular winner, starting at La Baule in 1926, a venue that would see him win again and again. Many more victories in races and hillclimbs followed, and he often travelled overseas specialising in the Algerian, Moroccan and Tunisian Grands Prix.

By 1933, when the Amilcars were no longer competitive, he switched to privately entered Alfa Romeo Monzas and Bugattis. By 1938 Scaron had teamed up with 'Le Sorcier' Amédée Gordini, racing Simca Gordini sports cars. When peace returned in 1946 he continued to race the Fiat-engined Gordini single-seaters and he finished third in the Belgian Grand Prix of 1946 and third again in the 1949 French GP. After a final race at Le Mans in 1952, and an entry in the Tour de France Automobile in a Simca Aronde, Scaron retired from racing and concentrated on his businesses in Le Havre, but he received his due recognition when he received the Legion of Honour medal in 1954. José Scaron died at Neuilly-sur-Seine on 17 July 1975.

José Scaron.

HENKEN WIDENGREN

Per Lars Henrik 'Henken' Widengren was born in Vingåker, Sweden, on 20 June 1910, the son of a successful textile manufacturer specialising in men's suits. Often known as 'Henk', he had raced in Britain since 1929 starting with an Austin Seven and in 1932 he entered the Monte Carlo rally with an Alvis and then finished fifth overall and won the 1.5-litre class at the Le Mans 24-hour race in an Aston Martin partnered by Sammy Newsome. He had already acquired an Amilcar C6 that he frequently raced at Brooklands. This car underwent several modifications and featured a streamlined body that suited the high speeds at Brooklands. With this car he also set a speed record at Montlhéry of 185.588 kilometres (115 miles) in one hour in 1933 and attempted other records at the Avus track in Berlin. A significant victory was at the Easter B.A.R.C. Brooklands meeting, when he won the Ripley Lightning Long Handicap at 107.81 mph on 2 April 1934, He had also competed in the Swedish Winter Grand Prix several times through the 1930s as well as the Finnish Grand Prix and other ice races.

He was made Vice-Managing Director of AB L & P Widengren in 1936, the same year he married and appears to have given up racing. His brother Per-Victor Widengren also raced with Mercedes SSK and an Alfa Romeo Monza. Henk Widengren died at Sotogrande in Spain on 23 October 1989.

Brian Twist, another Brooklands regular.

Henken Widengren.

CHAPTER 15

WHAT THE PRESS, AND OTHERS, SAID

Amilcars down the years generated much press coverage and what follows is a collection of reports and road tests from various publications around the world in roughly chronological order. Not surprisingly, most of the early press coverage of the sporty and light cars of the 1920s was full of praise, but later as things started to go wrong Amilcar came in for some criticism, one could say deserved.

1921

In one of the first reviews in the French press *Omnia – Revue Practique de l'Automobile* of October 1921 reported:

> *Don't believe as its name would seem to suggest, that this elegant voiturette dates back to the Carthaginian era. It appears for the first time at the Grand Palais. If we haven't spoken about Amilcar before, be sure we'll be talking about it again soon, and for good reason, you can be sure of that.*

The British magazine *Light Car & Cyclecar* of December 1921 in a road test of the CC described it as 'a fascinating machine to drive' while *The Autocar* at the same time found it 'impressive' with 'remarkable power developed by a very small engine, coupled with excellent brakes, were impressive features of a French voiturette', going on to say 'there was probably no main road in all England that the little car could not climb', but with some criticism reserved for the harsh ride and rattles from the bodywork.

Another French publication, *Moto-Revue* said, 'It is a very pretty cyclecar, very much a voiturette in construction, and only about 30kg short of being a small car'.

1922

Already alert to their potential in competition, *Cyclecars & Voiturettes* commenting on the UMF Endurance Trial in the Marly Forest noted:

> *Amilcar instantly commanded our attention. One of their vehicles, driven by Munch, finished with the leaders, while the other two were only penalised for stops to change a tyre and replace a spark plug. One even noticed the good roadholding of these vehicles on the worst parts of the course, thanks to a well-conceived, faultlessly executed suspension and a particularly well sorted mechanism.*

La Vie Automobile commenting on the new generation of cyclecars wrote of the Amilcar CC, 'Among those taking its place in the first rank the voiturette Amilcar.' Explaining the reasons the Amilcar was more than just a cyclecar; thus:

> *The first principle of the men who created the Amilcar was that they had to make a machine that you can get into without being a contortionist: the engineers who design small cars have a tendency to assume that the measurements of the passengers are in direct proportion to the engine size. Two routes are possible when you create an economy car: whether to leave things out, to conceive some new way of operating components like the clutch, the gear change or the transmission, or whether to make a big car in miniaturising conventional design methods, while carefully watching every detail in order to keep the price down. That was the route chosen by the technicians who created and developed the Amilcar.*

Further it praised: 'The general aspect of the vehicle, its dimensions, the comfort that it offers its occupants, the speed it is able to reach, the robustness of its components, it is almost as good as a voiturette as a cyclecar.' In comparing it to the idea of a cyclecar it goes on: 'The constructors of the Amilcar give the dimensions such that it offers the same comfort as a more powerful car.' More praise came from driving: 'Moreover, if one takes the wheel of this little car, one is first surprised by its perfect roadholding.'

The test driver for *Moto-Revue* wrote in October: 'A very pleasant vehicle to drive... the clutch was very progressive... extremely easy gear change... excellent roadholding... particularly tidy presentation', but also criticising a noisy back axle and again, as with *The Autocar* the year before, hard suspension. Over a 193-km (120-mile) test route, fuel consumption was recorded as 6.5 litres per 100km (43mpg) and a top speed of 82km/h (51mph). The driver also commented he found the gear lever a long way away, but he soon got used to it. Then finding the handbrake out of reach he tried something odd:

> *Now, I had the experience of driving for a whole day in Paris using only the handbrake as much as possible. During that day I only had to use the footbrake twice, once in danger of being pulled by a taxi against a kerb, and the other time as a result of the imprudence of a pedestrian.*

La Vie Automobile covered a 257-km (160-mile) route recording even better fuel consumption – 5.8 litres per 100km (49mpg) and a top speed of 83km/h (52 mph) – and echoed many of the same thoughts praising the engine, gearshift, brakes, suspension, roadholding and steering with the sole criticism noting the pedals were too close together.

So, for the early CC model the consensus was that it was well designed, well built, had decent performance and good brakes but a less than perfect ride. This would soon be improved.

On Thursday 12 October 1922, covering the Paris Salon, *l'Auto* wrote of the appearance of the E Type at the Salon: 'This brand, which has serious means, has just released a 10hp model which is among the most successful chassis on display. Its success is now as certain as that of the other models.'

1923

The fitting of Hartford shock absorbers seemed to have improved the ride, as noted in the report in *Cyclecars, Motos & Voiturettes* in July 1923:

> *All hills were climbed in top at a sparkling pace. The engine was responsive, very flexible with lively pick-up. The steering was very soft, the gearbox well sorted and the rear axle very silent. The perfect suspension was further improved by the famous Hartford shock absorbers – a standard fitting. Even on the worst roads, I never slowed down or even had a bolt to tighten. I arrived at the conclusion that the chassis was extremely robust, very well thought out and constructed.*

1924

In January 1924, *Autoleven*, a leading Dutch car magazine from that time, said:

> *When you see the small engine, you are amazed at the performance. They are equipped with a 4-cylinder engine, a multiple plate clutch, thermosyphon cooling. The chassis with 1100cc engine have pressure lubrication, the other lubrication according to the barbotage system. The gearbox is for three forward gears and one reverse. All have magneto ignition, cardan transmission, Rudge wire spoke wheels, also electric starter and lighting. The bodies are for 2, 3 or 4 seats. The Weymann bodies exhibited at the stand, being a torpedo, a conduite intérieur, a 2-seater Grand Sport and a convertible, are a perfect match for the fast cars.*

The February issue of *Autoleven* contains an advertisement with the text:

> *Out into the great outdoors at a time that suits you. It doesn't matter when, the Amilcar is always ready for you. No preparation, no objections, the costs of driving are minimal – expressed in a few cents. In ten minutes it takes you outside, where you can enjoy yourself to the fullest. After such a ride you come back, refreshed, charged with the same energy that lies in the spirited car.*

Another Dutch journal *Het Motorrijwiel en de Kleinauto* (The Motorcycle and the Small Car) wrote of the CGS in February 1924:

> *A competitor of Salmson, besides its neighbour at the Show, is the Amilcar, also of French origin, that is shown on the stand of the Automobiles Peltenberg Company. This voiturette of 6hp that has just been imported into Holland made an excellent impression. It has no differential, just like the Salmson, has extraordinary roadholding, possesses efficient brakes and its small powerful engine is especially good in tackling hills. In its standard version, equipped with electric lighting and starter as standard, it only costs 1855 florins. This particularly rapid little machine reached 85km/h. We had the opportunity of trying this 'lively little devil' and we have very good memories of it.... Here it is, right in front of me, the famous Amilcar, the lively French cyclecar, with such an impressive sporting record in France, country of cyclecar constructors par excellence, even to a foreigner. The pretty blue of its bodywork shines in the sun and the eye rests easy on its light yet robust silhouette. The Amilcar, seeming to guess my intentions, says to me with a knowing smile: 'Go on, climb aboard, I want to show you what I'm made of'.*

Meanwhile, back in France in March 1924, *Moto-Revue* tested a CS.

> *The average speed achieved was very markedly superior to what we experienced previously since from Paris to Etampes we averaged 72.58km/h and even on the Montlhéry to Etampes section of 23.6km the average was 82.8km/h. The maximum speed achieved on the level was 105.26km/h. The fuel consumption was around 8 litres per 100km.*

Presumably the increase in fuel consumption was due to the high speeds driven.

In Australia, *The News*, an Adelaide newspaper, wrote on 29 July 1924:

> *A new car in Adelaide. Automobiles Limited, which has the agency has fitted one chassis with an Australian sports body, and the whole is a remarkably neat job, with lines that any owner would be proud of. The Amilcar will be sold complete with sports body, enamelled blue or red, and five wire wheels and tyres.*

Also in Adelaide, *The Mail*, on 9 August 1924, reported:

> *One of the best-known light cars on the Continent is the Amilcar, the selling rights for which have been secured by Automobiles Limited, Grote Street, City, a new company formed to handle the car in this State. A demonstration run in a 7.5hp four-cylinder model driven by Mr J. E. Hennessy (Drummond's service manager) proved interesting. This model is low, graceful, and excellently finished. The test was over a variety of road surfaces, and the small engine seemed pleasantly lively, for it picks up unhesitatingly and quickly when negotiating traffic. Three-point suspension is provided and the springing was good, and the car as a whole comfortable. The steering was also easy, and there was about the whole vehicle a feeling of tightness and solidity which betokened first-class workmanship. The brakes were well up to their work. A roomy Australian two-seater body is fitted and the upholstery is of genuine leather.*

The magazine *Moto-Revue* reviewing the CGS observed in October 1924:

> *The Amilcar voiturette is the dream machine of anyone who loves fast, responsive cars. Vehicles with simple and robust mechanics and a finish that exceeds your expectations; those are the two points that strike you about the construction of the Amilcar. The speed with which this marque has conquered the public added to the extraordinary and still growing success that welcomed the famous voiturette when it was launched have been unprecedented in motoring history.*

1925

In Australia the fortnightly *Motor Life* magazine reported on an E-Type on 3 January 1925. Given the time it would have taken to ship cars around the world it is not surprising this one had the 1486cc engine, not the 1572cc unit as announced at the Paris Salon the previous October. It is thought too that the company were happy to offload unsold stocks on to the Australian market, which by dint of distance rarely did get the latest models on time. Whatever the relative modernity, the tester praised the car. 'In view of the fine performances put up by the little 6hp Amilcar in the competition world, more than ordinary interest attaches to the new 11hp model.' The report goes on to point out a couple of design advantages that would have been of interest to Australian motorists of the time, particularly in the country areas where roads could be very rough. 'The complete power unit is very neatly designed and is suspended in the frame at three points so that any flexing of the chassis will not strain the engine bearer arms' and (the rear) '... axle is equipped with spiral bevel gears and is of the fully floating type. This means that axle shaft breakage will not allow the rear wheels to "come adrift"'. Further praise for the front brakes:

> *These brakes deserve special mention. They are brought into action by pins which pass through the swivel bolts and operate the brake cams by small arms. As these pins pass directly through the turning centres, there is no possibility of the brakes being brought into action when the front wheels are turned.*

Motor Life concluded:

> *On the road the car is both steady and comfortable. It is capable of cornering at high speed without rolling or skidding. Possibly the Hartford shock absorbers which form part of the standard equipment have something to do with this. As a sporting car the 11hp Amilcar does not leave much to be desired, but its chassis is long enough to accommodate a very comfortable touring body, so that the tastes of the touring motorist and the competition enthusiast are catered for.*

Of the G-Type, *The Autocar* commented after testing an example with already over 60,000 miles on the clock: 'The Amilcar, even in saloon form, shows its sporting parentage. It is comfortable, well sprung for its weight, economical and has good road manners.'

The Autocar of 27 November 1925, reporting on Morel giving the CO its debut victory at Gaillon said, 'The first appearance of this car was at the Gaillon hillclimb, where, with Morel at the wheel, it beat all competitors….' (in its class). The same magazine called the CO, '…The first purely racing car of 1100cc as distinct from sports models adapted for racing.'

Light Car & Cyclecar commented: 'The car had been specially conceived with the aim of racing and record breaking… and it is not the intention of its creators to market a 6-cylinder model at present.' Of course, that intention soon turned out to be reversed.

In France *l'Auto* was also impressed: '…very favourable impression of the new Amilcar, a quite remarkable supercharged 6-cylinder of 1100cc'.

1926

Moto-Revue enthused of the CGSs: 'This thoroughbred car offers great speed with safety because it is provided with powerful front wheel brakes and its roadholding is impeccable, thanks to its suspension and its meticulously studied weight distribution.'

1927

In January 1927, excited by the prospect of the new C6, *Moto-Revue* announced: 'The Amilcar 6-cylinder client type has just been tested at Montlhéry and will be running there at 165km/h during the next season for the lucky and daring amateurs who are now ready to floor the accelerator. This will be the opportunity for fine battles between them.'

In September 1927, *La Vie Automobile* was impressed with the L-Type, saying:

> *The 8CV L Type allows you to undertake the longest journeys with the pleasure that comes from the use of a significant car, while offering the immense advantage of a speed comparable with that of a car of twice the capacity, allied to a substantial economy of fuel consumption and maintenance. It marvellously achieves the Amilcar formula of a light, fast and most spacious and comfortable car.*

Of the troubles facing the French automobile business in 1927, W. F. Bradley predicted in *The Autocar*: 'As far as France only is concerned the open car appears likely to go out of existence except as a sporting job. All the demand is for closed bodies.' *The Autocar* went on to comment of the new L-Type:

> *Slowly but surely the car once considered 'a baby' is being regarded more seriously both by manufacturers and buyers, and one hears less and less of the term 'baby' and all that the term inferred as applied to light cars. It is easy to start and control. It is responsive and powerful when hills heave in sight… The car holds the road splendidly and is stable on corners.*

1928

In October 1928, the *Edinburgh Evening News* wrote enthusiastically: '… Reverting to straight-eights, the new 55hp Amilcar is keenly sought out at Olympia by straight-eight enthusiasts…', but it was not all good news.

Of the intended alliance with W. C. Durant, *The Autocar* wrote:

> *While leaving the two companies financially independent, will provide for co-operation in marketing and production. Amilcar will market the Durant and Locomobile cars in France and also the Rugby lorries. Durant will manufacture parts in America for Amilcar and will sell the car in the United States.*

Well, we now know that was a waste of printer's ink!

Of the new M-Type, *Omnia* wrote:

> *…aimed at a clientele that looks to a car to provide a fast but very comfortable means of transport. The classic elegance of line of the Amilcar is now allied to a method of construction that is not only robust from the bodywork point of view but is also most comfortable and luxurious. The size of the seat, the depth of the cushions and the rake of the seatbacks have all been studied in detail in order to create bodywork that is as pleasant as possible to use.*

Omnia was also impressed by the new C8:

> *This car is essentially a fast grand tourer. The chassis will especially attract the full attention of connoisseurs by reason of the originality of its concept. Amilcar has remained true to its tradition of achieving with a small engine performance at least equal and often superior to that of cars of twice the capacity.*

1929

Famed French journalist and founder of the Le Mans 24-hour race, Charles Faroux visited the Salon in 1929 and was invited by Marcel Sée to test a C8 at Saint Denis. Writing in *L'Auto* he was full of praise.

> *Here I am in the presence of a chassis that is pleasing to the eye on first sight, and that a more detailed survey places even higher in our esteem. At the first touch of the starter the engine ran. I was already impressed: the tickover was perfectly slow and silent. Certainly there are a lot of good cars about presently and I am delighted that so many of them are French, but this straight-eight Amilcar has a vigorous personality… it has astonishing roadholding of the kind that you only find in very few cars, proving that, at Amilcar, they know how to learn from their many glorious involvements in racing… The steering combined precision with sweetness. The brakes, vigorous in action, are exceptionally good.*

1930

In 1930 *The Autocar* tested the new 8-cylinder Amilcar and seemed to like it:

> *The straight-eight Amilcar is a machine which breaks away completely from one's preconceived opinion of the make as a type, and in the breakaway has been improved very much indeed from practically every point of view.*

Impressed with its speed and handling they wrote, 'Very few cars are as good in this regard as the Amilcar eight….there is no roll or sway….and the road shock is not felt through the thin-rim wheel.' They were however critical of the French-made fabric body and suggested a chassis clothed with a British body would be better.

Faroux again, this time writing in *La Vie Automobile*, tested a CS8 in July and was still a fan:

> *As soon as you take the wheel of the straight-eight Amilcar you are immediately at one with the car. After a single kilometre you can feel every reaction and can then drive with perfect safety. That's the result of a perfect distribution of masses and a careful study of every organ in order to endow the car with the greatest possible safety.*

Of the rigorous testing done before delivery he wrote, 'Therefore all small imperfections will have been remedied and the car will be delivered in absolutely tip-top condition', concluding, 'Amilcar's eight-cylinder is indeed a high-class production.'

All of that praise did not help and there were problems. Of course, the erstwhile Amilcar agent and racer Vernon Balls famously said of the CS8 '…it wasn't a good car. The complicated valve gear gave trouble and it was never possible to keep it on eight cylinders'.

1931

Of the new M3-Type, the enthusiastic writer for *Automobilia* said, 'Six years of experience are reason enough to ensure the perfection of the famous Amilcar engine, so often imitated in recent years but still unequalled.'

1932

A short report in *Le Petit Marseillais* on 10 October said:

> *This marque which has always specialised in small, light, fast cars of great breeding launches this year a new model which extends a series whose success is far from being exhausted. It is a 4/5 CV established by the engineer Moyet creator of the previous models. This 4/5 CV is established to receive a two-seater convertible; its low lines have a rare elegance, and despite the cylinder capacity of 850 cubic centimetres we register 19CV at 3,750rpm. Here is a model that will be worth many sales.*

1933

A year later on 8 October, *Le Petit Marseillais* again wrote of the current Amilcar range:

> *The programme of Amilcar for 1934 comprises three chassis. These are the 5CV, the 7CV and the 9CV. The 5CV is a mechanical achievement of the very first order. The engine bore has been increased to 50 millimetres, in addition the power supply is ensured by a vertical carburettor, hence better power supply and more brilliant acceleration, while the elongated chassis allows it to receive three places. As for what concerns the road holding and the averages achieved, it is enough to be edified to address the numerous customers. We resume the study of the 7CV and especially the 9CV which deserve to be examined in their smallest details.*

Omnia in June 1933 gave a complimentary summary of the 5CV.

> *The 5 CV Amilcar is not a small car any more than a small car, it is a fully balanced 2-seater, depending on its destination. There is a basic characteristic that should always be considered in any comparison of cars between them, it is the power-weight ratio. A vehicle can be established for transport that meets a well-defined requirement. Its capacity will be 2 or 4 seats, depending*

on the service envisaged. Its power will be 5 or 6 fiscal CV. This vehicle cannot always be called a car in the full sense that custom gives to this term. We have seen many examples of this so far. Either the bodywork is ridiculously cramped, or the engine is clearly too weak. It is never advisable to sit between two chairs. Let us now consider the 850cc Amilcar. Its engine develops 21hp. The weight of the 2-seater car in running order is 510 kilograms. The power-weight ratio is therefore 25 kilogrammes per effective horsepower, an excellent ratio, an essential ratio for having a car and even here an excessively cheerful car. The 850cc Amilcar is therefore an exact solution for the rapid transport of two people. It is at the same time a solution at least as 'economical' in use, as the best that could be presented in the genre, because a very light vehicle and a small engine, lead to very low expenses. Six litres of gasoline per 100 kilometres, one litre of oil for 1,500 kilometres. What less do you want to allocate, if you want the comfort and the driving pleasure of a truly modern vehicle. This is the ideal car for a stroll in good weather. With the door windows up, you enjoy perfect protection.

1935

Amilcar effectively lost their way through the 1930s and seem to have generated very little coverage in the motoring press. With little or no distribution in the previous international markets, it was probably only the French press that would have commented, and by the time of the Pégase they were selling so few cars they may have been just about invisible to the rest of the motoring world. However, *Omnia* reporting on the Paris Salon on 1 October 1935, was full of praise for the latest model from Amilcar.

All fans of fast vehicles with perfect road holding safety know the Amilcar-Pégase model which continued the most brilliant year. Driving at 120 in complete tranquillity, feeling your car gripping the ground in the most difficult road conditions, being certain to stop in the minimum space while maintaining an impeccable line, are attractions to which the fine connoisseur gives all his sympathy. There is another attraction to which this demanding fine connoisseur is not indifferent, it is that this very safe vehicle is, at the same time, of beautiful line, that it is racy, that at a glance one judges that it is the exceptional and 'gay' model. If the Amilcar-Pégase proved its sporting qualities at the Circuit d'Orléans, the Course du Val de Cuech, the Grand Prix de Lorraine, the Circuit de l'Isère, the Rallye des Alpes Françaises by ranking first each time, it shone no less in the elegance competitions where the competitions are no less lively. For the elegance of the bodies, we have the confirmations of the International Trophy of feminine elegance in Bagatelle, the competitions of Laval, Deauville, Malo-les-Bains, La Baule. One does not seduce the juries, on all occasions, without having seriously deserved it.

1938

L'Automobile sur la Cote d'Azur reporting on the Paris Salon in October 1938 found the Compound interesting:

Amilcar – Last year we had the surprise of the new Amilcar 'Compound' which, by its special technique, was truly the highlight of the 1937 Salon. We have reviewed this car which uses aluminium alloys to the maximum and whose body is compounded with the chassis in Alpax (patent J.-A. Grégoire). With a power of 7hp it is equipped with a four-cylinder engine, a four-speed gearbox and reverse gear with helical pinions which, as well as the axle, is mounted in an aluminium casing. The designs of the new Amilcar with front-wheel drive eliminate the disadvantages of the vast majority of chassis which make the fixing of mechanical parts difficult and the repairs of chassis-bodies difficult. The use of the Alpax allows it to arrive at a weight of about 650 kgs for the chassis which, however, has four comfortable seats. The four wheels are independent and the braking is ensured by self-centring Bendix brakes. The engine has a displacement of 1185cc. This car built by Hotchkiss is easy to make, the price of the foundry tooling not reaching a tenth of that of the stamping tooling. The mechanical parts are fixed on bosses or judiciously reinforced parts of the foundry. The cast parts, which are machined, are easily interchangeable with the minimum of cost, solving the question of repair in a rational way. The rigidity of the carcass remains absolute whatever the torsional forces that the profile of the road makes the chassis undergo. To give an idea of the possibilities of this astonishing car, we will cite the raid carried out by one of them in North Africa and through the Balkans, covering 12,913 kilometres with an average consumption of 9.49 litres per 100 kilometres, finishing this journey at Montlhéry by covering 103.626 kilometres in one hour, completing a circuit at an average of 111.061km/h, a most satisfactory result if we consider that the engine had sucked up the sand of four deserts before this attempt.

1939

When *The Autocar* finally managed to test the Hotchkiss-Amilcar Ten as the Compound was called in Britain, they seemed impressed:

> *This is not just a 10hp car competitive in price and appeal with the general run of cars in similar rating, but an individualistic machine of decidedly interesting design. It is attractive, a good deal above the average for this size and class in handling characteristics, and at the same time rides comfortably.*

The above comments reflect Amilcar's superiority over the competition in the cyclecar sector through the 1920s, as well as their impressive sporting achievements. However, as they lost their way in the 1930s the various models faced stiffer opposition, particularly from Citroën, who had risked all on putting the Traction Avant into production and also had the Ford-like mass production ability to make them affordable. The Traction alone did a lot of damage to the rest of the French car industry and was another nail in Amilcar's coffin.

LATER QUOTES

In later publications those that were involved with Amilcars in their prime offered their memories. Writers today can often view vintage cars, particularly sporting ones, through rose-coloured glasses, or at least sepia-coloured nostalgia, while at the same time finding it easy to find fault and causes to blame for the failures. Amilcar through the years between 1921 and 1939 did not have the benefit of hindsight. The following comments are however nothing less than accurate.

Jean Albert Gregoire, who wrote of the Amilcar in his book *Fifty Years of the Automobile*, 'I loved the exhaust noise. It was slightly less deep than Bugatti's which rattled windows but so much better than the clickety, asthmatic Salmson. The exhaust note was always a strong commercial point Amilcar had in its favour.' Gregoire said of his chance to work with Amilcar, 'What an honour it was for me to follow Moyet, a great engineer and charming man at Amilcar, a marque I had dreamed about like all boys of my age.'

In *Classic Cars* of December 1974, Pierre Chan reminisced of his days in the drawing office:

> *Although the early Amilcar was extremely simple it had such handling and good roadholding that the young clientele persuaded the firm's directors to create a new vehicle derived from the original but suitable for more sporting use.*

He went on to tell of his memories when working on the 6-cylinder CO:

> *Chinon and I were so enthusiastic that we sometimes forgot the time when working at our drawing boards. What more intoxicating, indeed, for a technician than to be able to give free rein to his imagination, without taking account of the obsession with cost that was the chief bugbear when it came to production cars.*

Lord Montagu commented in his book *Lost Causes of Motoring* of the Compound, '...probably the most advanced creation to come out of France since André Citroën had shaken the wiseacres with his 7CV Traction four years before.'

Some of the best features in recent times have been in *Classic & Sports Car* magazine and in September 2014 Jon Pressnell sampled a rare surviving Compound and commented on the production problems that beset it. He at least got to drive it and offered a fair judgement on how it stacks up against its contemporaries:

> *...the Amilcar no more speedy than a much-cheaper Juvaquatre, and appreciably less lively than the zingy overhead-valve Simca Eight. There are 70 recorded survivors, a reflection upon the resistance to rust of the largely aluminium structure.... With domed-glass Marchal headlamps and proprietary Deco-like side-lights, the car lives up to its catalogue claim of offering "exceptional elegance for a small-capacity car".*

He summed up with criticism of the lack of performance, and the cable-operated gearchange, '...but the action is precise.' As for roadholding and comfort Pressnell wrote, '...the car bucks around on poor roads... relative to many a British small saloon of the time, its ahead of the game, but a Traction Avant shades it.'

Mick Walsh has long been *Classic & Sports Car's* ace tester of vintage racers and sampled a C6 in April 2022. Registered YW 91 this was the ex-Beris Harcourt-Wood and W. E. 'Bill' Humphreys car of Brooklands fame.

> *One glance into the tight footwell it's clear that narrow shoes are essential to work the centre-throttle pedal layout... gearbox requires careful feel to find first because it's easy to move the swept-back lever too far forward into reverse... once away the transmission is a total delight, fast and precise. The super-responsive engine makes it a treat to double-declutch, with the rapid downshifts into corners accompanied by that distinctive exhaust through the fishtail pipe close behind... the chassis is communicative. You really feel part of the car... is a joy to command, its delicate feel emphasising its neat, quality design and construction.*

CHAPTER 16

AMILCAR TRIVIA

What is trivia? The word comes from the ancient days of the Roman empire, 'at a place where three roads meet' (*tri via* means three ways in Italian). At these road junctions, it was common to put up notices of local interest: pig market this way; sandals re-soled; a chariot-mender this way; or gladiator fight at the arena on Saturday night. Such inconsequential information became known as 'trivia'. Well, here follows some Amilcar trivia.

THE SPECIALS

As often happened when a vintage sports car is getting left behind the competition or has blown its engine, an impecunious and inventive mechanic would install a more powerful engine and update the running gear to create what is generally referred to as a 'Special'. This was common practice even in the 1920s, and the tradition is still alive today. Amilcars with light and sharp handling chassis were

Ernest Eldridge in his Special at Indianapolis.

particularly suited to these later modifications and many are still out competing in historic speed events. Here a few examples.

The Eldridge Special

Ernest Eldridge sold his monstrous old Fiat aero-engined Mephistopheles to fund an entry into Grand Prix racing with cars of his own design, the Eldridge Specials. One of these was based on the narrow Amilcar 'False Tandem' chassis, the other a modified two-seater CGS frame into which he fitted Anzani 1500cc side-valve engines to which he added a DOHC cylinder head and a supercharger. He campaigned these cars at many races through the 1925 season including the San Sebastian, and the Italian Grands Prix, both of which he failed to finish. There were also appearances at Brooklands without much success and in 1926 he took two cars to America for an attempt at the 1926 Indy 500 – like many others, tempted by the prize money. Eldridge drove one car with Douglas Hawkes in the other. Again, with no success, the pair then entered a couple of other oval speedway races before seeing sense and buying a front-wheel-drive Miller with which he had been impressed.

The Amilcar Riley Kerr-Bate Special

In 1932 architect Stanley Chave Kerr-Bate, 26 years old at the time, started building himself a racing car with the intention of competing at Brooklands. He already had a Riley Nine, which although too heavy, did have an engine with the promise of some tunability. The search for a suitable chassis led him to a

Douglas Hawkes in the other Eldridge Special at Indianapolis.

The Amilcar Riley Kerr-Bate Special.

Vernon Balls in his streamlined Amilcar at Brooklands.

lightweight and sharp-handling Amilcar CGSs from 1928 into which the Riley engine, gearbox and front axle were fitted. The engine received a Laystall crankshaft, the flywheel was lightened and with various other modifications a set of four SU carburettors were persuaded to supply the fuel and air mixture. A simple single seat racing body was constructed and more suitable ratios were installed in the gearbox. The project took Kerr-Bate a few years to complete, but he did make a couple of appearances at Brooklands and Donington before war intervened, during which the car received some minor bomb damage. He sold the car on in the early 1950s and the next owner fitted a glass fibre two-seater body. Some years later in the hands of a VSCC member the car was rebodied again in aluminium and then sold on to owners in America and Australia before returning to the UK.

In need of care and attention by the late 1990s, the Special was entrusted to Ashton Keynes Vintage Restoration to undertake a full rebuild and it retains the registration TM 2771 for road use in the UK with chassis number 601159. Since then it has taken part in many historic events, including the Vintage Montlhéry revival meeting, before being sold on again by Brightwells Auctions and is still performing very well.

The Caldersmith Special

Another special created in Australia is Tony Caldersmith's Amilcar–Ford. Taking a G-Type chassis and fitting a Ford Model A engine, Brian added a Miller Schofield 1929 overhead valve cylinder head mated to the Ford's three-speed gearbox. Sparks are supplied by a special distributor made for using the Ford engine in aircraft, which has twin points. The back axle has a Holden crown wheel and pinion and strengthened half shafts. The body was then made by a craftsman in Melbourne and the car was finally finished in 1999, since when it has had some success on track.

There are many others and no limit to some people's imaginations. Of the other Amilcars still racing in Australia, the Snape Special has a Willys engine, the KB Special is powered

Frédéric de Coninck in his Amilcar-powered speedboat.

by an Overland Whippet motor. Also built in Australia an Amilcar G-Type chassis with a supercharged 6-cylinder AC-Bristol engine is now back competing in the UK where otherwise Riley engines, fours and sixes, seem a popular option, a few so powered still active in VSCC events. Prince Bira, a famous Grand Prix racer from the 1930s, started racing in an Amilcar-Riley at Brooklands in 1927. In the USA there are at least two Amilcars with, not surprisingly, Ford engines.

Then there are those that have been restored as well as possible from found parts, a common theme being to use larger capacity Amilcar side-valve fours with pressure-fed lubrication from the later models in the early CC and C4 chassis. Some of these are also used for competition and many are registered for road use as vintage Amilcars but often still referred to as 'Specials', as they are no longer as they were when they originally left the factory.

The Coninck racing boat

In 1906, Frédéric 'Gaston' de Coninck, founding member of the Yacht Club de France, and Knight of the Legion of Honor, bought a shipyard in Maisons-Laffitte, a suburb to the north-west of Paris. The business named G. de Coninck & Cie grew, and he produced sailboats, paddle boats, towing boats, lifeboats, ferries for the Suez Canal Company and motorboats that won many races in the 1500cc category. One of these with which he contested speedboat competitions was the 'Amilcar de Coninck'.

Competing in the then-popular Courses de Canot Automobiles, Coninck's speedboat is pictured racing at Monte Carlo in 1923 and was powered by an Amilcar engine. Later Coninck retired to Le Havre and sold the business to Ettore Bugatti, who also had an interest in power boats.

FAMOUS AMILCAR FANS

Isadora Duncan

On 14 September 1927, the legendary American dancer Isadora Duncan (1877–1927) died in a tragic accident in an Amilcar CGSs on a street in Nice.

Angela Isadora Duncan was born in San Francisco in 1877, started teaching dance at a young age and moved to London and then Paris in 1900. She was known as a pioneer of modern dance and performed throughout Europe and Russia. A life full of scandal followed her everywhere and as her fame waned in her later years she became notorious for her financial problems, running up debts at hotels, a well-publicised love life and public drunkenness.

Isadora Duncan, the famous dancer who met a tragic end in an Amilcar.

Benoît Pierre Falchetto was either a mechanic or a car salesman in 1927. Exactly what Falchetto was doing the day he picked up Duncan is the subject of some historical conjecture. One story has it that he was asked to demonstrate the Amilcar CGSs to Duncan, a prospective customer. Another was that they had planned to drive to a nearby hotel for romantic purposes; it was said that Duncan had a taste for younger lovers; Falchetto was almost half her age at the time. Whatever the purpose of the ill-fated trip, Duncan was wearing a long silk scarf gifted to her by her friend Mary Desti, who was standing by as the couple got in the car. Desti had suggested Duncan wore a cape in the open car but Duncan waved her off with the scarf around her neck saying *'Adieu, mes amis. Je vais à la gloire!'* ('Farewell, my friends. I go to glory!') although Desti is later reported to have said the actual farewell was ....*'Je vais à l'amour'* ('I am off to love'). As Falchetto drove away, the scarf became entangled around the spokes of the rear wheel and brake drum, immediately pulling Duncan from the car and breaking her neck. It was

Benoît Falchetto, who was Isadora Duncan's driver on that fateful day.

Desti who took Duncan's body to the hospital where she was pronounced dead.

Writer and Paris-based patron of the arts Gertrude Stein famously remarked that 'affectations can be dangerous'. Duncan was cremated, and her ashes were placed in Père Lachaise Cemetery in Paris.

Benoît Pierre Falchetto (1900–1983) subsequently started racing in 1928 with an Amilcar and later with Bugattis from 1930 onwards, switching to a Maserati in 1934.

Many subsequent reports have it that Duncan died in a Bugatti, a myth perpetuated by the 1968 film of Duncan's life. It has been claimed that the film producers either could not find an Amilcar at the time or considered the Bugatti added more glamour to the scene.

Jacques Henri Lartigue

This prolific French photographer and painter (1894–1986) was also a motoring enthusiast with a taste for sports cars and pretty girls.

Sir Peter Ustinov

Peter Ustinov (1921–2004) was an actor, film director, writer and favourite of television talk shows for many years. He recorded the comic commentary of the fictitious Grand Prix of Gibraltar, which was not a surprise, as he also had a famous affiliation with old sports and racing cars. At different times he owned Alfa Romeos, Aston Martins, Maseratis and famously a pair of Hispano-Suizas. He only qualifies for a mention here for the revelation in his last published interview when he asserted that as a child he remembered; 'there was no one yet qualified to exorcise an internal combustion engine from a small boy'. He, like many other boys pretended to be an imaginary car himself. 'I know to this day precisely what make of car I was – an Amilcar. At one period in my life, I switched

Jacques Henri Lartigue and one of his lady friends and his Amilcar.

on in the morning and stopped being a car at night only after I reversed into bed and cut the ignition.' The rather rotund Ustinov added, 'even at that age I had a presentiment that a certain portliness would be with me all my life. Amilcars appealed, for being waspish, athletic and slightly fragile'.

Horace Chase

There are various claims for who invented the Sidecar cocktail and one of them is probably true, but there is one story that involves an Amilcar. A young American in Paris, Horace Chase used to frequent the bar at the Ritz Hotel. The usual patrons meant there was always a line of Rolls-Royces, Hispano-Suizas and other such limousines in the street outside in the Rue Cambon. Horace's Amilcar was miniscule by comparison and the barman Frank joked, 'You call that thing a car? That's a child's toy, that's more like the size of a sidecar than a regular car.' From that remark, whenever Horace turned up he was greeted as 'Mr Sidecar'. One day Horace asked Frank to mix him a drink he remembered mixing himself at home in Florida; 'I used to mix Bacardi and lemon juice and a little Cointreau. Let's try that but use brandy instead.' Horace and Frank both agreed the new recipe was a success, so Frank named the cocktail the 'Sidecar' after Horace's little Amilcar's nickname.

Other claims dating back to 1922 suggest Pat MacGarry, the bartender at Buck's Club in London (creator of the Bucks Fizz cocktail) invented it, while Harry MacElhone of the famous Harry's Bar in Paris also takes the credit. For now, we can choose to believe the story of Frank at the Ritz with the Amilcar connection.

Howard Fowler was a flying ace with the American forces who achieved notoriety when, after a drunken bet on Armistice Day, he flew his biplane under the Arc de Triomphe. Horace Chase decided to emulate his feat by driving his Amilcar through the normally closed-off arch – maybe he had partaken of one too many Sidecars himself. One of Chase's friends, the wealthy American socialite and fellow Floridian, Alice DeLamar, also had a townhouse in Paris. She was also an Amilcar enthusiast and after the pair visited the factory she wrote to a friend:

> *They were all lined up on display in a large barn-like shed, rather like an airplane hangar. We fairly shouted with delight… there were black ones and red ones and blue ones and tooled aluminium jobs with mahogany trim, and in all manner of style they were incredibly chic. The car was a very good bet for exploring the byways of Europe in those early Twenties when the roads were none too good. They were so light in weight*

Suzy Vernon was one of Lartigue's favourite models, here in a CGS3.

you didn't have to get a horse to pull them out of the mud or sand if you got stuck.

Miss DeLamar had three Amilcars, which she preferred over her Bugatti, one reason being the smell of the castor oil the Bugatti required while the Amilcar ran on regular motor oil. DeLamar's partner, Broadway actress Eva Le Gallienne, also had a CGS of her own.

The Grand Duke Kirill Vladimirovich

Another famous Amilcar owner was Grand Duke Kirill Vladimirovich, who claimed to be the rightful successor to the Russian throne. He was exiled in France after the revolution in his home country.

Charles Nungesser

This Frenchman was a famous air ace in World War I, ranked third in terms of 'kills' and decorated many times. He was known to have a taste for fast cars and was a fan of the Amilcar, so in 1923 he bought a CC for his wife Consuelo, although he probably had a more powerful model. Nungesser died in 1927 while trying to be the first to fly across the Atlantic Ocean.

Jean-Paul Belmondo

In the 1982 film *Ace of Aces* starring Jean-Paul Belmondo, part of the story is based on Nungesser's wartime flying adventures. Belmondo was said to have borrowed this CGSs while filming and then drove it around on a holiday trip to Spain but blew up the engine, which he had rebuilt in Switzerland before returning it to its owner Jacques in France. Better known though is Belmondo's use of a CGS in the gangster film *Borsalino*.

Marthe Ferrare

This opera singer was popular around Paris in the 1920s and 1930s. Did she own this skiff-bodied Amilcar, or was she just asked to pose for the photo?

Exiled in Brittany, Grand Duke Kirill Vladimirovich and Princess Victoria take a drive in their Amilcar.

This CGSs has a film star past with Jean-Paul Belmondo.

Jacques Tati

Anyone interested in old French cars may also be a fan of Jacques Tati's films, particularly *Monsieur Hulot's Holiday* from 1952. In the Jacques Tati biography by David Bellos, he repeatedly refers to Tati driving an Amilcar when in fact it was a Salmson AL3, so rest assured no Amilcars were harmed in the production of this excellent comedy masterpiece!

Marthe Ferrare taking part in the '*Championnat des artistes*' (whatever that was), at the Parc des Princes on 23 May 1924.

Tintin

An Amilcar even featured in the *Tintin* cartoon comic book series in the tale *Tintin in the Land of the Soviets*, with the hero driving what appears to be a stylised version of a C6.

EPHEMERA

Amilcars can turn up in many strange places.

A print of a supercharged Amilcar CGSs of unknown origin.

An advertising poster in the typical Art Deco style of the period.

Amilcar CGSs on a Spanish postage stamp.

Danish sticker translates as something to do with 50 years of quality tyres in Viborg.

Skiff-type Amilcar artwork on a matchbook cover.

A C6 or CO racer on a Shell oil giveaway card.

Giant brand licorice collector's card.

Unusual cabriolet design on a Dutch cigarette card.

Atlantic petrol station collector's card.

Another cigarette card from The House of Craven.

SOCIÉTÉ NOUVELLE pour L'AUTOMOBILE

(SOCIÉTÉ ANONYME)

Statuts déposés en l'Étude de Mᵉ BARILLOT, notaire à Paris, le 29 Septembre 1921.

CAPITAL SOCIAL : TROIS MILLIONS DE FRANCS

DIVISÉ EN 30.000 ACTIONS DE 100 FRANCS CHACUNE

SIÈGE SOCIAL : 34, rue du Chemin-Vert, à PARIS (XIᵉ)

ACTION de CENT francs, Série B

AU PORTEUR

№ 018.877

ENTIÈREMENT LIBÉRÉE

PARIS, le 1ᵉʳ Septembre 1922.

UN ADMINISTRATEUR. UN ADMINISTRATEUR.

Share certificate for the Société Nouvelle pour l'Automobile dated 1921.

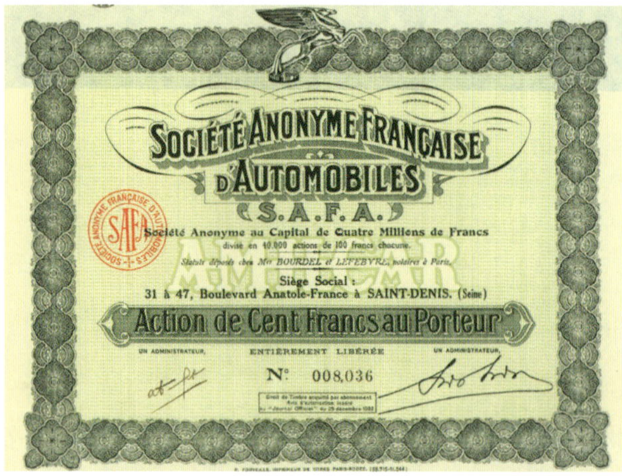

SOCIÉTÉ ANONYME FRANÇAISE D'AUTOMOBILES

(S.A.F.A.)

Société Anonyme au Capital de Quatre Millions de Francs

divisé en 40.000 actions de 100 francs chacune

Statuts déposés chez Mᵉˢ BOURDEL & LEFEBVRE, notaires à Paris.

Siège Social : 31 à 47, Boulevard Anatole-France à SAINT-DENIS. (Seine)

Action de Cent Francs au Porteur

UN ADMINISTRATEUR, ENTIÈREMENT LIBÉRÉE, UN ADMINISTRATEUR

N° 008,036

Share certificate for the Société Anonyme Française d'Automobile from 1932.

Warren Brown A.M. is a writer, journalist and well-known cartoonist in Australia who kindly sketched this writer in his Amilcar CS.

APPENDIX I

TECHNICAL SPECIFICATIONS

Through the eighteen years of Amilcar's existence there were several different families of models, some of which shared common parts, some being new designs with little in common with their predecessors. The following tables show the various early 4-cylinder models where evolution included common parts with minor changes. The later models that followed, being new designs, varied more in their equipment and the target market so there are more varied details and specifications.

Accessories were sourced from various suppliers as listed at the end of this chapter and were not always common to each model according to supplies available.

Body styles, too, could vary: some were standardised in house, but as chassis were often clothed by other coachbuilders there were always exceptions too.

Production numbers are shown where known. Factory records were lost long ago and all quoted figures should be taken as approximate.[(7)]

Note also the power figures quoted are as published by the factory in period. The motor industry has since devised several different formulae for measuring an engine's output dating back to the early days of steam power. Two common definitions used today are the imperial horsepower, which is about 745.7 watts, and the metric horsepower, which is approximately 735.5 watts. One imperial horsepower lifts 550 pounds (250kg) by 1 foot (30cm) in 1 second. Then there is brake horsepower – bhp – calculated on a load dynamometer, which can vary according to how it is measured, at the crankshaft, transmission output, or at the driven wheels. To confuse further, in modern times figures are quoted as DIN, PS, SAE, watts and kilowatts. Then there is taxable horsepower, which was purely used to estimate power for a taxable value and even then this would vary in different countries; RAC HP in Britain would not be the same as the French CV rating. So, for simplicity we will just use the original quoted hp numbers.

It would be normal practice here to include top speed and fuel consumption figures too. However, there were many variables – particularly the size and weight of the bodywork fitted – which would make a significant difference to the abilities of a small side-valve 4-cylinder engine. Where such information would be a case of averaging the guesswork of previously published figures I have left those specifications out rather than quote any inaccuracies. Those statistics that have been quoted in the original advertisements may be only taken as an optimistic sales pitch, although there were some efforts to accurately measure performance as reported in period road tests (see Chapter 15).

Amilcar CC, 1921–25

Production total: 5,000 including the CV and CS.
Chassis: Trapezoid two longitudinal rails, open ended with three crossmembers.
Engine rigid mounted to three points.
Wheelbase: 2.31 metres
Track: Front: 1.10 metres Rear: 1.10 metres
Engine: Four cylinder cast iron in unit with crankcase.
Bore 55mm Stroke 90mm – Capacity 903cc
Side-valve head, valves operated by camshaft and rocking cam followers acting on valve stem with single valve springs.
Crankshaft carried in two white metal 35mm bearings.
Big end bearing 35mm white metal.
Casting altered to allow fitting of starter in 1923.
Fuel system: Solex side-draught carburettor gravity fed from tank mounted on front bulkhead.
Ignition: Magneto with fixed advance.
Maximum power: 17hp at 2,300rpm.
Cooling: Thermo-syphon to front mounted radiator.
Transmission: Three speed and reverse gearbox.
Ratios: 12 to 1, 6.8 to 1 and 4.28 to 1
Clutch: three steel discs running in engine oil.
Driven through flexible Hardy Spicer joint and shaft in torque tube.
Rear axle: Straight-cut crown wheel and pinion with no differential and single axle shaft.
Banjo type from 1923 with two half shafts.
Front axle: U section pressed steel with wood insert. Drop forged from 1924.
Steering: Worm and sector in bronze casting.
Brakes: Ribbed cast iron 220mm diameter drums.
Rod operated by hand and foot controls.
Suspension: Quarter elliptic front and rear mounted on outside of chassis rails.
Friction shock absorbers.
Wheels and tyres: 40 spoke wire wheels on Rudge hubs; 50 spokes from 1924.
Beaded edge 700 × 80 tyres; 710 × 90 from 1924.
Electrical system: Acetylene lighting, 6-volt electric optional until standard in 1923 with dynamo driven by timing gears.
Starter optional from 1923.

Amilcar CV, 1922–23

Production total: Included in the CC and CS total.
Chassis: Trapezoid two longitudinal rails, open ended with three crossmembers.
Engine rigid mounted to three points.
Wheelbase: 2.31 metres
Track: Front: 1.10 metres Rear: 1.10 metres
Engine: Four cylinder cast iron in unit with crankcase.
Bore 57mm Stroke 90mm – Capacity 985cc
Side-valve head, valves operated by camshaft and rocking cam followers acting on valve stem with single valve springs.
Crankshaft carried in two white metal 35mm bearings.
Big end bearing 35mm white metal.
Casting altered to allow fitting of starter in 1923.
Fuel system: Solex side-draught carburettor gravity fed from tank mounted on front bulkhead.
Ignition: Magneto with fixed advance.
Maximum power: 18hp at 2,500rpm.
Cooling: Thermo-syphon to front mounted radiator.
Transmission: Three speed and reverse gearbox.
Ratios: 12 to 1, 6.8 to 1 and 4.28 to 1
Clutch: three steel discs running in engine oil.
Driven through flexible Hardy Spicer joint and shaft in torque tube.
Rear axle: Straight-cut crown wheel and pinion with no differential and single axle shaft.
Banjo type from 1923 with two half shafts.
Front axle: U section pressed steel with wood insert. Drop forged from 1924.
Steering: Worm and sector in bronze casting.
Brakes: Ribbed cast iron 220mm diameter drums.
Rod operated by hand and foot controls.
Suspension: Quarter elliptic front and rear mounted on outside of chassis rails. Friction shock absorbers.
Wheels and tyres: 40 spoke wire wheels on Rudge hubs.
Beaded edge 700 × 80 tyres.
Electrical system: Acetylene lighting, 6-volt electric optional until standard in 1923 with dynamo driven by timing gears. Starter optional from 1923.

Amilcar CS, 1923 –25

Production total:	Included in the CC and CS total.
Chassis:	Trapezoid two longitudinal rails, open ended with three crossmembers. Engine rigid mounted to three points.
Wheelbase:	2.31 metres
Track:	Front: 1.10 metres Rear: 1.10 metres
Engine:	Four cylinder cast iron in unit with crankcase. Bore 58mm Stroke 90mm – Capacity 1004cc Side-valve head, valves operated by camshaft and rocking cam followers acting on valve stem with single valve springs. Crankshaft carried in two white metal 35mm bearings. Big end bearing 35mm white metal.
Fuel system:	Solex side-draught carburettor gravity fed from tank mounted on front bulkhead.
Ignition:	Magneto with fixed advance.
Maximum power:	22hp at 3,000rpm.
Cooling:	Thermo-syphon to front mounted radiator.
Transmission:	Three speed and reverse gearbox. Ratios: 12 to 1, 6.8 to 1 and 4.28 to 1 Clutch: three steel discs running in engine oil. Driven through flexible Hardy Spicer joint and shaft in torque tube.
Rear axle:	Banjo type with no differential.
Front axle:	U section pressed steel with wood insert. Drop forged from 1924.
Steering:	Worm and sector in bronze casting.
Brakes:	Ribbed cast iron 220mm diameter drums. Rod operated by hand and foot controls.
Suspension:	Quarter elliptic front and rear mounted on outside of chassis rails. Hartford friction shock absorbers.
Wheels and tyres:	700 × 80 wheels and tyres until 1924. 710 × 90 then 715 × 115 Balloon tyres in 1925.
Electrical system:	6-volt electric lighting and starter motor. Dynamo driven by timing gears.

Amilcar C4, 1922–29

Production total:	4,950
Chassis:	Trapezoid two longitudinal rails, extended at rear to carry longer bodywork with four crossmembers. Engine rigid mounted to three points.
Wheelbase:	2.45 metres
Track:	Front: 1.10 metres Rear: 1.10 metres
Engine:	Four cylinder cast iron in unit with crankcase. Bore 58mm Stroke 90mm – Capacity 1004cc Side-valve head, valves operated by camshaft and rocking cam followers acting on valve stem with single valve springs. Crankshaft carried in two white metal 35mm bearings. Big end bearing 35mm white metal. Casting altered to allow fitting of starter in 1923.
Fuel system:	Solex side-draught carburettor gravity fed from tank mounted on front bulkhead.
Ignition:	Magneto with fixed advance.
Maximum power:	22hp at 3,000rpm.
Cooling:	Thermo-syphon to front mounted radiator.
Transmission:	Three speed and reverse gearbox. Ratios: 12 to 1, 6.8 to 1 and 4.28 to 1 Clutch: three steel discs running in engine oil. Driven through flexible Hardy Spicer joint and shaft in torque tube.
Rear axle:	Straight-cut crown wheel and pinion with no differential and single axle shaft. Banjo type from 1923 with two half shafts. Differential added 1925.
Front axle:	U section pressed steel with wood insert. Drop forged from 1923.
Steering:	Worm and sector in bronze casting. Larger steering box from 1926.
Brakes:	Ribbed cast iron 220mm diameter drums. Rod operated by hand and foot controls. Front brakes from 1928.
Suspension:	Quarter elliptic front and rear mounted on outside of chassis rails. Friction shock absorbers.
Wheels and tyres:	40 spoke wire wheels on Rudge or RAF hubs, beaded edge 700 × 80 tyres; 50 spokes 710 × 90 from 1924. 'Comfort' tyres from 1926.
Electrical system:	Acetylene lighting, 6-volt electric optional until standard in 1923 with dynamo driven by timing gears. Starter motor from 1923. 12-volt from 1928.

Amilcar CGS, 1923–26

Production total:	2,418 CGS and CGS3.
Chassis:	Pressed steel longitudinal rails, open ended with three crossmembers, tapering in at the rear with outwardly curved dumb irons at the front. For the CGS3 it was extended upward and closed at the rear to support the third seat. Engine rigid mounted to three points.
Wheelbase:	2.425 metres
Track:	Front: 1.09 metres Rear: 1.09 metres
Engine:	Four cylinder cast iron in unit with crankcase. Bore 60mm Stroke 95mm – Capacity 1075cc Side-valve head, valves operated by camshaft and rocking cam followers acting on valve stem with single valve springs. Crankshaft carried in two white metal 35mm bearings. Big end bearing 35mm white metal. Redesigned Ricardo cylinder head. Pressure lubrication from 1925.
Fuel system:	Solex side-draught carburettor gravity fed from tank mounted on front bulkhead.
Ignition:	Magneto with fixed advance.
Maximum power:	33hp at 3,700rpm.
Cooling:	Thermo-syphon to front mounted radiator.
Transmission:	Three speed and reverse gearbox. Ratios: 12 to 1, 6.8 to 1 and 4.28 to 1 Clutch: three steel discs running in engine oil. Driven through flexible Hardy Spicer joint and shaft in torque tube.
Rear axle:	Banjo type with no differential.
Front axle:	Drop forged I section beam axle.
Steering:	Worm and sector in bronze casting.
Brakes:	Ribbed cast iron 225mm diameter drums on the front wheels, 210mm diameter drums at the rear, rod operated by foot controls. Handbrake on rear wheels only.
Suspension:	Semi-elliptic springs front and quarter elliptic springs at the rear mounted on outside of chassis rails. Hartford friction shock absorbers.
Wheels and tyres:	40 spoke wire wheels on Rudge hubs; 50 spokes from 1924. Beaded edge 700 × 80, 700 × 85, 700 × 90 or 710 × 90 tyres. Later 27 × 4 well-base tyres.
Electrical system:	6-volt electric lighting and starter motor. Dynamo driven by timing gears.
Accessories:	Jaeger or OS gauges for speedometer, oil pressure, ammeter, rev counter and clock. Nivex fuel gauge. Ignition advance and retard control.

Amilcar CGSs, 1926–29

Production total:	885
Chassis:	Pressed steel longitudinal rails, open ended with three crossmembers, tapering in at the rear with outwardly curved dumb irons at the front. Wheelbase reduced by shortening the rear leaf springs. Engine rigid mounted to three points.
Wheelbase:	2.323 metres
Track:	Front: 1.045 metres Rear: 1.090 metres
Engine:	Four cylinder cast iron in unit with crankcase. Bore 60mm Stroke 95mm – Capacity 1075cc. Side-valve head, valves operated by camshaft and rocking cam followers acting on valve stem with single valve springs. Crankshaft carried in two white metal 35mm bearings. Big end bearing 35mm white metal. Same as CGS except modified camshaft allowing higher engine speed and larger capacity 6 litre sump pan.
Fuel system:	Solex side-draught carburettor gravity fed from tank mounted on front bulkhead.
Ignition:	Magneto with variable advance.
Maximum power:	35hp at 4,500rpm.
Cooling:	Thermo-syphon to front mounted radiator.
Transmission:	Three speed and reverse gearbox. Ratios: 12 to 1, 6.8 to 1 and 4.28 to 1 Clutch: three steel discs running in engine oil. Driven through flexible Hardy Spicer joint and shaft in torque tube.
Rear axle:	Banjo type with differential added in 1928.
Front axle:	Drop forged I section beam axle with new profile to lower the car.
Steering:	Worm and sector in new larger steering box as fitted to the G Type with improved turning circle.
Brakes:	Ribbed cast iron 260mm diameter drums all round operated by steel ribbons at the front, rod operated at the rear. Handbrake on rear wheels only.
Suspension:	Semi-elliptic springs front and shortened quarter elliptic springs at the rear mounted on outside of chassis rails. Hartford friction shock absorbers.
Wheels and tyres:	Rudge wheels with 27 × 4 tyres.
Electrical system:	6-volt electric lighting and starter motor. Dynamo driven by timing gears. 12-volt from 1928.
Accessories:	Jaeger or OS gauges for speedometer, oil pressure, ammeter, rev counter and clock. Nivex fuel gauge. Ignition advance and retard control.

Amilcar 10CV E Type, 1923–25

Production total: 500

Chassis: Pressed steel longitudinal rails with four crossmembers.

Wheelbase: 2.97 metres.

Track: 1.25 metres

Engine: Four cylinder cast iron in unit with crankcase.
Bore 65mm Stroke 112mm, capacity 1486cc
Bore 67mm Stroke 112mm, capacity 1575cc for 1925
Side-valve head, valves operated by camshaft and rocking cam followers acting on valve stem with single valve springs.
Crankshaft carried in two white metal 46mm bearings.
White metal big end bearings.
Splash fed lubrication.

Fuel system: Solex side-draught carburettor gravity fed from tank mounted on front bulkhead.

Ignition: Magneto with variable advance.

Maximum power: 42hp at 3,500rpm 1468cc, then 46hp at 3,500rpm for 1575cc.

Cooling: Thermo-syphon to front mounted radiator.

Transmission: Four speed and reverse gearbox.
Clutch: three steel discs running in engine oil.
Driven through flexible Hardy Spicer joint and shaft in torque tube.

Rear axle: Banjo type with helical gear crown wheel and pinion with differential.

Front axle: Drop forged steel.

Steering: Worm and sector in bronze casting.

Brakes: Rod operated cast iron 350mm diameter drums.

Suspension: Semi elliptic springs front and cantilever springs rear.
Hartford friction shock absorbers.

Wheels and tyres: Wire wheels with Rudge hubs with 765 x 105 tyres.

Electrical system: 6-volt electric lighting and starter, dynamo driven by timing gears.

Amilcar 11CV J Type, 1925–28

Production total: 300

Chassis: Pressed steel longitudinal rails with four crossmembers.

Wheelbase: 3.0 metres

Track: 1.273 metres

Engine: Four cylinder cast iron in unit with crankcase.
Bore 73mm Stroke 112mm, capacity 1878cc
Side-valve head, valves operated by camshaft and rocking cam followers acting on valve stem with single valve springs.
Crankshaft carried in two white metal 46mm bearings.
White metal big end bearings.
Pressure fed lubrication.

Fuel system: Solex side-draught carburettor gravity fed from rear mounted tank by Weymann Exhauster pump.

Ignition: Magneto with variable advance.

Maximum power: 46hp at 3,500rpm.

Cooling: Thermo-syphon to front mounted radiator.

Transmission: Four speed and reverse gearbox.
Clutch: Ferodo dry plate.
Driven through flexible Hardy Spicer joint and shaft in torque tube.

Rear axle: Banjo type with helical gear crown wheel and pinion with differential.

Front axle: Drop forged steel.

Steering: Worm and sector in bronze casting.

Brakes: Rod operated cast iron 350mm diameter drums.

Suspension: Semi-elliptic springs front and cantilever springs rear.
Hartford friction shock absorbers.

Wheels and tyres: Wire wheels with Rudge hubs with 765 × 105 or 775 × 145 tyres.

Electrical system: 12-volt electric lighting and starter, dynamo driven by timing gears.

Amilcar 7CV G Type, 1924–27

Production total: 2,500
Chassis: Pressed steel longitudinal rails with four crossmembers,
Engine rigid mounted to three points.
Wheelbase: 2.60 metres
Track: 1.19 metres
Engine: Four cylinder cast iron in unit with crankcase.
Bore 60mm Stroke 95mm – Capacity 1075cc
Side-valve head, valves operated by camshaft and rocking cam followers acting on valve stem with single valve springs.
Crankshaft carried in two white metal 35mm bearings.
Big end bearing 35mm white metal.
Pressure lubrication.
Fuel system: Solex side-draught carburettor gravity fed from tank mounted on aluminium front firewall.
Ignition: Magneto with variable advance.
Maximum power: 28hp at 3,500rpm.
Cooling: Thermo-syphon to front mounted radiator.
Transmission: Three speed and reverse gearbox.
Clutch: three steel discs running in engine oil.
Driven through flexible Hardy Spicer joint and shaft in torque tube.
Rear axle: Banjo type, spiral bevel gears with differential.
Front axle: Drop forged I section beam axle.
Steering: Worm and sector in new larger steering box with improved turning circle.
Brakes: Ribbed cast iron 260mm diameter drums on all four wheels, Handbrake on rear wheels only.
Suspension: Semi-elliptic springs front and cantilever springs at the rear with Hartford friction shock absorbers.
Wheels and tyres: Wire wheels on Rudge or RAF hubs; 715 × 115 tyres.
Electrical system: 12-volt electric lighting and starter motor. Dynamo driven by timing gears.
Accessories: Jaeger or OS gauges for oil pressure, ammeter, rev counter and clock.
Ignition advance and retard control.

Amilcar 8CV L Type, 1927–28

Production total: 2,500
Chassis: Pressed steel longitudinal rails with four crossmembers. Engine rigid mounted to three points.
Wheelbase: 2.65 metres
Track: 1.19 metres
Engine: Four cylinder cast iron in unit with crankcase.
Bore 60mm Stroke 105mm – Capacity 1190cc
Side-valve head, valves operated by camshaft and rocking cam followers acting on valve stem with single valve springs.
Crankshaft carried in two white metal 35mm bearings.
Big end bearing 35mm white metal.
Pressure lubrication.
Fuel system: Solex side-draught carburettor gravity fed from tank mounted on aluminium front firewall.
Ignition: Magneto with variable advance.
Maximum power: 28hp at 3,500rpm.
Cooling: Thermo-syphon to front mounted radiator with fan driven off the dynamo.
Transmission: Three speed and reverse gearbox.
Clutch: three steel discs running in engine oil.
Driven through flexible Hardy Spicer joint and shaft in torque tube.
Rear axle: Banjo type, spiral bevel gears with differential.
Front axle: Drop forged I section beam axle.
Steering: Worm and sector in new larger steering box with improved turning circle.
Brakes: Ribbed cast iron 260mm diameter drums on all four wheels. Handbrake on rear wheels only.
Suspension: Semi-elliptic springs front and cantilever springs at the rear with Hartford friction shock absorbers.
Wheels and tyres: Wire wheels on Rudge or RAF hubs; 715 × 115 tyres.
Electrical system: 12-volt electric lighting and starter motor. Dynamo driven by timing gears.
Accessories: Jaeger or OS gauges for oil pressure, ammeter, rev counter and clock. Ignition advance and retard control.

Amilcar C6, 1927–30

Production total: 40 to 60, exact total not known.
Chassis: Ladder frame with two curved side members and five crossmembers stiffened by solid engine mounting.
Wheelbase: 2.195 metres
Track: 1.09 metres front and rear.
Engine: Six cylinder cast iron block with aluminium crankcase.
Bore 56mm, Stroke 74mm – Capacity 1094cc
Double overhead camshaft cast iron cylinder head.
30mm diameter valves with three concentric springs.
Crankshaft machined from solid billet carried in seven bearings, five white metal and two roller bearings.
White metal big end bearings.
Gear driven timing gears at the rear of the block driving the magneto and water pump.
High pressure lubrication by dry sump system with two-stage pump fed from 12 litre oil tank at front of the chassis.
Fuel system: Bronze 40mm Solex and Roots type supercharger running at 900 grams (13psi) pressure. 100 litre fuel tank in the tail.
Ignition: Scintilla magneto.
Maximum power: 62hp at 5,600rpm.
Cooling: Front mounted radiator with centrifugal pump.
Transmission: Four speed and reverse gearbox. Ferodo dry plate and steel disc clutch.
Rear axle: Banjo type, straight cut gears with differential.
Front axle: Reversed U-section beam axle with dropped centre.
Steering: Worm and sector in bronze steering box.
Brakes: Ribbed cast iron 260mm diameter drums on all four wheels cable operated. Handbrake on rear wheels only mounted outside the body.
Suspension: Semi-elliptic springs fixed at the front and sliding in trunnions at the rear, quarter elliptic rear springs pivoting on rear axle casing with four friction shock absorbers.
Wheels and tyres: 50 spoke wire wheels with Rudge hubs, 27 × 4 or 4.00 × 19 tyres.
Accessories: Two rev counters, oil pressure gauge, clock and fuel pressure gauge, ignition advance control. Hand pump to pressurise the fuel tank.

Amilcar 7CV M and M2 Type, 1928–31

Production total: 1,174 M Type and 2,651 M2 Type = 3,825 total.
Chassis: Pressed steel longitudinal rails with four crossmembers, Engine rigid mounted to three points.
Wheelbase: 2.65 metres
Track: 1.19 metres
Engine: Four cylinder cast iron in unit with crankcase.
Bore 60mm Stroke 110mm – Capacity 1244cc
Side-valve head, valves operated by camshaft and rocking cam followers acting on valve stem with single valve springs.
Crankshaft carried in two white metal 35mm bearings.
Big end bearing 35mm white metal.
Pressure lubrication.
Fuel system: Solex side-draught carburettor gravity fed from tank mounted on aluminium front firewall.
Ignition: Magneto with variable advance.
Maximum power: 28hp at 3,500rpm.
Cooling: Thermo-syphon to front mounted radiator with fan driven off the dynamo.
Transmission: Three speed and reverse gearbox. Four speed gearbox for M2.
Clutch: three steel discs running in engine oil.
Driven through flexible Hardy Spicer joint and shaft in torque tube.
Rear axle: Banjo type, spiral bevel gears with differential.
Front axle: Drop forged I section beam axle.
Steering: Worm and sector in new larger steering box with improved turning circle.
Brakes: Ribbed cast iron 260mm diameter drums on all four wheels, Handbrake on rear wheels only.
Suspension: Semi-elliptic springs front and cantilever springs at the rear with Hartford friction shock absorbers.
Wheels and tyres: Wire wheels on Rudge or RAF hubs; 715 × 115 tyres.
Electrical system: 12-volt electric lighting and starter motor. Dynamo driven by timing gears.
Accessories: Jaeger or OS gauges for oil pressure, ammeter, rev counter and clock. Ignition advance and retard control.

Amilcar C8, 1929–30

Production total:	Less than 800 produced of all eight-cylinder cars, exact total not known. One source says no more than 350.
Chassis:	Trapezoidal frame with pressed steel side members with rivetted crossmembers with a tube at each end.
Wheelbase:	3.0 metres
Track:	1.325 front and rear.
Engine:	Eight cylinder cast iron block with integral crankcase. Bore 62mm, Stroke 75mm – Capacity 1811cc – 10CV Prototype Bore 63mm, Stroke 80mm – Capacity 1995cc – 11CV C8 Overhead camshaft cast iron cylinder head driven by gears at the back of the block. 30.2mm diameter valves with double springs. Crankshaft carried in five main 55mm bearings. White metal 48mm big end bearings. High pressure lubrication by vane type oil pump. Engine mounted on three Silentbloc bearings.
Fuel system:	Double choke Solex carburettor fed by an electric pump from a 65 litre fuel tank in the tail.
Ignition:	Scintilla magneto with automatic advance.
Maximum power:	Not recorded.
Cooling:	Front mounted radiator with thermostatically controlled fan.
Transmission:	Four speed and reverse gearbox. Ferodo dry plate clutch.
Rear axle:	Banjo type with differential.
Front axle:	Drop forged I section beam axle.
Steering:	Worm and sector steering box.
Brakes:	Cast iron drums on all four wheels cable operated.
Suspension:	Semi-elliptic springs front and rear with four friction shock absorbers.
Wheels and tyres:	Wire wheels with Rudge hubs, 14 × 45 or 5.50 × 18 tyres.
Accessories:	Central Alcyl lubrication system operated by a hand pump on the dashboard.

Amilcar CS8, 1929–33

Production total:	Less than 800 produced of all eight-cylinder cars, exact total not known. One source says no more than 350.
Chassis:	Trapezoidal frame with pressed steel side members with rivetted crossmembers with a tube at each end.
Wheelbase:	3.0 metres
Track:	1.325 front and rear.
Engine:	Eight cylinder cast iron block with integral crankcase. Bore 66mm, Stroke 85mm – Capacity 2326cc – Rated at 13CV Overhead camshaft cast iron cylinder head driven by gears at the back of the block. 30.2mm diameter valves with double springs. Crankshaft carried in five main 55mm bearings. White metal 48mm big end bearings. High pressure lubrication by vane type oil pump. Engine mounted on three Silentbloc bearings.
Fuel system:	Double choke Solex carburettor fed by an electric pump from a 65 litre fuel tank in the tail.
Ignition:	Scintilla magneto with automatic advance.
Maximum power:	58hp at 4,000rpm.
Cooling:	Front mounted radiator with thermostatically controlled fan.
Transmission:	Four speed and reverse gearbox. Ferodo dry plate clutch.
Rear axle:	Banjo type with differential.
Front axle:	Drop forged I section beam axle.
Steering:	Worm and sector steering box.
Brakes:	Cast iron drums on all four wheels cable operated.
Suspension:	Semi-elliptic springs front and rear with four friction shock absorbers.
Wheels and tyres:	Wire wheels with Rudge hubs and 5.50 × 18 tyres.
Accessories:	Central Alcyl lubrication system operated by a hand pump on the dashboard.

Amilcar 7CV M3 Type, 1931–34

Production total: 2,725

Chassis: Heavy gauge longitudinal rails with six crossmembers in trapezoidal form. Engine mounted to three points with two Silentbloc bearings at the rear.

Wheelbase: 2.675 metres

Track: 1.21 metres front, 1.24 metres rear.

Engine: Four cylinder cast iron in unit with crankcase.
Bore 60mm, Stroke 110mm – Capacity 1244cc
Side-valve head, valves operated by camshaft and rocking cam followers acting on valve stem with two concentric valve springs.
Crankshaft carried in two white metal 37mm bearings.
37mm white metal big end bearings.
Pressure lubrication.

Fuel system: MO type Solex side-draught carburettor gravity fed from tank fixed to sheet metal front firewall.

Ignition: Magneto with variable advance.

Maximum power: 27hp at 3,700rpm.

Cooling: Thermo-syphon to front mounted radiator with fan.

Transmission: Four speed and reverse gearbox.
Double plate clutch running in oil.
Driven through flexible Hardy Spicer joint and shaft in torque tube.

Rear axle: Banjo type, helical gears with differential.

Front axle: Drop forged I section beam axle.

Steering: Worm and sector in new cast-iron steering box with improved turning circle.

Brakes: Ribbed cast iron 260mm diameter drums on all four wheels. Handbrake on rear wheels only.

Suspension: Semi-elliptic springs front and rear with Hartford friction shock absorbers.

Wheels and tyres: 12 × 45 wire wheels on Rudge hubs.

Electrical system: 12-volt electric lighting and starter motor. Dynamo driven by timing gears.

Accessories: Gauges for speedometer, oil pressure, clock and fuel level. Ignition advance and retard control.

Amilcar 5 CV, 1932–34

Production total: 2,456 all types.

Chassis: Trapezoidal pressed steel, inverted U-section longitudinal rails with three crossmembers.

Wheelbase C Type: 2.15 metres

Track: 1.06 metres front, 1.08 metres rear.

Wheelbase C3 Type: 2.25 metres

Track: 1.06 metres front, 1.08 metres rear.

Wheelbase C5 Type: 2.37 metres

Track: 1.06 metres front, 1.10 metres rear.

Engine: Four cylinder cast iron in unit with crankcase.

C Type: Bore 58mm Stroke 80mm – Capacity 845cc

C3 Type: Bore 59mm Stroke 80mm – Capacity 877cc

C5 Type: Side-valve head.
Crankshaft carried in two white metal 37mm bearings.
Camshaft driven by two gears off crankshaft.
White metal big end bearings.
Pressure lubrication by vane type pump.
Mounted on three Silentbloc bearings.

Fuel system: Solex side-draught carburettor gravity fed from tank.

Ignition: Distributor with battery.

Maximum power: C Type: 19hp at 3,750rpm.
C3 Type: 21hp at 4,000rpm.
C5 Type: 22hp at 4,000rpm.

Cooling: Thermo-syphon to front mounted radiator with fan.

Transmission: Three speed and reverse gearbox.
Ferodo clutch.
Driven through flexible Hardy Spicer joint and driveshaft in torque tube.

Rear axle: Helical gears running in tapered bearings with differential.

Front axle: Solid beam axle with inclined kingpins.

Steering: Worm and sector in steering box.

Brakes: Drums on all four wheels, cable operated.

Suspension: Semi-elliptic springs front and quarter elliptic springs at the rear with RAXEF shock absorbers.

Wheels and tyres: Steel disc wheels; 110 × 40 tyres.

Electrical system: 6-volt battery, 12 volt on Aerodynamic models. Belt driven Dynastart starter dynamo unit.

Amilcar 9CV M4 Type, 1933–34

Production total: 2,725

Chassis: Heavy gauge longitudinal rails with six crossmembers in trapezoidal form.
Engine mounted to three points with two Silentbloc bearings at the rear.

Wheelbase: 2.675 metres

Track: 1.21 metres front, 1.24 metres rear.

Engine: Four cylinder cast iron in unit with crankcase.
Bore 72mm, Stroke 100mm – Capacity 1629cc
Side-valve head, valves operated by chain driven camshaft and rocking cam followers acting on valve stem with double valve springs.
Crankshaft carried in three white metal bearings.
White metal big end bearings.
Pressure lubrication.

Fuel system: MO type Solex side-draught carburettor gravity fed from tank mounted at the rear of the chassis with electric pump.

Ignition: Distributor and coil.

Maximum power: 37hp at 3,700rpm.

Cooling: Thermo-syphon to front mounted radiator with fan.

Transmission: Four speed and reverse gearbox.
Ferodo dry plate clutch.
Driven through flexible Hardy Spicer joint and shaft in torque tube.

Rear axle: Banjo type, helical gears with differential.

Front axle: Drop forged I section beam axle.

Steering: Worm and sector in new cast-iron steering box with improved turning circle.

Brakes: Ribbed cast iron 260mm diameter drums on all four wheels. Handbrake on rear wheels only.

Suspension: Semi-elliptic springs front and rear with Hartford friction shock absorbers.

Wheels and tyres: 130 × 140 wire wheels.

Electrical system: 12-volt electric lighting and starter motor. Belt driven dynamo.

Accessories: Gauges for speedometer, oil pressure, clock and fuel level.

Amilcar Pégase, 1934–37

Production total: Approximately 300 of all types.

Chassis: Bought in from Delahaye, pressed steel, inverted U-section longitudinal rails with crossmembers.

Wheelbase: 2.80 metres

Track: 1.30 metres front, 1.35 metres rear.

Engine 11CV Prototype: Four cylinder overhead valve designed by Grillot.
Bore 80mm, Stroke 100mm – Capacity 2011cc
Balanced crankshaft carried in three bearings.
Camshaft driven by chain off crankshaft.
Pressure lubrication by mechanical pump.

Fuel system: Side-draught carburettor fed by mechanical pump.

Ignition: Distributor with 12-volt battery.

Maximum power: 50hp at 3,800rpm.

Engine 12CV N7 Normale: Four cylinder overhead valve, same as Delahaye 134.
Bore 80mm, Stroke 107mm – Capacity 2151cc
Balanced crankshaft carried in three bearings.

Fuel system: Downdraught carburettor with automatic choke fed by mechanical pump.

Ignition: Distributor with 12-volt battery.

Maximum power: 58hp at 3,750rpm.

Engine 12CV N7 Sport: Four cylinder overhead valve, same as Delahaye 134.
Bore 80mm, Stroke 107mm – Capacity 2151cc
Balanced crankshaft carried in three bearings.

Fuel system: Twin carburettors fed by mechanical pump.

Ignition: Distributor with 12-volt battery.
Altered ignition timing.

Maximum power: 58hp at 3,750rpm.

Engine 14CV Competition: Four-cylinder overhead valve designed by Grillot.
Bore 89mm, Stroke 100mm – Capacity 2488cc
Balanced crankshaft carried in three bearings.
High pressure lubrication.

Fuel system: Downdraught carburettor fed by mechanical pump.

Ignition: Distributor with 12-volt battery.
Altered ignition timing.

Maximum power: 75hp at 5,000rpm.

Cooling: Radiator with pump and fan.

Transmission: Four speed synchronised gearbox.
Dry plate clutch.
Driven by tubular driveshaft with two joints.

Rear axle: Helical gears with differential.

Steering: Worm and sector in steering box.

Brakes: Bendix patent drums on all four wheels, cable operated except hydraulic system on Competition model.

Suspension: Independent front and semi-elliptic springs at the rear with shock absorbers, uprated for Competition model.

Wheels and tyres: Pressed steel wheels, light alloy wheels optional at extra cost.

Amilcar Compound, 1937–42

Production total: Less than 900.
Chassis: Alpax alloy castings; two side longerons, two crossmembers and front bulkhead. Reinforced with steel panels above rear crossmember.
Wheelbase: 2.50 metres (2.65 metres for commercial chassis).
Track: 1.19 metres
Engine 5CV Prototype: Four cylinder cast iron block in unit with crankcase.
Bore 59mm, Stroke 85mm – Capacity 929cc
Side-valve head.
Crankshaft carried in two white metal 37mm bearings.
Camshaft driven by two gears off crankshaft.
White metal big end bearings.
Pressure lubrication by vane type pump.
Fuel system: Solex side-draught carburettor fed by mechanical pump from tank.
Ignition: Coil and distributor with automatic advance.
Maximum power: 22hp at 4,000rpm.
Engine 7CV B 38: Four cylinder cast iron block.
Bore 63mm, Stroke 95mm – Capacity 1185cc
Cast iron side-valve head.
Fuel system: Solex side-draught carburettor fed by mechanical pump from tank.
Ignition: Coil and distributor with automatic advance.
Maximum power: 33hp
Engine 8CV B 67: Four cylinder cast iron block.
Bore 67mm, Stroke 95mm – Capacity 1340cc
Cast iron overhead valve head.
Maximum power: 45hp
Cooling: Thermo-syphon to front mounted radiator with fan.
Transmission: Four speed and reverse gearbox. Single plate clutch. Front wheel drive by shafts with double Cardan joints.
Steering: Rack and pinion.
Brakes: Cast iron 205mm diameter drums on all four wheels. Self-adjusting.
Suspension: Two transverse springs front and torsion bars at the rear.
Wheels and tyres: Pierced steel disc wheels with 5.25 × 15 tyres.
Electrical system: 6-volt electric lighting, dynamo and starter motor.

APPENDIX II

COMPETITION RESULTS

The following list of results from races, hillclimbs and other events up to 1939 is compiled from many old motoring magazines, books and online sources, but cannot claim to be the definitive collection of all competition results for Amilcars worldwide.

I have found some online sources differ in their given results and where necessary I have referred back and confirmed results as published in magazines of the period, *Moto Revue, Motor Sport, Omnia*, etc. There may be many more minor events not recorded and of course other post-World War II and modern-day historic races. Results shown are for top three placings and class victories except where noted; other results are listed where an Amilcar scored a minor place in one of the more significant events such as the Le Mans 24-hour race, the Bol d'Or or a Grand Prix. Which model Amilcar is noted where known. There were several different forms of competition at the time. Races were held on a mix of road and closed circuits. Sprints and some speed records were for a 'flying' start through a measured distance, some were standing start, while D.A. is the abbreviation for '*Départ Arrete*', which required a standing start and braking to a stop at the defined distance. '*Course de Côte*' is French for a hillclimb. Speed records are noted as such. Many other amateur drivers entered competitions in Amilcars without any significant results but often securing the minor places. In France there were: Emile Contet, Emile Dourel, Benoît Falchetto, Armand Girod, Gaston Réveiller (also an Amilcar dealer), Marcel Rouleau, Mme Fernande Roux (the wife of Maurice Mestivier), Vincent Tersen, Emile Tetaldi and Louis Trintignant, although standing out among them Robert Jeuffrain did manage to collect a few trophies along the way. In Italy, Attilio Barbieri, Umberto Capello, Pietro Cattaneo, Tommaso Saccomani, Filippo Sartorio and Alfonso Zampieri. At Brooklands in England, although few at the time would have claimed to be professional racing drivers, there was certainly a good number of wealthy amateurs who were brave enough to rack up a few good results; H. T. H. Clayton, A. T. 'Goldie' Gardner, Beris Harcourt-Wood, W. E. 'Bill' Humphries, A. B. Pemberton and Brian Twist. Heinrich Joachim von Morgen and Willy Scholl did well in Germany, where Willy Briem was a regular winner. Francisco Castelló, Oscar Leblanc, Miguel Matas and Angel Rodríguez in Spain and Helmer Carlsson in Sweden were also successful in local events.

Events listed were in France except where identified otherwise. All of these results go some way to show how successful these cars were in various competitive events, which must have had a significant effect on sales, especially in Europe and Great Britain.

1921
23 October
André Morel entered a flying kilometre speed trial at Lyon in 1921 and took a class victory with an average speed of 90.5km/h.

1922
19 February
Munch shared victory at the Concours d'Endurance de l'UMF at the Circuit de Marly near Versailles.
30 April
Course de Côte du Camp hillclimb, Marseille: 1st Fernand Michel – Amilcar.
1 May
Brooklands, England, Junior Car Club 1-litre Handicap: 1st A.E. Bull – Amilcar CC; 2nd C.A.H. Mason – Amilcar CC 'Special'.
7 May
Limonest, Lyon: 1st André Morel – Amilcar CC – under 1500cc class at 73km/h.
21 May
Moto Club de Lyon at Saint-Andre-de-Corcy. Cyclecars 1100cc - 2nd André Morel - Amilcar CC.
27–29 May
Saturday and Sunday, 27-28 May - Bol d'Or - Clichy Vaujours -
1st André Morel - Amilcar 1.1-litre - 1,450.658km in
24 Hours = 60.447km/h;
5th in class, 7th overall - Marius Mestivier - Amilcar 1.1-litre.
5 June
Course de Côte Pont-Réan, Rennes - 1st Maurice Boutmy - Amilcar.
12 June
Flying kilometre speed trial at Lyon - André Morel - Amilcar - 1st in class at 120km/h.
2 July
Crochat, Limoges, Limousin - 1st Maurice Boutmy - Amilcar - 1100cc cyclecars class
Val de Suzon hillclimb, Dijon - 1st André Morel - Amilcar - 1100cc cyclecars class.
27–30 July
Boulogne-sur-Mer - organised by the Automobile Club du Nord.
The Thursday started with a 3km race in heavy rain, in which André Morel won the 1100cc class. He followed that with a victory in the standing kilometre and a second in the 500 metre hillclimb. These combined results meant Morel was classified first overall with Boutmy finishing third.

28 August
Laffrey, Grenoble - 1st 'Ladiv' (Marcel Vidal) – Amilcar.
17 September
Cyclecar Grand Prix at Le Mans - 3rd Fratissier - Amilcar;
4th André Morel - Amilcar
Morel and Amilcar were crowned 1922 Champion of France in the 1100cc class.
24 September
Circuit des Routes Pavées - 19 laps, 247km
1100cc class - 2nd André Morel - Amilcar.
500 metre sprint - 1st André Morel - Amilcar.
Morel overall winner.
1 October
Gaillon hillclimb, Rouen - Touring Cars 1100cc: 1st Fratissier – Amilcar Cyclecar 1100cc; 4th Marius Mestivier – Amilcar; 5th André Morel – Amilcar.
Amilcar claimed 47 victories that year.

1923
28 January
Allauch-Pailladou hillclimb, Marseille - 1st André Morel - Amilcar 1.1-litre.
17 February
Paris-Nice race - 1st in class André Morel - Amilcar 1.1-litre.
23 February
La Turbie hillclimb, Nice - 1st André Morel - Amilcar 1.1-litre.
5 March
Course de Côte du Camp hillclimb, Marseille - 1st André Morel - Amilcar 1.1-litre.
11 March
Coeur-Volant hillclimb, St. Germain Forest - 1st Marius Mestivier - Amilcar 1.1-litre.
25 March
Concours d'Endurance de l'UMF at Malmaison, Paris - 1st Marius Mestivier - Joint class win with Benoist and Bueno in Salmsons and Sénéchal in a Sénéchal.
29 April
Brooklands, England, Junior Car Club - 1-litre Handicap - 2nd Vernon Balls - Amilcar CS.
Ladies Handicap - 2nd Mrs G. Duller - Amilcar CV.
Spring Sweepstakes - 2nd Vernon Balls - Amilcar CS.
12 May
Brooklands, England, Ealing & District MCC - Touring Car Handicap - 1st Mrs G. Duller - Amilcar CV.
19–20 May
Bol d'Or, Saint-Germain-en-Laye - 5th Fratissier - Amilcar CS.
26–27 May
Le Mans 24-hour race - 18th overall - 3rd in 1.1 litre class - Maurice Boutmy / Jérôme Marcandanti – Amilcar CV.
27 May
Limonest, Lyon - Cyclecars 1st Courbet – Amilcar - 2nd Rodensky - Amilcar -
Touring cars 1000cc - 1st Lapaire – Amilcar.
2 June
Brooklands, England, Essex Junior Short Handicap - 1st Vernon Balls - Amilcar CS.
3 June
Planfoy, St. Etienne - 1st André Morel - Amilcar 1.1-litre.
10 June
Vendranges, Roanne - 1st André Morel - Amilcar 1.1-litre.
24 June
Val de Suzon hillclimb, Dijon - 1st André Morel - Amilcar 1.1-litre.
30 June
Brooklands, England, Surbiton Junior Short Handicap - 1st Mrs G. Duller - Amilcar CV.
15 July
Engelberg, Lucerne, Switzerland - 1st Max Schlotterbeck - Amilcar 1.1-litre.
19 August
Mont Ventoux hillclimb - new record in the 1.1 litre Racing car class for André Morel.
1100cc Touring car class - 1st Riviera – Amilcar.
26 August
Val de Cuech, Salon-de-Provence - 4.2km - 1st 'Ladiv' (Marcel Vidal) – Amilcar.
29 September
Brooklands, England, Essex Junior Short Handicap - 2nd Mrs G. Duller - Amilcar CV.
30 September
Circuit des Routes Pavées - 1st in class, 7th overall - André Morel - Amilcar CS.
Chrischona, Basel, Switzerland - 1st Max Schlotterbeck - Amilcar 1.1-litre.
7 October
Gaillon hillclimb, Rouen - 1100cc Cyclecar class - 1st Marius Mestivier at 82km/h.
1100cc Touring class - 2nd André Morel at 71.7km/h.
25 November
Circuito del Garda, Salo, Italy - 1st in class, 4th overall - Giulio Binda - Amilcar C4.

1924
27 January
Allauch-Pailladou hillclimb, Marseille: 1st 1100cc Racing class, 2nd overall – André Morel – Amilcar. 1.1-litre – 1st 1100cc Touring class – 1st Orello – Amilcar.
10 February
Paris-Saint-Cyr Rally - 1st Robert Jeuffrain – Amilcar.
2 March
La Turbie hillclimb, Nice - 1st André Morel - Amilcar 1.1-litre.
23 March
Ballon Rally, Versailles - Voiturette Class: 1st Robert Jeuffrain – Amilcar.
30 March
Coeur-Volant hillclimb, St. Germain Forest - 2nd Marius Mestivier - Amilcar 1.1-litre.
6 April
Course de Côte du Camp, Marseille - 1st André Morel - Amilcar 1.1-litre.
13 April
Course de Côte Chateau Thierry - 1km sprint - 1st Marius Mestivier - Amilcar 1.1-litre.
20–21 April
Rallye Bayeaux - St-Lô - 1st Maurice Boutmy – Amilcar.
27 April
Targa Florio, Sicily, Italy - 1st in 1100cc class, 19th overall - Domenico Gamboni - Amilcar CGS.
10 May
Paris-Roubaix-Paris Rally: 1st Robert Jeuffrain – Amilcar.
18 May
Rallye Tours-Poitiers - Gymkhana - 1st Couturier - Amilcar.
The gymkhana in the Parc de Blossac included several tests, race between flags, a race carrying a glass of water, a race in reverse and more with aggregate times deciding the result.
24 May
Côte de Massillan, Nîmes, Gard - 1st André Morel - Amilcar 1.1-litre.
25 May
Limonest, Lyon - Cyclecar class: 1st André Morel – Amilcar 1.1-litre 'Tandem'.
Racing class 1100cc - 1st Jean Lapeyre - Amilcar CGS - Touring class 100cc - Durieux – Amilcar.
1 June
Planfoy, St. Etienne - André Morel - Amilcar 1.1-litre.
9 June
Seiberer Road, Weißenkirchen, Wachau, Austria - 1st Bernhard Kandl - Amilcar 1.1-litre.
14–15 June
Le Mans 24-hour race - 14th Maurice Boutmy / Jérôme Marcandanti - Amilcar CV.
15 June
Navacerrada, Madrid, Spain - 2nd Jean Mauvais - Amilcar 1100cc.
22 June
Val de Suzon hillclimb, Dijon - 1st André Morel - Amilcar 1.1-litre.
Rheineck-Walzenhausen-Lachen, Switzerland - 1st Frau Rothenbach - Amilcar.
6 July
Côte du Ballon d'Alsace - 1st André Morel - Amilcar 1.1-litre.
13 July
Côte de Laffrey, Grenoble - 1st André Morel - Amilcar 1.1-litre.
20 July
Spa 24 Hour race - Grand Prix of Belgium.
1st 1100cc class, 12th overall - Joseph Reinartz / Charles Libovitch - Amilcar CGS;
3rd 1100cc class, 17th overall - Roger Rouleau - Amilcar CGS.
16–17 August
Côte Internationale du Klausen, Switzerland: 1st Frau Rothenbach – Amilcar 1.1-litre.
At the same venue for a 13% hillclimb; 1st André Morel – Amilcar 1.1-litre – new 1100cc record.
Côte de la Croix-Saint-Robert, Puy-de-Dôme; 1st Bastide – Amilcar.
31 August
Coupe du Canigou, Vernet-Les-Bains, Pyrénees - 1st Ané d'Ormoy - Amilcar 1.1-litre.
7 September
Chazeron, Châtel-Guyon, Riom - 1st Brenly - Amilcar 1.1-litre.
28 September
Gaillon hillclimb, Rouen - 1km D.A. - 1st Marius Mestivier - Amilcar 1.1-litre.

29 September
Schälk Hillclimb, Iserlohn-Letmathe Germany - 1st Wilhelm Jüttermann - Amilcar.
5–6 October
Circuit des Routes Pavées - 2nd Marius Mestivier - Amilcar 1.1-litre.
11 November
Coupe de l'Armistice, Versailles - Gold Medal - Robert Jeuffrain – Amilcar.

1925
25 January
Allauch-Pailladou hillclimb, Marseille - 1st André Morel - Amilcar 1.1-litre.
22 February
Montserrat Hillclimb, Barcelona, Spain: 1st Ricardo Balletbó – Amilcar.
1 March
Plâtrières, Aix-en-Provence, 1st André Morel - Amilcar 1.1-litre.
Côte d'Argenteuil, Paris - 1st Marius Mestivier - Amilcar 1.1-litre.
14 March
Nice - 1km Standing Start Sprint - 1st André Morel - Amilcar 1.1-litre.
15 March
Côte de la Turbie hillclimb, Nice - 1st André Morel - Amilcar 1.1-litre.
Amélie-Les-Bains, Roussillon - 1st Ané d'Ormoy - Amilcar 1.1-litre.
Grâce-Berleur, Liège, Belgium - 1st Elcé - Amilcar 1.1-litre.
21 March
Moyenne Corniche hillclimb, Monaco - 1st André Morel - Amilcar 1.1-litre.
26 March
Côte de l'Estérel hillclimb, Nice - 1st André Morel - Amilcar 1.1-litre.
29 March
Hestreux, Béthane, Dolhain, Verviers, Belgium - 1st Feredy - Amilcar 1.1-litre.
5 April
Course de Côte du Camp hillclimb, Marseille - 1st André Morel - Amilcar 1.1-litre.
12 April
Zbraslav-Jiloviste hillclimb, Czechoslovakia - 1st André Morel - Amilcar 1.1-litre.
16 April
Côte de la Mi-Corniche hillclimb, Monaco - 1km D.A. - 1st André Morel - Amilcar 1.1-litre.
19 April
Côte à Château-Thierry - 1km D.A.
1100cc Single seater class - without passenger - 1st Marius Mestivier - Amilcar 1.1-litre.
1100cc Sports car class - with passenger - 1st Marius Mestivier - Amilcar 1.1-litre.
25 April
Brooklands, England, Surbiton Junior Long Handicap - 3rd Mrs G. Duller – Amilcar.
26 April
Côte des Alpilles, Avignon - 1st André Morel - Amilcar 1.1-litre.
10 May
Rainerbergrennen, 5.2km hillclimb, Germany - Sportscars – up to 1100cc: 1st Josef Schwarzenbrunner – Amilcar.
17 May
Grand Prix de l'Ouverture, Montlhéry - 4th Ernest Eldridge - Eldridge Amilcar Special.
21 May
Les 17 Tournants hillclimb, Paris - 1st Marius Mestivier - Amilcar 1.1-litre.
24 May
Massillan, Nîmes, Gard - 2nd André Morel - Amilcar 1.1-litre.
2 June
Bol D'or Saint-Germain-en-Laye - 1100cc Racing Class.
1st 1100cc Racing Class, 2nd overall - André Morel - Amilcar 1.1-litre;
2nd 1100cc Racing Class, 4th overall - Chanu - Amilcar 1.1-litre.
6 June
Brooklands, England, Sutton & Cheam Short Handicap - 3rd R.G. Petitt - Amilcar CGS.
7 June
Limonest, Lyon - 1st in class, 2nd overall - André Morel - Amilcar 1.1-litre.
14 – 15 June
Le Mans 24-hour race - DNF - André Morel / Marius Mestivier - Amilcar CGS – Accident.
27 June
Brooklands, England, BARC Long Handicap - 3rd Vernon Balls - Amilcar CGS.
5 July
Val de Suzon hillclimb, Dijon - 2nd André Morel - Amilcar 1.1-litre.
12 July
Castrejana Hillclimb, Bilbao, Spain: 1st Joaquín Palacio y Power – Amilcar.
12–13 July
Spa 24 Hour race - Grand Prix of Belgium - 9th in class - Roger Rouleau / Marcel Rouleau - Amilcar CGS; 10th in class - Coene / Joseph Reinartz - Amilcar CGS.
DNF - André Morel / Charles Libovitch - Amilcar CGS.
9 August
Mont Ventoux hillclimb - 1st André Morel - Amilcar 1.1-litre.
14 August
Seiberer Road, Weißenkirchen, Wachau, Austria - 1st Max Hoffmann - Amilcar 1.1-litre.
6 September
Ferrier, Nice - 1st Signoret - Amilcar 1.1-litre.
28 September
Brooklands, England, Junior Car Club 200 Mile Race - 3rd R.G. Petitt – Amilcar CGS.
18 October
Gaillon hillclimb, Rouen - 1km D.A. - 1st André Morel - Amilcar CO.

1926
20 February
Moyenne Corniche hillclimb, Monaco - 1st André Morel - Amilcar CO.
21 February
Côte du Mont Agel, Nice - 1st André Morel - Amilcar CO.
25 February
Côte de la Turbie hillclimb, Nice - 1st André Morel - Amilcar CO.
28 February
Course de l'Estérel hillclimb, Cannes - 1st André Morel - Amilcar CO.
7 March
Côte d'Argenteuil, Paris - 1st André Morel - Amilcar CO.
28 March
Grand Prix de Provence, Miramas - Voiturette Class - 1st André Morel - Amilcar CO;
2nd Charles Martin - Amilcar CO.
3 April
Brooklands, England, BARC Short Handicap - 2nd Vernon Balls - Amilcar CGS.
11 April
Grâce-Berleur, Liège, Belgium - 1st Hugh - Amilcar 1.1-litre.
17 April
Brooklands, England, Junior Car Club Novices Handicap -
1st A. Pemberton - Amilcar CGS;
3rd J.L. Chadwick - Amilcar CGS.
24 April
Brooklands, England - Surbiton Junior Short Handicap – 2nd Vernon Balls - Amilcar CGS.
Surrey Senior Long Handicap - 1st Vernon Balls - Amilcar CGS.
Surbiton All Comers Handicap - 3rd H. Dawson - Amilcar CGS.
25 April
Côte des Alpilles, Avignon - 1st André Morel - Amilcar CO.
Targa Florio, Sicily, Italy - 5th in 1100cc class - Francesco Starrabba - Amilcar CGS.
9 May
Arpajon Speed Records.
Flying km - 1st André Morel - Amilcar CO - 18.235 seconds.
Flying mile - 1st André Morel - Amilcar CO - 29.565 seconds.
1km D.A. - 1st Charles Martin - Amilcar CO - 28.555 seconds.
Rabassada hillclimb, Barcelona, Spain - 1100cc Sports: 1st P. Soler – Amilcar.
10 May
Avenida Brigadeiro Luiz Antonio, Sao Paolo, Brazil: 1st Wladimir Rezende – Amilcar.
16 May
Côte de Limonest, Lyon - 1100cc Sports Car - 1st André Morel - Amilcar CO.
1100cc Touring Car - 4th Robert Jeuffrain - Amilcar 1.1-litre.
23 May
Les Dunes, Poitiers, Sprint - 1st André Morel - Amilcar CO.
30 May
Côte du Calvaire, Fontainebleau - 1st Charles Martin - Amilcar CO.
Montagne Saint-Nicolas, La Louvière, Belgium - 1st Arthur Legat - Amilcar 1.1-litre.
31 May
Indianapolis 500, USA.
Classified 14th DNF - Douglas Hawkes - Eldridge Amilcar Special.
Classified 19th DNF - Ernest Eldridge - Eldridge Amilcar Special

6 June
Côte de Poix, Amiens - 2km D.A. - 1st André Morel - Amilcar CO; 2nd Charles Martin - Amilcar CO.
4 July
La Cruche, Renaix, Ronse, Belgium - 1st Robert Saey - Amilcar 1.1-litre.
Circuit des Gattières, Nice - 1100cc Sports Car: 1st Tamme – Amilcar 1.1-litre.
11 July
Côte de Pourville, Dieppe - 2km Standing start - 1100cc Racing Car – 1st Charles Martin - Amilcar CO.
1100cc Sports Car - 1st Robert Jeuffrain - Amilcar C6; 2nd Lipman - Amilcar CGSs.
17 July
Brooklands, England, Junior Car Club Production Car Race - 2nd in class, 3rd overall - Vernon Balls - Amilcar CGS.
18 July
Laffrey, Grenoble - 1st Charles Martin - Amilcar CO.
25 July
Cran d'Escalles, Calais - 1st Vandamme - Amilcar 1.1-litre.
Planfoy, St. Etienne - 1st Charles Martin - Amilcar CO.
G. P. de Saint Sébastien, Spain
Heat 1 - 1st Charles Martin - Amilcar CO; 2nd Arthur Duray - Amilcar CO.
Heat 2 - 1st Arthur Duray - Amilcar CO.
Heat 3 - 1st Arthur Duray - Amilcar CO.
8 August
Côte du Klausen, Switzerland - 1st André Morel - Amilcar CO.
15 August
Broche à Rôtir, Le Havre - 1st Charles Martin - Amilcar CO.
16 August
Côte de La Croix Saint Robert au Mont d'Or, Auvergne - 1st André Morel - Amilcar CO.
22 August
Malchamps Spa, Belgium - 1st Joseph Reinartz - Amilcar 1.1-litre.
Grand Prix des Frontières, Chimay, Belgium – 3rd Arthur Legat - Amilcar CGS.
25 August
La Baule, Brittany - 1km Sprint - 1st José Scaron - Amilcar C6.
28 August
La Baule, Brittany - Grand Prix de La Baule - 1st André Morel - Amilcar CO.
29 August
Col des Montes, Chamonix - 1st D. Lobré - Amilcar 7hp.
5 September
Italian Voiturette Grand Prix, Monza - 1st André Morel - Amilcar CO - 2nd Arthur Duray - Amilcar CO.
12 September
Côte des Moulineaux, Rouen - 1100cc Racing Car - 1st Charles Martin - Amilcar CO.
1100cc Sports Car - 1st Robert Jeuffrain - Amilcar C6. 1100cc Touring Car - 1st José Scaron - Amilcar C6.
19 September
Buckower Dreieck-Rennen, Germany - 100km, 8 laps - 1100cc Sports Cars: 1st Willy Scholl – Amilcar.
25 September
Brooklands, England, Junior Car Club 200 Miles - 1st in class, 4th overall - Charles Martin - Amilcar CO.
2nd in class, 5th overall - Arthur Duray - Amilcar CO; 3rd in class, 7th overall - André Morel - Amilcar CO;
5th in class - R. Bond - Amilcar CGS.
26 September
Montlhéry Speed Tests - 1100cc Racing Car - 1st André Morel - Amilcar CO;
2nd Charles Martin - Amilcar CO. 1100cc Sports Car - 1st Robert Jeuffrain - Amilcar C6.
3 October
Gaillon hillclimb, Rouen - 1km D.A. - 1100cc Racing Car – 1st André Morel - Amilcar CO.
1100cc Sports Car - 1st Charles Martin - Amilcar CO – Short Chassis.
17 October
GP du Salon Montlhéry - 1st Arthur Duray - Amilcar CO; 4th Robert Jeuffrain - Amilcar C6.
24 October
Côte des 17 Tournants hillclimb, Paris - 1.8km D.A. - 1100cc Racing Car - 1st André Morel - Amilcar CO.
1100cc Touring Car - 1st André Morel - Amilcar C6.
11 November
Coupe de l'Armistice, Versailles - Gold Medal - Robert Jeuffrain - Amilcar C6.
Amilcar claimed 74 victories for the 6-cylinder cars in 1926.

1927
12–15 January
Monte Carlo Rally - 1st Marcel Lefebrve-Despeaux - Amilcar G Type Sedan s/c.
30 January
Boulevard Michelet, Marseille - 1km Sprint - 1st André Morel - Amilcar CO.
6 March
Geneva Speed Trials - Flying kilometre 1100cc - Charles Martin - Amilcar CO.
13 March
Côte de la Turbie hillclimb, Nice - 1st André Morel - Amilcar CO.
20 March
Argenteuil, Paris - 1.8km Sprint - 1st Charles Martin - Amilcar CO.
27 March
Grand Prix de Provence, Miramas - 2nd André Morel - Amilcar CO; 5th Arthur Duray - Amilcar CO.
3 April
Tourist Trophy of France, Montlhéry - 1st André Morel - Amilcar CO; 5th Charles Martin - Amilcar CO.
10 April
Grand Prix de Vitesse, Montlhéry - 1st André Morel - Amilcar CO; 2nd Charles Martin - Amilcar CO.
18 April
Grand Prix de 1100cc, Montlhéry - 1st Arthur Duray - Amilcar CO; 4th Vincent Tersen - Amilcar CGSs.
Brooklands, England - Easter Monday
BARC Short Handicap - 4th Vernon Balls - Amilcar C6
BARC Long Handicap - 1st Vernon Balls - Amilcar C6.
23 April
Brooklands, England - Surbiton Junior Short Handicap - 2nd Vernon Balls - Amilcar C6.
Surbiton Junior Long Handicap - 2nd Vernon Balls - Amilcar C6.
50 Mile Handicap - 4th A.B. Elford - Amilcar CGS.
1 May
Côte des Plâtrières, Aix-en-Provence - 1st André Morel - Amilcar CO.
8 May
Course de Côte du Camp hillclimb, Marseille - 1st André Morel - Amilcar CO.
15 May
Harfleur, Le Havre - 1st Charles Martin - Amilcar CO.
18 May
La Rampe du Calvaire, Fontainebleu - 1st Charles Martin - Amilcar CO.
22 May
Côte de Monrepos, Bordeaux - 1st in 1100cc Racing class, 2nd overall - André Morel - Amilcar Offset CO.
2nd in 1100cc Sports class, 3rd overall - André Morel - Amilcar CO.
29 May
Grand Prix des Frontières, Chimay, Belgium - 1st Arthur Legat - Amilcar CGS;
4th Chaudier - Amilcar CGS.
6 June
Brooklands, England - BARC Short Handicap - 3rd Vernon Balls - Amilcar C6.
19 June
Planfoy, St. Etienne - 1st Charles Martin - Amilcar CO.
Circuito di Bologna, Italy - 1100cc class, 1st Alfonso Zampieri - Amilcar C6.
Opening Race, Nurburgring, Germany - 1100cc class 1st - Jules von Krohn – Amilcar.
1100cc Sports Car class - 1st Robert Gockenbach - Pluto Amilcar;
3rd Hans-Joachim von Morgen – Amilcar.
1100cc Racing Car class - 1st Hermann Freiderich - Pluto Amilcar.
Some sources list Jules von Krohn as the winner instead of Freiderich.
26 June
Laffrey, Grenoble - 1st Charles Martin - Amilcar CO.
10 July
Côte de Pourville, Dieppe - 2km D.A.
Racing Car - 1st Charles Martin - Amilcar CO.
Sports Car - 1st Robert Jeuffrain - Amilcar C6.
25 July
San Sebastion Grand Prix, Lasarte Circuit, Spain - 1100cc class - 1st in class, 6th overall - Charles Martin - Amilcar Offset CO.

14 August
Paris Grand Prix, 24 hours, Montlhéry - 1st Charles Martin - Amilcar MCO; 2nd André Morel - Amilcar MCO.
28 August
Wavre, Belgium, 1st Emile Cornet - Amilcar 1.1-litre
One Hour Records, Chimay, Belgium - 1100cc Racing Class - 1st Marcel Rouleau - Amilcar C6.
4 September
Côte de la Valette, Rouen, 1km + 1 mile - 1st Robert Jeuffrain - Amilcar C6.
10 September
Boulogne sur Mer Grand Prix des Voiturettes - 1st 1100cc class, 4th overall - Arthur Duray - Amilcar Offset CO.
18 September
Buckower Dreieck Race, Germany: 1st 1100cc Racing Cars – Willy Scholl – Amilcar.
25 September
Gaillon hillclimb, Rouen - 1km D.A. - 1st André Morel - Amilcar Offset CO.
26 September
Montlhéry Speed Tests
Racing Car - 1st André Morel - Amilcar Offset CO - 2nd Charles Martin - Amilcar Offset CO.
16 October
Brooklands, England, Junior Car Club 200 Mile Race - 1st André Morel - Amilcar Offset CO; 2nd Vernon Balls - Amilcar CO; 3rd Charles Martin - Amilcar Offset CO.
17 October
Critérium Salon Automobile, Montlhéry.
Race 1 - 1st Charles Martin - Amilcar Offset CO; 2nd Arthur Duray - Amilcar Offset CO; 6th Robert Jeuffrain - Amilcar C6.
Race 2 - 1st Arthur Duray; 6th Robert Jeuffrain - Race 3 - 1st Arthur Duray; 6th Robert Jeuffrain.
Overall result - 1st Arthur Duray; 4th Robert Jeuffrain.
11 November
Coupe de l'Armistice, Versailles - Gold Medal - Robert Jeuffrain - Amilcar C6.

1928
14–18 January
Monte Carlo Rally - 7th Fernand Pousse / M. Herteau - Amilcar L Type: 10th Desestre – Amilcar.
3 March
Inter-Varsity hillclimb, Ewelme Down, Wallingford, England.
1100cc class - 1st Arthur Llewellin - Amilcar C6.
18 March
Geneva Speed Trials
Flying kilometre 1100cc - Charles Martin - Amilcar MCO - 179.73km/h.
25 March
Argenteuil, Paris 1.8km Sprint - 1st Charles Martin - Amilcar MCO 1270cc.
9 April
Grand Prix d'Antibes - 1st 1100cc class, 4th overall - Jules Moriceau - Amilcar Offset CO.
Torigni, Saint-Lô - 1km hillclimb - 1st José Scaron - Amilcar C6.
21 April
Brooklands, England - BARC Junior Long Handicap - 2nd Vernon Balls - Amilcar C6.
Royal 50 Mile Handicap - 2nd Vernon Balls - Amilcar C6.
28 April
Brooklands, England - Junior Car Club Short Handicap - 2nd Vernon Balls - Amilcar C6.
Junior Car Club Long Handicap - 3rd W.B. Scott - Amilcar C6.
29 April
Côte des 17 Tournants hillclimb, Paris 1.8km D.A. - 1st André Morel - Amilcar Offset CO 1270cc.
6 May
Vernon, Normandy 1km Sprint - Touring Car - 1st Robert Jeuffrain - Amilcar C6.
Racing Car - 1st José Scaron - Amilcar C6.
Algerian Grand Prix, Staouéli Circuit - 1st Guy Cloître - Amilcar C6.
2nd Emile Dupont - Amilcar C6; 3rd Jacquin - Amilcar C6.
20 May
Grand Prix des Frontières, Chimay, Belgium - 4th Emile Cornet - Amilcar CGSs.
28 May
Brooklands, England BARC Long Handicap - B.H. Wood - Amilcar C6.
Eifelrennen, Nurburgring, Germany - 1100cc Sports Car class - 1st Ernst von Halle – Amilcar.
3 June
Côte de Limonest, Lyon - 1st André Morel - Amilcar Offset CO.
Münnerstadt Schweinfurt, Germany: 1st Hans von Meister – Amilcar.
Grand Prix of Tunisia - 1st Guy Cloître - Amilcar C6; 2nd Emile Dupont - Amilcar C6; 3rd Jacquin - Amilcar C6.
10 June
Rome Royal Grand Prix, Italy - 1st André Morel - Amilcar Offset CO; 2nd Alfonso Zampieri - Amilcar C6.
Grand Prix de Thuin, Charleroi, Belgium
Race 1 - 1st Arthur Legat - Amilcar C6. Race 3 - 1st Marcel Rouleau - Amilcar C6.
17 June
Ballon d'Alsace, Vosges - 1st José Scaron - Amilcar C6.
24 June
Moto Club de France, Montlhéry - Sports Car 1100cc - 1st Robert Jeuffrain - Amilcar C6.
30 June
Brooklands, England - Middlesex AC Long Handicap - 1st Mrs J. Scott - Amilcar C6.
Middlesex 50 Mile Handicap - 2nd W.B. Scott - Amilcar C6.
7 July
Brooklands, England - Surbiton Junior Short Handicap - 1st Mrs J. Scott - Amilcar C6.
Surbiton Junior Long Handicap - 2nd W.B. Scott - Amilcar C6.
8 July
Grand Prix de la Marne, Reims - 1st José Scaron - Amilcar C6; 2nd Antonio Valette - Amilcar C6.
21 July
Brooklands, England - Junior Car Club 200 Mile Race - 1st Vernon Balls - Amilcar C6; 2nd W.B. Scott - Amilcar C6.
22 July
La Baraque, Clermont-Ferrand - 1st André Morel - Amilcar 1270cc MCO.
27 July
Croix-Sorme, Trouville - 1st José Scaron - Amilcar C6.
29 July
Côte de la Croix Sonnet. Calvados 1km Sprint - Sports Car - 1st José Scaron - Amilcar C6.
Touring Car - 1st Robert Jeuffrain - Amilcar C6.
5 August
Freiburg Schauinsland hillclimb, Germany - 1100cc - 1st Heinrich Joachim von Morgen - Amilcar C6.
6 August
Brooklands, England, BARC Long Handicap - 3rd W.B. Scott - Amilcar C6; 4th Vernon Balls - Amilcar C6.
Ladies Handicap - 1st Miss M.J. Maconochie - Amilcar C6.
15 August
Torvillier, Troyes, Union des Motos Speed Trials - 208km/h recorded by Andre Morel - Amilcar 1270cc MCO (unofficial).
19 August
Buckower Dreieck-Race, Germany - 1st Willy Scholl - Amilcar;
2nd Eichmann - Amilcar;
3rd Heinrich Joachim von Morgen - Amilcar C6.
23 August
Grand Prix de La Baule - 100km race: 1st José Scaron – Amilcar C6; 3rd Robert Jeuffrain - Amilcar C6.
25 August
Brooklands, England, Cyclecar Grand Prix - 3rd H.A. Smythe - Amilcar CGS.
26 August
Arpajon Speed Event.
Flying kilometre - 1st André Morel - Amilcar 1100cc MCO - 206.895km/h.
Flying mile - 1st André Morel - Amilcar 1100cc MCO - 206.032km/h.
Flying kilometre - 1st André Morel - Amilcar 1500cc MCO - 210.770km/h.
Standing kilometre - 1st André Morel - Amilcar 1500cc MCO - 133.729km/h.
6 September
Boulogne-sur-Mer, Mont Lombert 1km - 1st José Scaron - Amilcar C6.
16 September
Moulineaux, Rouen - 1 Mile Sprint - 1st José Scaron - Amilcar C6.
Aš, Bohemia, Czech Republic - 1st Erich Ploß – Amilcar.
22 September
Brooklands, England, BARC Ladies Handicap - 3rd Miss M.J. Maconochie - Amilcar C6.
30 September
Gaillon hillclimb, Rouen 1km D.A. - 1st André Morel - Amilcar 1270cc MCO.
27 December
Morlaas: Pau 1.4km – 1st André Morel – Amilcar 1270cc MCO.

1929
27 January
Boulevard Michelet, Marseille - 1km Sprint - 1st André Morel - Amilcar 1270cc MCO.
17 March
Geneva Speed Trials - Flying kilometre - 1st André Morel - Amilcar 1270cc MCO.
24 March
Argenteuil, Paris - 2nd Robert Jeuffrain - Amilcar C6.
1 April
Grand Prix d'Antibes - 1st José Scaron - Amilcar C6.
7 April
Algerian Grand Prix, Staouéli Circuit - 1st Guy Cloître - Amilcar C6; 2nd Lucien Desvaux - Amilcar C6.
21 April
Pietro Bordino Cup - Alessandria, Italy - 1100cc class 1st Luigi Castelbarco - Amilcar C6.
28 April
Course de Côte de Champillon, Marne - 1st Robert Jeuffrain - Amilcar C6.
20 May
Brooklands, England, BARC Long Handicap - 3rd B.H. Wood - Amilcar C6.
26 May
Côte de la Valette, Rouen - Racing Car - 1st José Scaron - Amilcar C6.
Touring Car - 1st Robert Jeuffrain - Amilcar C6.
Lückendorf hillclimb - 1st Heinrich Joachim von Morgen - Amilcar C6.
Eifelrennen, Nurburgring, Germany: 1st Walter Bartsch – Amilcar C6; 2nd Fings – Amilcar.
29 May
Indianapolis 500, USA - Jules Moriceau - Amilcar 1270cc MCO - Retired: accident.
8 June
Grand Prix de Picardie, Péronne - 4th Treffel - Amilcar C6.
16 June
Grand Prix de Lyon - 1st José Scaron - Amilcar C6.
23 June
Grand Prix de Thuin, Charleroi, Belgium - 3rd Georges Télesphore - Amilcar C6; 4th Emile Cornet - Amilcar C6.
24 June
Moto Club de France, Montlhéry - Sports Car 1100cc - 1st Robert Jeuffrain - Amilcar C6.
30 June
Fichtelberg, Chemnitz, Germany - 1st Heinrich Joachim von Morgen - Amilcar C6.
7 July
Dieppe Grand Prix - 1st José Scaron - Amilcar C6.
Prix de la Ville de Reims - 2nd Emile Dupont - Amilcar MCO.
21 July
Scheideck, Lörrach, Germany 2.7km: 1st Haas – Amilcar.
18 August
Comminges Grand Prix, Saint Gaudens - 1st Pierre Darroman - Amilcar C6; 2nd José Scaron - Amilcar C6.
22 August
Grand Prix de La Baule - 1km Sprint - 1st José Scaron - Amilcar C6; 4th Robert Jeuffrain - Amilcar C6.
31 August
Brooklands, England, Cyclecar Grand Prix - 2nd A.T.G. 'Goldie' Gardner - Amilcar C6.
21 September
Brooklands, England, BARC Short Handicap - 1st A.T.G. 'Goldie' Gardner - Amilcar C6.
29 September
Circuito di Cremona, Italy - 1st Filippo Sartorio - Amilcar C6.
10 October
G. P. du M.C.F. Montlhéry - 1100cc Racing Car - 1st Robert Jeuffrain - Amilcar C6.
17 November
Grand Prix of Tunisia - 1st José Scaron - Amilcar MCO - 2nd Jacquin - Amilcar C6.

1930
9 February
Garmisch Winterfahrt, ADAC, Germany - Ice Races
Sportscars up to 1100cc - 2nd O.Schlicht - Amilcar; 3rd L.Hofmann – Amilcar.
22 March
Brooklands, England, BARC Essex Long Handicap - 1st Vernon Balls - Amilcar C6 s/c.
30 March
Montserrat, Barcelona, Spain: 1st in class, 5th overall – Francisco Castelló – Amilcar.
21 April
Grand Prix d'Anfa, Morocco - Racing 1100cc: 1st Charles Bénitah – Amilcar.
Sports 1100cc: 1st Saint-Geines – Amilcar.
27 April
Grand Prix d'Oranie, Algeria - 1st Emile Dupont - Amilcar C6; 4th Petrigi - Amilcar C6.
11 May
Grand Prix of Algeria - 4th José Scaron - Amilcar C6.
Côte de Zbraslav-Jiloviste, Czechoslovakia - 1100cc Racing cars: 1st Schmidt – Amilcar.
1100cc Sportscars: 2nd Novak – Amilcar.
24 May
Brooklands, England, BARC Racing Long Handicap - 1st Brian P.W. Twist - Amilcar C6.
25 May
Rome Grand Prix, Italy - 4th F. Sartorio - Amilcar 1100cc; 6th A. Attili - Amilcar 1100cc.
8 June
Iselsta Brink, Stockholm, Sweden: 1st Per Nas – Amilcar.
8–9 June
Bol d'Or, St, Germain - 6th in class - C.A. Martin - Amilcar CO Spéciale Martin.
9 June
Brooklands, England, BARC Devon Junior Long Handicap - 1st A.T.G. 'Goldie' Gardner - Amilcar C6 s/c.
Grand Prix des Frontières, Chimay, Belgium - 1st Marcel Rouleau - Amilcar CS8.
Curiously the organisers asked Rouleau to enter his 2.3 litre CS8 in the race for 750cc cars just to make up the numbers and, unsurprisingly, even on handicap he completed seven laps against the smaller cars, which only managed five.
29 June
Montjuïch Park, Barcelona, Spain - 2km Hillclimb: 2nd Angel Rodríguez – Amilcar.
18–19 July
Irish Grand Prix - Class G - 2nd, 9th overall, A.T.G. 'Goldie' Gardner - Amilcar C6.
20 July
Grand Prix du Matin, Dieppe - 1st José Scaron - Amilcar C6.
26 July
Brooklands, England, Light Car Club Long Handicap: 3rd A.T.G. 'Goldie' Gardner – Amilcar C6 s/c.
Light Car Club Grand Prix - 3rd A.T.G. 'Goldie' Gardner - Amilcar C6 s/c.
4 August
Brooklands, England, BARC Mountain Racing Handicap - 2nd Vernon Balls - Amilcar C6 s/c.
10 August
Circuit du Dauphiné, Grenoble - 1st José Scaron - Amilcar C6.
17 August
Grand Prix de Comminges - 1st in class, 3rd overall - José Scaron - Amilcar C6;
2nd in class, 6th overall - Emile Dourel - Amilcar C6.
24 August
Mont Ventoux hillclimb - Sports 1100cc: 1st Jacomin – Amilcar. Racing 1100cc - 1st Jean Lapeyre – Amilcar.
7 September
Voiturette Grand Prix of Monza - 1100cc class - 2nd José Scaron - Amilcar C6;
5th - Emil Dourel - Amilcar C6.
14 September
Circuit des Routes Pavées - Sport 1100cc class - 3rd C.A. Martin - Amilcar CO Spéciale Martin.
20 September
Brooklands, England, BARC Middlesex Junior Long Handicap.
2nd A.T.G. 'Goldie' Gardner - Amilcar C6 s/c.
Middlesex T.T. Handicap - 2nd A.T.G. 'Goldie' Gardner - Amilcar C6 s/c.
Mountain Speed Handicap - 3rd A.T.G. 'Goldie' Gardner - Amilcar C6 s/c.
4 October
Brooklands, England, BARC 500 Mile Race - 1st in class G, 5th overall - Brian P.W. Twist / Bob Porter - Amilcar C6 s/c.

1931
14 March
Brooklands, England, BARC Lincoln Junior Short Handicap - 2nd Brian P.W. Twist - Amilcar C6 s/c.
29 March
Grand Prix of Tunisia - 1st 1500cc class, 10th overall - José Scaron - Amilcar C6.
12 April
Mille Miglia, Italy - 3rd in sports car 1.1 litre class, 46th overall - Sergio Carnevalli / Conconi - Amilcar CGSs.

26 April
Circuito di Pietro Bordino - Alessándria, Italy - 2nd 1100cc class - Benoit Falchetto - Amilcar 1100cc.
17 May
Grand Prix of Casablanca, Morocco - 1st 1100cc class, 4th overall - 1st José Scaron - Amilcar C6. 4th 1100cc class, 9th overall - Emile Dourel - Amilcar C6.
24–25 May
Bol d'Or, Saint-Germain-en-Laye - 1st 1100cc class, 4th overall - C.A. Martin - Amilcar CO Spéciale Martin.
7 June
Grand Prix of Geneva, Switzerland - 1100cc class - 1st Benoit Falchetto - Amilcar C6; 3rd Emile Dourel - Amilcar C6.
28 June
Harfleur, Le Havre 1km - 1st José Scaron - Amilcar C6.
5 July
Grand Prix du Vaucluse, Avignon - 1100cc Supercharged class - 1st Benoit Falchetto - Amilcar C6.
2nd Gaston Réveiller - Amilcar C6; 3rd Emile Dourel - Amilcar C6.
6 July
Rome Grand Prix, Italy - 1st José Scaron - Amilcar C6.
19 July
German Grand Prix, Nurburgring - 2nd Englebert Graf von Arco-Zinneberg - Amilcar C6; 3rd - José Scaron - Amilcar C6; 4th Marcel Rouleau - Amilcar C6.
26 July
Freiburg-Schauinsland Hillclimb, Germany - Sports cars 1100cc: 1st Herzberg – Amilcar.
2 August
Circuit du Dauphiné, Grenoble - 1st José Scaron - Amilcar MCO; 3rd Emile Dourel - Amilcar C6.
3 August
Brooklands, England, BARC London Junior Short Handicap - 1st W.E. Humphreys - Amilcar C6 s/c.
BARC London Junior Short Handicap - 3rd H.T.H. Clayton - Amilcar C6 s/c.
30 August
Mont Ventoux hillclimb.
Racing Cars 1500cc - 2nd Louis Trintignant - Amilcar 1270cc MCO.
6 September
Grand Prix of Monza, Italy - 1st José Scaron - Amilcar MCO; 3rd Englebert Graf von Arco-Zinneberg - Amilcar C6; 5th Emile Dourel - Amilcar CO.
13 September
Grand Prix de La Baule - 4th José Scaron - Amilcar MCO.
27 September
Grand Prix de Brignoles - 1500cc class - 1st Louis Trintignant - Amilcar 1270cc MCO.
1100cc class - 1st Emile Dourel - Amilcar C6.
Masaryk Grand Prix, Brno, Czechoslovakia – 2nd Englebert Graf von Arco-Zinneberg - Amilcar C6.

1932
4 April
Grand Prix of Tunisia - 1st in class, 12th overall - José Scaron - Amilcar MCO.
24 April
Grand Prix d'Oranie, Algeria - 1st in class, 9th overall José Scaron - Amilcar MCO.
Läggestabacken, Mariefred, Sweden - 1st Börje Dahlin - Amilcar C6.
30 April
Brooklands, England, BRDC British Empire Trophy - Heat 2 - 1st W.E. Humphreys - Amilcar C6 s/c.
5 May
Wiesbadener Automobil Competition, Erbenheim Airfield, Germany.
2.0km grass track race - 1500cc class - 1st Rudolf Steinweg – Amilcar.
15 May
Grand Prix de Frontières, Chimay, Belgium - 1100cc class 1st Georges Bultot - Amilcar CGS.
16 May
Provence Trophy, Nîmes - 1st José Scaron - Amilcar MCO.
Bol d'Or, Saint-Germain-en-Laye.
1st 1100cc class - C.A. Martin - Amilcar CO Spéciale Martin.
2nd 1100cc class - Auguste Bodoignet - Amilcar CO Spéciale Martin.
5th 1100cc class - Raph - Amilcar CO Spéciale Martin.
29 May
Mazamet, Tarn 2km - 3rd Emile Dourel - Amilcar C6.
Circuit de Torvilliers, Troyes 7.6km - 3rd Ralph Gilbert - Amilcar C6.
18–19 June
Le Mans 24-hour race - 1st in class, 8th overall - C.A. Martin / Auguste Bodoignet - Amilcar CO Spéciale Martin.
10 July
Spa 24-Hours, Belgium: 2nd in class, 9th overall – van Hove / Havelange – Amilcar.
31 July
Circuit de Nice - 2nd Gaston Réveiller - Amilcar C6.
1 August
Brooklands, England, BARC Hereford Senior Short Handicap - 1st H.T.H. Clayton - Amilcar C6 s/c.
14 August
GP du Comminges - 2nd Emile Dourel - Amilcar C6.
Coppa Acerbo, Pescara, Italy - 1100cc class - 1st José Scaron - Amilcar MCO.
28 August
Bellevue hillclimb, Avignon - 1100cc 1st Gaston Réveiller - Amilcar. 1500cc 1st Leurquin – Amilcar.
Sallies-de-Bearn hillclimb, Pau 6.7km - 1100cc Racing - 1st Emile Dourel - Amilcar C6.
4 September
Mont Ventoux hillclimb - 1100cc Racing 1st Gaston Réveiller - Amilcar C6.
10 September
Brooklands, England, BARC Yorkshire Junior Long Handicap - 1st Henken Widengren - Amilcar C6 s/c.
BARC Yorkshire Senior Long Handicap - 1st H.T.H. Clayton - Amilcar C6 s/c.
22 September
G. P. du M.C.F. Montlhéry - Racing Car 1100cc - 2nd Robert Jeuffrain - Amilcar C6.
28 October
Gaillon hillclimb, Rouen - Racing 1100cc - 1st José Scaron - Amilcar MCO.
Sports 1100cc - 1st Robert Jeuffrain - Amilcar C6.

1933
21–25 January
Monte Carlo Rally.
2nd in under 1500cc class, 6th overall - Roger Bravard - Amilcar M Type.
6th in under 1500cc class, 12th overall - Fernand Pousse - Amilcar M3.
2–5 February
Garmisch Winterfahrt, ADAC, Germany - Ice Races - Sportscars up to 1500cc: 2nd Willy Briem – Amilcar.
26 March
Chanteloup, Paris 1.2km - 1st José Scaron - Amilcar C6.
16 April
Brooklands, England, BARC Addlestone Senior Long Handicap - 2nd Henken Widengren - Amilcar C6 s/c.
6 May
Brooklands, England, International Trophy - 4th in class, 7th overall - Henken Widengren - Amilcar C6 s/c.
14 May
Côte de la Valette, Rouen - 1st José Scaron - Amilcar C6.
28 May
La Tranchée, Tours - 1st José Scaron - Amilcar C6.
Circuit d'Orleans - 2000cc class:
2nd Georges Boursin - Amilcar CO Spéciale Martin; 3rd Deschamps - Amilcar CO Spéciale Martin.
1100cc class:
2nd C.A.Martin - Amilcar CO Spéciale Martin; 3rd Fernand Pousse - Amilcar CO Spéciale Martin; 4th Jean Nadeau - Amilcar CO Spéciale Martin.
4 June
Provence Trophy, Nîmes - 4th Gaston Réveiller - Amilcar C6.
4–5 June
Bol d'Or, Saint-Germain-en-Laye - 1st Jean de Gavardie - Amilcar CO Spéciale Martin;
4th Poulain - Amilcar CO Spéciale Martin;
5th Blot - Amilcar CO Spéciale Martin;
6th Camille Poiré - Amilcar CO Spéciale Martin.
5 June
Brooklands, England, BARC Cobham Senior Long Handicap - 2nd H.T.H. Clayton - Amilcar C6 s/c.

17–18 June
Le Mans 24-hour race - 5th in class, 12th overall - Jean de Gavardie / Henri de Gavardie - Amilcar CO Spéciale Martin.
18 June
Ars-La Châtre, Châteauroux - 2nd José Scaron - Amilcar CO.
Mazamet, Tarn, 2km Hillclimb - 1st Emile Dourel - Amilcar C6.
25 June
Grillenberger Sachsenring, Germany - 1100cc class 1st Helmut Schellenberg – Amilcar.
2–3 July
Spa 24-hour race, Belgium.
1st 1100cc class, 14th overall - Arthur Duray / Jean de Gavardie - Amilcar CO Spéciale Martin.
9 July
La *Baraque*, Clermont-Ferrand: 1st José Scaron Amilcar CO; 2nd Leurquin – Amilcar.
3 September
Mont Ventoux - 1100cc Racing - 1st Leurquin – Amilcar.
27 September
Brooklands, England - H.T.H. Clayton - Amilcar C6 s/c – Standing Mile Record.
1 October
Argenteuil. Paris - 1st José Scaron - Amilcar CO.
22 October
La Mata, Mataró near Barcelona, Spain - 1st Miguel Matas - Amilcar 1100cc.
28 October
Montlhéry Record - Henken Widengren - Amilcar C6 s/c - 185.588km in 1 Hour.
5–6 December
Montlhéry Record - Arthur Duray / Jean de Gavardie / Henri de Gavardie.
24 Hour Record, 3,285.643km = 136.902km/h - Amilcar CO Spéciale Martin.

1934
4 February
Titisee Ice Races, Germany - Sportscars up to 1500cc: 1st Willy Briem - Amilcar.
18 March
Chanteloup, Paris - 1st José Scaron - Amilcar CO.
2 April
Brooklands, England, BARC Ripley Lightning Long Handicap - 1st Henken Widengren - Amilcar C6 s/c.
20 May
Grand Prix des Frontières, Chimay, Belgium - 1st Marcel Rouleau - Amilcar C6; 2nd Joseph Deshormes - Amilcar CGS; 4th Paul Baudart - Amilcar CGSs.
20–21 May
Bol d'Or, Saint-Germain-en-Laye - Racing class 1100cc: 4th Poulain - Amilcar CO Spéciale Martin; 5th Delpech - Amilcar CO Spéciale Martin; 7th Blot - Amilcar CO Spéciale Martin.
Sport class 1100cc - 2nd Camille Poiré - Amilcar CO Spéciale Martin.
16–17 June
Le Mans 24-hour race - 14th Arthur Duray / Jean de Gavardie - Amilcar CO Spéciale Martin;
20th C.A. Martin / Fernand Pousse - Amilcar CO Spéciale Martin;
22nd Camille Poiré / Gaston Robail - Amilcar CO Spéciale Martin.
1 July
Karlforsbacken, Sweden - 1st Helmer Carlsson - Amilcar C6.
22 July
Mosserudsbacken, Sweden - 1st Helmer Carlsson - Amilcar C6.
6 August
Brooklands, England, BARC Esher Senior Short Handicap - 2nd H.T.H. Clayton - Amilcar C6 s/c.
12 August
Dreifaltigkeitsberg, Germany: 1st Willy Briem – Amilcar.
13 October
Brooklands, England, BARC First Kingston Junior Long Handicap - 1st R.F. Oats - Amilcar C6 s/c.
BARC Second Kingston Junior Long Handicap - 3rd R.F. Oats - Amilcar C6 s/c.

1935
22 April
Brooklands, England, BARC Easter Junior Long Handicap - 3rd F.J. Monkhouse - Amilcar C6 s/c.
5 May
Röforsloppet, Sweden - 1st Helmer Carlsson - Amilcar C6.
26 May
Circuit d'Orleans - 2500cc Sports - 1st Maurice Mestivier - Amilcar MCO.
Klevaliden, Sweden - 1st Helmer Carlsson - Amilcar C6.
30 June
Grand Prix de Lorraine, Seichamps-Nancy - Touring Cars: 1st Maurice Mestivier – Amilcar.
7 July
Mosserudsbacken, Sweden - 1st Helmer Carlsson - Amilcar C6.
13–15 July
Rallye des Alpes Françaises - 1st in class - Charles Roch - Amilcar Pégase.
14 July
Öjebergsbacken, Sweden - 1st Helmer Carlsson - Amilcar C6.
1 September
Freiburg-Schauinsland hillclimb, Germany: 2nd Willy Briem – Amilcar.

1936
23 February
Winter Grand Prix of Sweden, Lake Rämen on ice: 6th Karl-Emil Rolander - Amilcar C6.
3–8 March
Paris-Saint Raphael Féminin Rally - 3rd in 2200-3000cc class, 18th overall - Mme Fernande Roux - Amilcar Pégase Racer.
30–31 May
Bol d'Or, Saint-Germain-en-Laye - Racing class 1100cc: 2nd Grignard – Amilcar.
Sports class 1100cc: 4th Horvilleur – Amilcar.
1 June
Brooklands, England, BARC, Fourth Whitsun Mountain Handicap - 3rd H.T.H. Clayton - Amilcar C6 s/c.
5 July
Grand Prix de la Marne, Reims - 14th Marcel Contet - Amilcar Pégase Lightweight Racing.
3 August
Brooklands, England, BARC, Third August Mountain Handicap - 1st H.T.H. Clayton - Amilcar C6 s/c.
30 August
Freiburger Bergrekord hillclimb, Germany: 1st Willy Briem – Amilcar.
6 September
Grand Prix de France du MCF, Montlhéry - 3rd Mme Fernande Roux - Amilcar Pégase Racer; 4th Emile Contet - Amilcar Pégase Racing Lighweight.

1937
10 July
Brooklands, England, BARC, First July Short Handicap - 2nd H.T.H. Clayton - Amilcar C6 s/c.
12 September
Prebichl, Styria, Austria - 1st Robert Fleischanderl - Amilcar supercharged.
16 October
Brooklands, England, BARC, Second October Long Handicap - 3rd H.T.H. Clayton - Amilcar C6 s/c.

1938
15–20 February
Paris-Saint Raphael Féminin Rally.
1st in 3.0 litre class, 10th overall - Mme Fernande Roux - Amilcar Pégase Racer.
8 May
Coupes de Paris, Montlhéry - 2nd René Biolay - Amilcar C6.
5 June
Grand Prix des Frontiéres, Chimay, Belgium - 4th René Biolay - Amilcar C6.
11 September
12 h de Paris, Montlhéry, 1st 3,0 litre class, 5th overall - Maurice Mestivier / Mme Fernande Roux - Amilcar Pégase Racing Lightweight.
24 September
Brooklands, England, BARC, Third Dunlop Outer Circuit Race - 3rd P. Courtney - Amilcar C6 s/c.
15 October
Brooklands, England, BARC, Second October Long Handicap - 3rd P. Courtney - Amilcar C6 s/c.

1939
29 May
Brooklands, England, BARC, Locke King Trophy - 2nd P. Courtney - Amilcar C6 s/c.
6 August
Grand Prix de Comminges - 12th Maurice Mestivier - Amilcar Pégase.

APPENDIX III

THE ORIGINAL PARTS SUPPLIERS

Larger companies such as Citroën, Peugeot and Renault of course had the ability to produce component parts. However, when Amilcar started they were just one of many new operations getting into the cyclecar boom and most of their rivals were merely assembling cars from mechanical parts bought in from various suppliers. Amilcar, unlike many other small manufacturers, did make most of their cars entirely in-house, only buying in specialist components, especially electrical equipment, as needed. Consumables like spark plugs and tyres came from any available stocks.

The following is a list of the suppliers that they sourced key parts from.

Blériot

Louis Blériot was best known for his pioneering aircraft and his Type XI with which he became famous for being the first to fly across the English Channel. He had already established a business making car headlamps with an integral acetylene generator. These were standard equipment on Panhard et Levassor and Renault cars. After World War I he made a Blériot motorcycle and by 1921 he had joined the ranks of cyclecar builder as well as his aircraft manufacturing business. He had factories in France and England. Amilcar sourced dynamos, lamps and starter motors from Blériot.

Bosch

German Robert Bosch, a trained engineer, had previously worked for Thomas Edison in the USA and Siemens in London before he founded his eponymous company in Stuttgart in 1886. A year later Gottlieb Daimler asked him to design a magneto for use in his early automobiles. From that start both his expertise and his business grew and he set up the Automatic Magneto Electric Ignition Company in France in 1899. In the 1920s Amilcar sourced RB magnetos from the Bosch company. Of course the name Bosch later became a household name worldwide.

Chausson

Gaston and Jules Chausson set up a company, Ateliers Chausson Frères, in 1907 in Asnières-sur-Seine. They supplied radiators for the growing French motor industry; their early customers included Berliet, and Clément, Corre La Licorne, Mors and Panhard et Levassor. Between the two world wars their business expanded into metal stamping, making bodies for various car manufacturers. Chausson took over the Swiss radiator manufacturer Gallay, and car maker Chenard & Walcker. In later years they were absorbed into the Peugeot company and then taken over as a sub-brand of Trigano motorhomes.

Cozette

The 'Société du Carburateur Cozette' of 34, Avenue de Roule, Neuilly-Sur-Seine offered improved cylinder heads, carburettors and superchargers to boost the performance of Amilcars. Engineer Harry Ricardo had worked on improving the efficiency of a combustion chamber by inducing turbulence to speed up the burning of the incoming fuel-air mixture. This process – known as the 'squish effect' – allowed for an increase in compression ratio without causing pre-ignition, and by burning all of the petrol probably even improved fuel consumption. In 1926 René Cozette took out a licence for Ricardo's patent of 1919 to produce an improved cylinder head for Amilcar engines. Cozette also manufactured an eccentric vane-type supercharger with a built-in oil pump. In a test, *Omnia* magazine claimed the power increased from 33hp at 3,700rpm on a standard engine to 53hp at 4,000rpm with the supercharger fitted without any noticeable increase in fuel consumption. Amilcar driver Fernand Pousse had a word of warning though, reporting that on two attempts with a CGSs at a hillclimb he blew the engine up both times saying 'I did not think it worth trying the experiment a third time'. Cozette also offered their own carburettors for use with the supercharger and models for unblown Amilcars and other marques.

Ducellier

Ducellier was a French company specialising in the production of automotive lighting and electrical components, with origins dating back to 1830. The company founded by Gabriel Ducellier initially produced candle lanterns for horse-drawn carriages. By 1900 Ducellier had a showroom in the centre of Paris at 25 Passage Dubail in the 10th arrondissment. In 1911, Ducellier created the Phares Ducellier brand and introduced the first electric headlamps for automobiles. The company is now part of the Valeo group. Ducellier supplied Amilcar with dynamo generators, lamps, starters and other electrical components.

Ferodo

Ferodo was founded in 1897 by Herbert Frood in England. Ferodo was the first company to use asbestos for brake linings and developed the first modern brake friction materials. Eugène Buisson formed the Société Anonyme Française du Ferodo (SAFF), with headquarters at 64, Avenue de la Grande-Armée, Paris, producing the first friction materials made in France. Ferodo supplied brake and clutch linings to Amilcar.

Gallay

Jean Gallay started making radiators in Switzerland for use in biplanes in the 1914–18 war and, when peace returned, like many others in manufacturing and engineering, moved into supplying automobile companies including Amilcar. Gallay was later taken over by Chausson.

Hartford

The Truffault-Hartford Shock Absorber, made by the Hartford Suspension Company, was the first ever true shock absorber. It was invented by a Frenchmen, J. M. M. Truffault. In 1904, Edward V. Hartford and Truffault created the Hartford Suspension Company in New York, later, in 1908 relocating to New Jersey. By the time Amilcar became a customer, Hartford shock absorbers were the most common type used in the industry. Often referred to by the brand André Hartford, this was only relevant in the UK after 1926 when Theodore Bernard André of T. B. André & Co. Ltd took on the rights for the local market.

Jaeger

Paris-based watchmaker Edmond Jaeger is world famous for his partnership with Swiss company LeCoultre & Cie making high-end watches under the combined Jaeger-LeCoultre name. Edmond Jaeger started producing aviation instruments made at the Swiss factory in Vallée de Joux for English and French pilots in World War I. The quality of these became so famous, that enemy German pilots began removing the Jaeger instruments from planes they had shot down. Post-war a switch to supplying the growing automobile industry lead to the establishment of a factory at Le Vallois and, to get around protectionist measures, a London-based workshop making every type of automotive gauge required. So, these British-made instruments also found their way into many Amilcars. Jaeger and LeCoultre merged as one brand in 1937.

Marchal

In 1923, industrialist, motor racing enthusiast and inventor Pierre Marchal started a company La Société pour la Fabrication de Projectors et Lanternes Électriques in Pantin, north-east of Paris, dedicated to electric lighting. Immediately successful, Marchal lighting adorned not only Amilcars; Bugatti, Delage, Delahaye and Hotchkiss were also customers. In 1963 Marchal merged with SEV (Société d'Équipements pour Véhicules), which was in turn taken over by SAFF (Société Anonyme Française du Ferodo). Ferodo became Valeo who also own Ducellier, and the Marchal name disappeared (at least until a Japanese company bought the rights to the name in 2009).

O.S.

Otto Schulze patented an eddy current speedometer in 1902 and from 1908 these were made by O.S. Autometerwerke E. Seignol in Frankfurt, Germany. O.S. gauges were made in France at Ateliers Seignol, Neuilly sur Seine and sold through a shop E. Seignol, 17, Rue Duret, Paris. Later merged with VDO and then Siemens, the O.S. brand still exists today.

RAF Wheels

The RAF wheel (Roue Amovible Francais) was a common fitment especially in France made by CAM, 15, Avenue de la Grande-Armée, Paris. RAF hubs differ from the Rudge-Whitworth type in that they have square splines. Apart from Amilcar they were also used on early Bugattis, Hotchkiss's, Minervas and Panhards and some of the smaller Rolls-Royces.

Rudge-Whitworth Wheels

When the Whitworth Cycle Co. of Birmingham founded by Charles Henry Pugh merged with Rudge Cycle Co. of Coventry to form the Rudge-Whitworth company, it quickly became a leading supplier of centre-lock wire wheels. The Rudge-Whitworth QD (Quickly Disconnectable) system was first patented in 1908. The hub is splined to positively locate the wheel held on by a single central nut. The wheels on the right side of the car have a left-hand thread on the nut and vice versa, so effectively self-tightening. Their sales motto was 'Rudge it, do not trudge it'. Rudge-Whitworth quickly became standard fitment on many cars until the rights to manufacture were taken over by Jaguar after World War II. In April 1922, Carlo Borrani set up a new company called Rudge-Whitworth Milano in Milan, Italy. Borrani wheels are today well known for supplying wire wheels to some of the leading sports car manufacturers, not least Ferrari.

Solex

The Solex company was founded by Marcel Mennesson and Maurice Goudard, making radiators supplying early car manufacturers including the prestigious Delaunay-Belleville. Their radiators were also used by the Paris General Omnibus company. After the war and competing with Chausson, they diversified into making carburettors, buying the rights to the Jouffret and Renée patents. Solex carburettors were probably the most widely used by many manufacturers from the 1920s to the 1980s. The Solex name is now part of the Magneti Marelli concern.

PHOTOGRAPHIC CREDITS

Auto Restorations Ltd New Zealand: p.89 (all).
Alf van Beem/Wikimedia: p.67 (bottom).
Pierre Balian: p.45 (all).
Nick Bell: p.72 (bottom left and bottom right), p.73 (top and bottom).
Joris Bergsma: p.2.
Klaus Bremer: p.92 (all).
Brightwells.com: p.42 (all), p.61 (top and bottom), p.171 (top).
Han Brouwers: p.103 (bottom), p.104 (top).
Warren Brown, p.180 (bottom right) .
Brian Chisholm: p.46, p.47 (all).
Buch-t/Wikimedia: p.27 (top and bottom), p.137.
Von Buch-t – Eigenes Werk/Wikimedia: p.54 (top and bottom), p.98 (bottom), p.107, p.108 (top and bottom), p.109 (top and middle).
Charles01/Wikimedia, p.11 (right), p.108 (middle), p.131.
conceptcarz.com: p.125 (top right and middle).
Jos Cox: p.23 (all).
Croquant/Wikimedia: p.39 (top), p.121.
Ted Cross: p.63 (top left).
Doningtons Auctions: p.63 (top right, bottom left and bottom right).
Olivier Dumoulin: p.133, p.134 (top and bottom), p.135 (top).
Alain Ducrot: p.40 (top left), p.55, p.56.
Fortgens Photography: p.76 (top and bottom), p.77 (all).
Ted Geermans: p.105 (top right and bottom right), p.106 (top left, top right and bottom right).
Simon Goodman: p.141.
Neil Heilbrunn: p.24 (top and bottom), p.25 (top and bottom).
Hyman Ltd. Classic Cars: p.74 (top and bottom), p.75 (all), p.138 (top).
Jacques: p.177 (top).
Detlef Kayser: p.41 (all), p.64, p.65 (all).
Jean Louis Limbourg: p.115 (all).
Luzzago.com: p.80 (top and bottom), p.81 (top and bottom).
Chris Martin: p.30 (top and bottom), p.48 (top right), p.49 (all).
Karen Martin: p.48 (top left).
Ross Menz: p.40 (top right, bottom left and bottom right), p.51 (bottom), p.52 (top and bottom), p.53 (top and bottom), p.67 (top), p.78 (top and bottom), p.79 (all), p.105 (top left), p.106 (bottom left).
Alexander Migl/Wikimedia: p.91 (top).
Shannons.com.au: p.62 (all).
Tamorlan/Wikimedia: p.69 (top).
Von Thesupermat – Eigenes Werk/Wikimedia: p.90 (top and bottom).
Hugues Vanhoolandt: p.124, p.125 (top left and bottom), p.132 (top and bottom).
Peter White: p.93 (left and right), p.94 (top and bottom), p.95 (all).
Front cover photo: Chris Martin. Back cover photos (top to bottom): Peter White, Agence Roi (public domain) and Karen Martin.

BIBLIOGRAPHY, REFERENCES, SOURCES AND NOTES

BIBLIOGRAPHY

These are a few of the books and magazines in my collection that have helped with the research. As with all sources there may be differences in the stated facts and information. I do not claim to be infallible and the new 'expert' on every detail of Amilcar history, but my methods of research have tried to verify everything so far believed to be correct which may be questionable. Where there is reason to doubt something I have investigated all available sources to find evidence to either confirm or correct the previously held beliefs.

Boldiston, Bill, *The Amilcar in New South Wales*

Burgess-Wise, David, *Encyclopedia of Supercars* (Orbis, 1993)

Fouquet-Hatevilan, Pierre *Salmson – Toute* (E.P.A., 1986)

Fournier, Gilles and Burgess-Wise, David, *Amilcar*

Georgano, G. N., *The New Encyclopedia of Motorcars 1885 to the Present*

Grayson, Stan, *Automobile Quarterly* Vol. 13 no. 1

Nicholson, T. R., *The 4-cylinder Amilcar, 1920–1929* (Profile Publications)

Pritchard, Anthony, *Small Cars, Big Ideas* (*Motor Sport*, June 2004)

Schramm, Philippe, *L'Epopée de la Société Le Zèbre*

Wood, Jonathan, *Morgan – Performance Plus Tradition*

Bolides de l'Age d'Or, compiled by *L'Automobiliste*

Rétroviseur – March 1992

ONLINE RACE RESULT SOURCES

I started with the collection of old magazines in the library at the Australian Motorlife Museum and used a lot of other online sources to cross-reference the facts; not all agree but I managed to sort out what I believe to be correct.

Motorsport magazine, page http://www.motorsportmagazine.com/database/drivers/7906-arthur-legat

The Golden Era of Grand Prix Racing 1934–1940 by Leif Snellman, page https://www.goldenera.fi/

Conceptcarz.com, page http://www.conceptcarz.com

Racing Sports Cars, page http://www.racingsportscars.com/

Indianapolis 500 History

https://www.indianapolismotorspeedway.com/events/indy500/history/home

La Bérézina, https://www.laberezina.com/index.html

Speedfreaks, http://www.dlg.speedfreaks.org/archive/gen/1922.html

There is no index for this site, change year in address for required results.

NOTES

1 – Page 15

Did Morel and Moyet know each other prior to the meeting at the Excelsior restaurant in 1919? Some sources say Moyet had worked at Le Zèbre anyway, in which case they must have known each other working in what was a small operation. Some suggest Moyet was a prodigy of Salomon at Citroën when he was introduced to Morel, but whatever the truth of either story, one would think that within the relatively close community of the Parisian automobile industry each man would have been aware of the other.

2 – Page 20

It is strange that Fournier, a Frenchman himself, printed the claim that Amilcar and Duval were neighbours in the same street. This is because it is quite clear from early advertisements that Amilcar were based in the 11th arrondissement commonly referred to as the Bastille district. It is equally clear from the body plates affixed by Duval, who were based in Boulogne-sur-Seine, the industrial district across the Seine on the west side of Paris where they stayed even after moving from the original Rue de Chemin-Vert address. Was Fournier not familiar with the geography of Paris, had he been given some false information, or was it just a guess, as they shared a similar street name?

3 – Pages 28 and 35

The first appearance of the E-Type chassis at the October 1922 Paris Salon displayed the new front wheel brakes, which seems odd as the patent was not applied for until October 1923 and granted in May 1924. The magazine *L'Auto* did mention a new 10hp chassis on show at the 1922 Salon, although sales did not start until much later. The E-Type went on sale some time in 1923, possibly, as was the normal industry practice, not until the Salon of that year, so we may question if the 1922 chassis did actually have the fully working new front brakes. Also, that same photo of the E-Type chassis on page 56 in the Fournier book is also shown on page 32 captioned as the CC chassis at the 1922 Salon, which it obviously is not.

4 – Page 116

When exactly did Chinon leave Amilcar to go to Citroën? For the new TPV (Toute Petite Voiture) which was to become the 2CV, André Lefèbvre led the project team and had by the autumn of 1935 appointed Chinon to co-ordinate the bodywork and mechanical components. This confusion could be explained by the presence of the similarly-named Marcel Junion, who worked under Hotchkiss chief designer Vincenzo Bertarione at the time Hotchkiss were working with Grégoire on the forthcoming Compound.

5 – Page 116

In 1923 Ernest Schmid had, along with Ernest Henry, designed a 2.0-litre, 6-cylinder sleeve-valve engine, which was installed in a Rolland-Pilain racing car, which had no success. He later added superchargers and entered the cars under the Schmid name. Sleeve-valve engines of course do not have any conventional poppet valves and associated operating mechanisms. The straight-eight engine as designed by Grillot had overhead camshafts and poppet valves. Schmid had no connection with the straight-eight engine. Various other sources credit the Pégase engine to Grillot.

6 – Page 118

In the Fournier book, on page 100 he lists the Saint-Hubert Pégase option as a pillarless four-door saloon, but the illustration clearly shows a normal four-door with a centre pillar.

7 – Page 181

The Fournier book has a higher number based on engine numbers in sequence. There are other production numbers shown at: https://fr.wikipedia.org/wiki/Amilcar_(entreprise)

Later research by Jean Marie Lallouette published in *Le Pégase 94*, the members magazine of the Cercle Pégase Amilcar, shows slightly lower production numbers. The report acknowledges the available records as follows: sales records kept by André Morel; the catalogue of the Chambre Syndicale des Constructeurs (the union of French automobile manufacturers); records kept by Schlotterbeck the Swiss importer; some registration records and various publications from the period covered. The reality could be either one is correct or an approximate mix of each.

USEFUL CONTACTS

Amilcar Clubs

These clubs all have some information on their websites and members have access to valuable resources and other members who may be able to help with technical and historical questions.

The Amilcar Salmson Register	www.amilcar.co.uk
Cercle Pegase Amilcar	www.amilcar.net
Club Amilcar Cyclecar Suisse	www.amilcar.ch/index.html

Parts suppliers that may be useful

Auto Electric Supplies
Granville House, 11 Cross Street, Tenbury Wells, Worcestershire WR15 8EF, UK
www.autoelectricsupplies.co.uk

Depanoto
4 rue de la Malerie, 28400 Nogent le Rotrou, France
www.depanoto.fr

The Complete Automobilist
Crosswinds, Happisburgh, Norwich, Norfolk NR12 ORX, UK
www.completeautomobilist.com

The Amilcar Salmson Register
www.amilcar.co.uk/spares

PreWarCar.com
www.prewarcar.com

INDEX

First published in 2025 by
The Crowood Press Ltd
Ramsbury, Marlborough
Wiltshire SN8 2HR

enquiries@crowood.com
www.crowood.com

British Library Cataloguing-in-Publication Data
A catalogue record for this book is available from the British Library.

For product safety-related questions, contact:
productsafety@crowood.com

ISBN 978 0 7198 4510 9

Picture page 2: Joris Bergsma's fine CGSs in a picture-postcard Dutch setting.
Picture page 4: A famous Amilcar poster designed by Geo Ham.

Typeset by Simon and Sons

Cover design by Keith Wootton

Printed and bound in India by Parksons Graphics Pvt Ltd

Acknowledgements

At the time this writer was preparing the research for this book, two of the leading experts in the Amilcar history passed away. All Amilcar enthusiasts owe a great debt to both Desmond Peacock and Gilles Fournier. I do not pretend to fill their shoes here but gladly acknowledge their past efforts, without which my research would have been a more difficult task.

Thanks to those who contributed photos or some historical details; others just pointed me in the right direction with useful sources and links to follow up. Richard Fewster, Ted Geermans and Doug Gordon in Australia; Hugues Vanhoolandt in Belgium; Pierre Balian, Olivier Chabanne and Michel Marteling in France; Klaus Bremer and Detlef Kayser in Germany; Joris Bergsma, Henk Fortgens and Jos Cox in the Netherlands; Peter White in New Zealand; Rod Martin in the UK; and Peter Vack in the USA.

Last, but by no means least, the biggest thanks go to The Crowood Press for having faith in this project and patience when dealing with my emails, and of course my wife Karen, who puts up with my lack of interest in anything like real life while I am chained to the keyboard and for diligently proofreading my text, which must be quite hard work for someone not interested in the minutiae of vintage motoring.